A Garden *of* One's Own

A GARDEN of ONE'S OWN

Writings of

ELIZABETH LAWRENCE

Edited by Barbara Scott & Bobby J. Ward

The University of North Carolina Press

Chapel Hill & London

© 1997
The University of North Carolina Press
All rights reserved
Designed by Richard Hendel
Set in Centaur type
by Keystone Typesetting, Inc.
Manufactured in the United States of America

The paper in this book meets the guidelines for permanence and
durability of the Committee on Production Guidelines for Book Longevity
of the Council on Library Resources.

FRONTISPIECE: Elizabeth Lawrence at her garden gate.
This photograph appeared with the first of Lawrence's columns published in
The Charlotte Observer in 1957. Photograph courtesy of *The Charlotte Observer*.

Acknowledgments of permission to reprint previously published material
appear at the end of the book, following the index.

Library of Congress Cataloging-in-Publication Data
Lawrence, Elizabeth, 1904–1985.
[Selections. 1997]
A garden of one's own : writings of Elizabeth Lawrence / edited by
Barbara Scott and Bobby J. Ward.
p. cm.
Includes bibliographical references (p.   ) and index.
ISBN 978-0-8078-2349-1 (cloth : alk. paper)
ISBN 978-0-8078-5978-0 (pbk. : alk. paper)
ISBN 978-1-4696-4931-3 (ebook)
1. Gardening—Southern States.   2. Gardening—North Carolina.
3. Gardening.   4. Lawrence, Elizabeth, 1904–1985.   I. Scott,
Barbara, 1948–   Sept. 30–   II. Ward, Bobby J.   III. Title.
SB453.2.S66L382   1997
635.9—dc21   96-39348

CIP

To the memory of

Linda Mitchell Lamm

and

William Lanier Hunt,

friends of Elizabeth and

members of her circle

of gardeners,

and

J. C. Raulston,

a Brother of the Spade

CONTENTS

Introduction, xi

1. BEGINNINGS

Elizabeth Lawrence—An Autobiography, 3
Twenty-One Plant Facts for Gardeners in the Middle South, 5
The Onset of Spring, 12

2. TREES & SHRUBS

Broad-Leaved Evergreens for the Mid-South, 17
Here Are Blossoms for Southern Evergreens, 25
Pinkneya pubens, 29
Butcher's-Broom—*Ruscus aculeatus*, 31
Some Trees and Shrubs of the Southeast, 33

3. BULBS

Summer-Flowering Bulbs, 41
Outdoor Hardy Crinums, 43
Diverse Bulbs for the South, 45
Narcissi for Next Spring's Garden, 51
Amaryllids in a Southern Garden, 60
In Quest of Autumn-Blooming Bulbs, 74
Ornamental Alliums in North Carolina, 77
Hybrid Crinums, 79
Further Notes on Hybrid Crinums, 83
A Review of the Iris Family, 86
Tender Bulbs for Summer Bloom, 92
Habranthus, 94
Zephyranthes smallii in North Carolina, 96

4. PERENNIALS & ANNUALS

Perennials Suitable for the Mid-South, 99
Annuals Down South, 106

Garden Phlox, 113
Torenia bailloni, 116
Some Crotalarias for the Mid-South, 117
Permanent Perennials, 119
My Best Twenty-Five Daylilies, 125
The Curtain in Your Garden, 128
Groundcovers, 130
Ivy: Cool Green in Summer, Warm Green in Winter, 133

5. NATIVE PLANTS

Handsome Wild Indigos, 139
Native Plants for the Country Doctor's Garden, 141
Pennyroyal, 144
Southern Endemics, 146
Neglected Natives, 149
Morrow Mountain, 151
A Wildflower Garden in August, 153
Trilliums, 155

6. ROCK GARDENS

Rock Garden Plants for the Mid-South, 161
Rules for Rock Gardens, 168
Rock Garden Conifers in Southern Nurseries, 172
Some Small Members of the Iris Family, 174
More about Violets, 176
A Review of Little Daffodils, 178
Some Notes on Species Tulips, 181
Rock Gardens in Winter, 184
Two Wonders, 186

7. BROTHERS OF THE SPADE

Miss Jekyll of Munstead Wood, 191
Friends in Oregon, 201
Letters from the West, 206
Brothers of the Spade, 214
In Memory of Dr. Edgar T. Wherry: No Phlox without a Salutation, 218
On William Lanier Hunt, 227

CONCLUSION
A Garden of One's Own:
Letters from Elizabeth Lawrence to a Friend, 235

Appendix 1:
Bibliography of Elizabeth Lawrence's Published Works, 247

Appendix 2:
A Circle of Gardeners, 251

Bibliography
Works Referred to by Elizabeth Lawrence, 259
Works Used by the Editors, 261

Index, 263

Permissions, 277

I know a bank where the wild thyme blows,

Where ox-lips and the nodding violet grows,

Quite over-canopied with luscious woodbine,

With sweet musk-roses and with eglantine:

There sleeps Titania, sometime of the night,

Lull'd in these flowers with dances and delight.

WILLIAM SHAKESPEARE

A Midsummer Night's Dream

INTRODUCTION

In his introduction to *Gardening for Love*, Allen Lacy remarked that he never knew Elizabeth Lawrence and that his life was the poorer for it. All of us who missed knowing her but who love to read her words and envision her gardens feel that poverty. But we do know Miss Lawrence through her writing, and our lives are the richer for it. In it we find a template for what it takes to be a gardener and a garden writer—an alchemy of art, science, and poetry.

When Elizabeth (as she preferred to be called) grew a plant, she noted its shape and the general impression it made in the garden, and she recorded subtle details of its color and smell. In *A Southern Garden*, she noted: "With silver bells, one must plant the early single blue hyacinths. These too, can be bought with the butter, and much more readily than silver bells for they increase well. Their fragrance is of cinnamon, and their color that of the periwinkle which usually serves as a ground-cover for them. The hyacinths and pale daffodils are a cool blue and silver that reminds one of things past."

She combined plants with an artist's sense of color and form, but she kept ordered records of their effect in her garden with a scientist's discipline. The tables of blooming dates in *A Southern Garden* show her thoroughness.

At the same time, she developed a prose style that captured her subjects and carried her voice. These lines in the opening pages of *A Southern Garden* reflect her refined style: "A gnarled rosemary is one of my chief treasures. I treasure it for the charm of its irregular outline, for the pale blue of its flowers in very early spring, and for the refreshing odor of its foliage as I brush against it in passing."

In *American Women Writers*, Beverly Seaton called her the South's "most distinguished writer on modern southern gardening" and remarked that "all of her works are written in a prose style reminiscent of the age of 'polite letters.'"

Like Emily Dickinson, Elizabeth Lawrence wrote a letter to the world. And the world wrote back to her. Reading her writing is like reading an open letter to a friend with whom she shares a love of books and a heightened sensitivity to nature. This style came naturally to her; she traded letters with other writers like Katharine White and Eudora Welty, with gardeners who knew the Latin names of every plant they grew, and with farm women who identified plants by regional common names passed along from gardener to gardener like the plants they grew and loved. Miss Lawrence's books and the writings in this collection are filled with conversations from those letters and quotations from garden writers in Great Britain and America. As she explains in *Gardens in Winter*, "I am not writing of my garden alone. I am writing of all those that I have seen, all those that I have read about in books, and all those that I know through letters."

When she quotes the words of Gertrude Jekyll and E. A. Bowles of Great Britain with the same polite familiarity with which she reports the latest confidences from Mr. Tong or Miss Isabel Busbee in Raleigh, she creates a timeless circle of people who love plants and the gardens that shelter them. This circle of gardeners crosses boundaries of time, space, and class; it is all-inclusive and ongoing. Equally intimate with writers of poetry, essays, and fiction, she cites Matthew Arnold, Thoreau, and Jane Austen with the same ease as she does garden writers and her correspondents, many of whom were farm women who advertised plants and bulbs in market bulletins. By weaving together references to gardens from so many different sources, she widens the circle, and embraces gardening as an art that is both refined and primitive.

Had Miss Lawrence chosen to write in another genre, she might be better known outside gardening circles. She chose, however, to write about what she loved and knew best, a choice that limited her audience but not her power of expression. All of her writings set a stage, which happens to be in the garden. The characters in her drama are plants, and she describes them with affection, including the seasons and conditions of their successes and failures and which ones marry well with which.

Although she wrote little about herself directly, her tone is always personal: small pieces of her daily routine surface in her books between observations about plants and their seasons of bloom. She came from a gardening family. Her grandmother grew "sweet white violets" (a sonnet about them appears in *A Southern Garden*), and her mother kept a "series of small black diaries" that recorded the bloom dates of everything she grew. Elizabeth kept her own garden diaries in her books and letters.

In *Gardens in Winter*, she writes of watching a cardinal, who "would arrive at the window every afternoon at tea time, and flutter and twitter and peer inside. When it grew dark he would settle on the cane of bamboo nearest the house, and when we sat down to dinner he would be fast asleep. We could see him by the candle light, handsomely red on his green perch. Sometimes in midwinter when I was up before daylight, I would find him there, still asleep. One morning he came to the window, and found us sitting by the fire having elevens. After that he made a habit of coming to the bamboo every morning at eleven."

This collection of pieces originally written for magazines and journals provides more of the same. Miss Lawrence writes about colchicums and how she used to bring them from the "five-and-ten" to bloom on the parlor table. "Afterward we planted them in a dank spot under the refrigerator drip, and they continued to bloom season after season." She recommends breakfast in the garden to fully appreciate *Linum perenne*, with its "pale blue flowers that fade by the middle of the morning." She notes the two small bulbs of *Zephyranthes smallii* planted just outside her studio window, where she could see a "scrap of yellow" whenever she looked up from her work. And she describes garden beds "so full that I cannot thrust the trowel into the soil to make a hole for some new treasure without cutting into the white flesh of a dormant bulb or digging up a plant whose top has died down."

Her many garden interests are reflected in this collection, which ranges from her series of articles in *House & Garden* on plants and practices for the mid-South to her careful descriptions of all the bulbs and rock garden plants that would grow in a climate that "changes from one extreme to the other" so suddenly. In editing the collection, Bobby Ward and I were at first inclined to arrange the essays chronologically to show how Miss Lawrence's gardening interests varied over time. But as we worked together on the pieces, we decided that arranging them by subject would make them more useful to readers.

In addition to magazine and journal articles, this collection includes Miss Lawrence's introductions to books by Gertrude Jekyll and William Lanier Hunt. We thought that combining this material in one volume would give readers a good look at all the writing Miss Lawrence produced apart from her books and newspaper columns.

The pieces in this collection have been left as originally written, except for a few small changes in punctuation and capitalization. Styles of punctuation and capitalization varied from publication to publication, and accordingly it appears that some publishers edited Miss Lawrence's work to conform to their standards. When we have felt it necessary to make minor changes, we have edited the articles to conform to the standards outlined in *The Chicago Manual of Style*.

Nomenclature has changed for many of the plants Miss Lawrence mentions, so, where necessary, we have updated the nomenclature by adding current designations in brackets after those she used. Our primary sources for current nomenclature were the Royal Horticultural Society's *Dictionary of Garden Plants* (1994), *A Synonymized Checklist of the Vascular Flora of the United States, Canada, and Greenland* by John Kartesz (1994), and *Hortus Third* (1976). The latter helped to bridge the nomenclature gap between *Hortus Second*, which Elizabeth Lawrence used, and the modern references.

There may be more writings from garden journals and bulletins by Elizabeth Lawrence that cannot be traced because they do not appear in any reference listings. The *Reader's Guide to Periodical Literature* included only a few listings under her name during the late 1930s. The *Bibliography of Agriculture*, however, listed many more of her contributions to magazines and plant journals.

Many of the articles reproduced here were not listed in any of the periodical indexes available in libraries. We happened upon them accidentally, while looking for something else, such as when Bobby found the article entitled "The Onset of Spring" by chance in an old copy of *The Home Garden* that he bought in a used bookstore. Likewise, I accidentally happened upon copies of a short-lived Raleigh magazine entitled *Southern Home and Garden* on a library shelf next to another publication that I was investigating. The magazine printed its first issue in April 1938 and ceased publication two years later. During its brief existence, William Lanier Hunt, Charlotte Hilton Green, and Elizabeth Lawrence all contributed articles about the plants they grew.

Elizabeth's work also appeared in national magazines like *House & Garden* and *American Home*. She wrote for *Flower Grower* and *Horticulture* and contributed often to the *Bulletin of the American Rock Garden Society*, *The American Horticultural Magazine*, and *Herbertia*, the journal of the International Bulb Society (formerly the American Amaryllis Society). She also wrote for newsletters such as *Garden Gossip*, published by the Garden Club of Virginia, and the *Newsletter of the North Carolina Wild Flower Preservation Society*. These publications were directed at readers with different levels of interest in gardens, but she wrote for all of them in the same clear voice that characterizes her books.

Based on all the material that we have found, it appears that Elizabeth Lawrence's first contribution to a periodical was the following short note entitled "A Good Flower Show Exhibit" that was printed in the July 1932 issue of *Garden Gossip*:

> At a large and successful flower show in Greensboro, North Carolina, was shown an interesting, small, formal, walled garden, which made such an impression that I am offering the description as a suggestion to chairmen of garden club flower shows.
>
> It was paved, and the walls were whitewashed brick; a lovely little piece of statuary (bronze) was set in an evergreen niche with a cool green pool below, fringed with forget-me-nots. No color, but two clumps of yellow *Hemerocallis flava* [*H. lilio-asphodelus*], and wisteria on a tree whose branches spread over one side of the garden. Line, form, and cool greenery were featured with the use of pointed evergreens. There was a seat on one side.

After writing articles on bulbs and crinums for *Garden Gossip*, she turned her attention to writing for magazines. From what we can glean from the periodical listings, Elizabeth Lawrence began writing for magazines in 1936, six years after she graduated with North Carolina State University's first class in landscape architecture. Between January of that year and October of the next, she wrote a series of articles for *House & Garden* that focused on plants for the mid-South and laid the groundwork for *A Southern Garden* (which was published by the University of North Carolina Press in 1942).

In 1943, she received the Herbert Medal from the American Amaryllis Society "in recognition of her important contributions to the advancement of horticulture, particularly the amaryllids." In the same year, the Tenth Anniversary Issue of *Herbertia*, the society's journal, was dedicated to Elizabeth Lawrence. She wrote a brief autobiography for the issue, in which she describes how she came to feel the "relation between poetry and the soil" and how she came to choose gardening as a profession and acquired such a compulsion to study plants for the South. That autobiography begins this collection, along with two other articles that represent beginnings—the first article that Elizabeth wrote for a magazine and an article that she wrote about the beginning of spring.

In 1945, Miss Lawrence created a study guide for the University of North Carolina's Library Extension Service to help garden clubs educate their members about the region. It is not part of this collection because its format is quite different from that of the materials included—it contains short chapters of text, each followed by a list of suggested readings—but it is worth noting as an example of Elizabeth's varied interests and services to fellow gardeners.

There are years when few listings appear under Elizabeth Lawrence's name in the periodical indexes. They seem to coincide with her move to Charlotte in 1948 and the periods just before the appearances of her books, and it is easy to imagine that she was focusing her attention on these other projects at those times. The last periodical listing that we could find for Elizabeth was in 1978 for an article in *Pacific Horticulture* entitled "Letters from the West." But when we wrote for permission to use it in this collection, Olive Rice Waters at *Pacific Horticulture* sent two more articles written in 1977 and 1981 about Miss Lawrence's gardening correspondence with friends in California, Oregon, and Washington.

The contributions to *Pacific Horticulture* reflect her long correspondence with other gardeners, which became the focus of *Gardening for Love*, the first book published from her papers and notes after her death, which was edited by Allen Lacy and published by Duke University Press in 1987. The "polite letter" that Miss Lawrence began writing with her first newsletter contribution in 1932 continues today because she left so much behind.

In 1990, *Through the Garden Gate*, a collection of her garden columns for *The Charlotte Observer* edited by Bill Neal, was published by the University of North Carolina Press. Later the same year, Duke University Press released *A Rock Garden in the South*, a collection of pieces in which she describes her rock garden in Raleigh and the saxatile plants she found to be adaptable to gardens in the mid-South. Three long articles that she wrote for bulletins published by the North American Rock Garden Society (formerly the American Rock Garden Society) were published as chapters in *A Rock Garden in the South*, so they are not included in this collection. All of her other contributions to the society's bulletin are included.

When she died in 1985, Elizabeth Lawrence was eighty-one years old. In her autobiography published some forty-two years earlier, she said that her ancestors were people who lived to be very old and she hoped to inherit their longevity so she could see many years of bloom in garden flowers.

Little is left of her garden in Raleigh, where a university fraternity now occupies the house she lived in for thirty-two years. The stone wall that bounded the back of the Lawrence property is falling down, and a basketball goal dominates the yard where her garden must have been. But, as she wrote in *A Southern Garden*, "What has gone before is not lost: the future is the past entered by another door."

As in Elizabeth's own garden, a rosemary bush grows in the Elizabeth Lawrence Memorial Border at the North Carolina State University Arboretum. Like all gardens, this one is still evolving. Curators Edith Eddleman and Doug Ruhren are establishing a mix of plants that will adapt to the site and provide pleasing contrasts in texture. They are selecting plants that Elizabeth Lawrence would have grown on such a site: one of the plants in the border, for example, is butcher's-broom, *Ruscus aculeatus*, which she often praised for being so persistent. And in keeping with her inquiring spirit, they are also trying new ones that might adapt to it. Some of the plants now in place came from people who knew her. Some came from her own garden.

Just as plants are traded from gardener to gardener for the love of it, the articles in this collection are gathered here because of many hands. Bobby and I discovered our mutual interest in researching Elizabeth's writing through our membership in the Piedmont Chapter of the North American Rock Garden Society, and we worked together to find the articles that Elizabeth wrote. Edith Eddleman told J. C. Raulston at the North Carolina State University Arboretum about our research, and he discussed it with David Perry of the University of North Carolina Press. David pursued the idea of publishing this collection and worked to make it happen.

All of the publishers and plant societies who gave their permission for essays to be reprinted also made the collection possible. Olive Rice Waters of *Pacific Horticulture* and R. Mitchel Beauchamp of the

International Bulb Society helped to locate articles that could not have been found elsewhere.

Linda Mitchell Lamm of Wilson, North Carolina, graciously shared her copies of the North Carolina Wild Flower Preservation Society's newsletter with us. She also allowed Bobby to read letters from Miss Lawrence that she has saved. They were the basis for Bobby's article, "A Garden of One's Own: Letters from Elizabeth Lawrence to a Friend," which was published in a memorial edition of *The Trillium*, the newsletter of the Piedmont Chapter of the North American Rock Garden Society. That article, which gives a taste of what it must have been like to get a letter from Elizabeth Lawrence, concludes this collection.

We thank Paul Jones, curator of the Asiatic Arboretum at the Sarah P. Duke Gardens at Duke University, for reviewing the text and recommending plant nomenclature updates. We also thank Tom Stuart of the Hudson Valley Chapter of the North America Rock Garden Society for reading the manuscript and offering constructive comments. Likewise, the two anonymous reviewers who evaluated the manuscript for the University of North Carolina Press made invaluable contributions to its final form.

Special thanks should be given to Warren Way and Elizabeth Rogers, Elizabeth Lawrence's nephew and niece, for their cooperation in allowing this work to be published and shared with all the gardeners who love to read Elizabeth.

Barbara Scott
Raleigh, North Carolina
October 1996

1 : Beginnings

*For many years my mother has kept
a record of the first flowers of each season,
writing down the blooms in the garden day by
day in a series of small black diaries.*
A Southern Garden

Elizabeth Lawrence—An Autobiography

When I was a little girl, my mother took great pains to interest me in learning to know the birds and wildflowers and in planting a garden. I thought that roots and bulbs and seeds were as wonderful as flowers, and the Latin names on seed packages as full of enchantment as the counting-out rhymes that children chant in the spring. I remember the first time I planted seeds. My mother asked me if I knew the Parable of the Sower. I said I did not, and she took me into the house and read it to me. Once the relation between poetry and the soil is established in the mind, all growing things are endowed with more than material beauty.

When I was twelve we came to live in Raleigh, in a house with an already established garden. It was fall when we came, and there was not much in bloom—only some old-fashioned roses and chrysanthemums that the frost had not caught. But the first spring was like living my favorite book, *The Secret Garden*. Every day the leaves and flower buds of some plant that we did not know was there would break through the cold earth. There were snowdrops under the hedge and crocuses in the grass, and the garden pattern was picked out in daffodils. And under the eaves of the summerhouse, a single fat white hyacinth bloomed. No other spring has ever been so beautiful, except the spring of the year I came home from college. The first spring in the South after four years in New York led me to choose gardening as a profession.

In the fall, a course in landscape architecture (the first in the South) was started at the North Carolina State College [North Carolina State University, Raleigh, N.C.], and I started with it, the only girl in the class. One morning a visitor came into the drafting room and stopped at my drawing table in passing and said, "I know another Miss Lawrence who is a landscape architect. She knows as much about plant material as anyone in the profession." I felt as if the mantle of the other Miss Lawrence had been thrown across my shoulders. I had never heard of her before, and I have never heard of her since; but, because of her, I felt a compulsion to study plants. I soon learned, however, that a knowledge of plant material for the South could not be got in the library, most of the literature of horticulture being for a different climate, and that I would have to grow the plants in my garden and learn about them for myself.

My ancestors were people who lived to be very old, and it encourages me to know that that I may have inherited their longevity and that I have many years ahead to see bloom in garden flowers that I have never seen in bloom before and have only just heard of.

The difficulty is not that it is too hot or too cold, or too wet or too dry, but that the changes from one extreme to the other are so frequent and so sudden.
A Southern Garden

Twenty-One Plant Facts for Gardeners in the Middle South

1. In Southern gardens, it is certainly better to use plant material adapted to mild climates than to struggle with varieties that will only thrive where the summers are cool. On the other hand, we should not be too sure that desirable plants will not grow in the South until we have given them a fair trial. Many plants that fail do so not because of the hot weather, but because they are not watered and not planted in a soil with sufficient humus. Many plants that do well in the North in full sun can be grown here if given some shade.

2. Two favorite perennials definitely not for the South are hybrid delphinium and Oriental poppies. While Chinese delphinium, especially the dwarf types, will do fairly well, other strains must be treated as annuals or biennials, and even then will be poor things compared to those grown in the North. We can console ourselves with larkspur, which reaches its perfection with us, especially since the large stock-flowering varieties have been developed. Baby's breath is also a doubtful subject for Southern flower borders, but we can substitute the charming wild spurge, *Euphorbia corollata*, which responds to cultivation when brought into the garden.

3. The controversy is still going on as to whether the French hybrid lilacs are worthwhile for the South. The general opinion seems to be that they are, if well watered and given a northern exposure. Certainly we should not give up all hope of having them, if they can be grown by taking a little extra trouble. Those who fail with them may do so because they have not given them the proper care, and not because of the exigencies of the climate. The Persian lilacs are unquestionably

the best species for the South. They have the added advantage of being free from attacks of insects and diseases. There are white and purple forms of *Syringa × persica*, and the dainty cut-leaf Persian lilac (*Syringa × persica laciniata*) [*Syringa × laciniata*] is very desirable for the fine texture of its foliage.

4. *Nandina domestica*, the heavenly bamboo of China and Japan, is hardy in the mid-South and root hardy in protected places in the Northern states. It is considered an evergreen, and no doubt it is in the far South. But in North Carolina, it sometimes drops its leaves. Nandina is a small, slender shrub resembling a bamboo in form and foliage. Its leaves turn red before they fall. The enormous bunches of brilliant red berries persist all winter and even in the spring, when they are likely to detract from the effect of early-flowering shrubs if planted too near them. Nandina will thrive in sun or partial shade. It is said to require a great deal of moisture, but it does very well for me without it. It is a favorite shrub for foundation planting, which is to be regretted when the house is of certain shades of brick.

5. As it is unquestionably the best practice for them, Southern gardeners need not take part in the arguments for and against fall planting. Here perennials planted in the spring do not have time to get established before the hot weather. November is the best month for remaking the borders and setting out most perennials because the early fall is likely to be dry. Annuals, if sown in the fall, should be sown in October or in December, not in November. I think December preferable, as the beds will be ready for the winter then and the seeds will not be disturbed.

6. About two inches of well-rotted manure and compost spread on the top of the flower beds in the fall will break down during the winter and be available for food when the plants begin their growth in the spring. In the South, many plants keep their green tops and continue to make new growth all winter. They cannot be mulched heavily, as is the practice where the ground freezes, but they need some protection against sudden freezes after very mild weather. It is a good plan to watch the weather reports and put a light covering of broom straw over the beds when a heavy freeze is predicted. This should be taken off when it turns warm again and put back when there is another sudden drop in temperature. This is not much trouble, as it will only be necessary once or twice during the winter.

7. The mimosa (*Albizia julibrissin*), a graceful tree from the Orient,

has become naturalized along the highways in the South, and is hardy to Washington. It is a perfect tree for flower gardens because its shade is too light to keep flowers and shrubs from blooming and because, being a legume, it adds nitrogen to the soil. In addition to its resistance to disease and insects,[1] it has a characteristic and interesting form, fine fern-like foliage, and delicate, silky rose or yellow flowers borne profusely in June and sparsely throughout the rest of the summer. Their tropical fragrance is delightfully refreshing on hot summer nights.

8. Roses should be pruned and given a dormant spray when the buds begin to swell. In the North this happens in March; in the South in February. They should be sprayed with a fungicide when the flower buds appear, and again when the buds show color. I don't know why the Radiance roses are so looked down upon by connoisseurs. They are certainly the best group for the South. In addition to 'Pink Radiance' and 'Red Radiance', there is the exquisite 'Mrs. Charles Bell' and the brilliant 'American Flower Guild'. The last has a slenderer bud than most of its group and is the shade of the 'American Beauty', with the same unfortunate habit of fading to a washed-out magenta. Those Southerners who are above growing these easy and satisfactory varieties will find that the 'Duchesse de Brabant', 'Killarney Queen', the 'Duchess of Wellington', 'Kardinal Piffl', and 'Antoine Rivoire' will do well for them.

9. Although the winter jasmine (*Jasminum nudiflorum*) is the only one commonly planted, there are several other species available. The winter jasmine is hardy to New York. It blooms off and on all winter and profusely in the spring. The drooping green branches give it the effect of an evergreen during the winter. It will grow anywhere, sun or shade, and in any soil. It is especially good to plant where the soil washes because the tips of the branches take root wherever they touch the ground. *Jasminum primulinum* [*Jasminum mesnyi*], blooming in May, is evergreen in the far South. *Jasminum floridum*, hardy to Maryland, blooms in the summer.

10. German iris are particularly adapted to planting in the South

---

1. When this article was written in 1936, it was not known that the mimosa is subject to mimosa wilt disease and webworms. The varieties 'Charlotte' and 'Tryon' are wilt-resistant, according to R. Gordon Halfacre, *Carolina Landscape Plants* (Raleigh, N.C.: Sparks Press, 1971), p. 192.

because the hot dry summers are needed to ripen the rhizomes. Some of the tenderer varieties, such as 'Purissima', cannot be grown in the North. Because German iris should not be watered during the summer and because they like lime, it is best to keep them out of the perennial border and give them a place to themselves. Drought-resistant annuals that are not tall enough or heavy enough to shade the rhizomes may be planted between them for summer bloom. Portulaca, California poppies, or nemophila will do very well. Immediately after the blooming period is considered the time to divide iris. However, in this climate, where it is apt to be dry at that time, the months of July, August, or September are safer. Those set out in July and August will make the best bloom the following year.

11. Northern gardeners will tell you that peonies should be set out on September the fifteenth; not the fourteenth, not the sixteenth—the fifteenth. One even goes so far as to say that peonies should be set out at nine o'clock on September the fifteenth. Since peonies must be taken up only when they are dormant, the best time for the South is the middle of October. They should not be allowed to bloom the first year after they have been divided. Late varieties will not thrive in the South. One of the best for this climate is 'Edulis Superba'. Others that will do well are 'Festiva Maxima', 'Felix Crousse', 'Baroness Shroeder', 'M. Jules Elie', 'Mikado', and 'Louis Van Houtte' [varieties of *Paeonia lactiflora*]. They should be protected from the hot afternoon sun.

12. The most important factor in gardening in the South is the length of the blooming season. We cannot have the burst of bloom that is possible in cold climates where everything comes out all at once. But we can have flowers nearly every month in the year. Usually there is one month when the gardens are bare. Some years it is November, and some years it is January. We should make the most of this long season by using late-blooming varieties of fall flowers and early-blooming varieties of spring flowers. If the seeds of *Crotalaria spectabilis*[2] are sown in June, the magnificent yellow spikes will begin to bloom the first of October and will last until late in November, unless there is an early frost. The little unidentified early trumpet narcissus that can be bought so cheaply by the bushel will bloom long before the larger, later varieties.

---

2. Since this article's publication in 1936, crotalaria has been banned from seed stores because the plant is toxic to livestock.

13. The ginger lily (*Hedychium coronarium*), an herbaceous perennial from tropical Asia, is hardy in Virginia. It is a valuable plant for the borders in late summer and fall, blooming from the middle of August until frost. The delicate, very fragrant white flowers are borne in terminal spikes. The plant is rather like a cornstalk in appearance, and the heavy tropical foliage makes a strong accent. The roots are fleshy. The ginger lily, or butterfly lily as it is sometimes called, requires a rich soil and plenty of water before blooming.

14. Cassias are invaluable for the mid-South because they withstand the summer drought and bloom gaily in September and October. The yellow, pea-shaped flowers and pale green leaves are as fresh as the spring flowers, no matter how shriveled everything else in the garden is. *Cassia marilandica* [*Senna marilandica*] grows to three or four feet. *Cassia corymbosa* [*Senna corymbosa*] is taller. Both may be used in a wide perennial border or in the shrubbery. Orange marigolds and white zinnias planted late in June will bloom in time to make a charming foreground for them.

15. I have heard various and conflicting reports as to the success of the Chinese elm [*Ulmus parvifolia*] in the South: that it is a very desirable tree and has all of the virtues claimed for it as to rapid growth and resistance to disease, or that it is not at all attractive and is so riddled by beetles and infested with disease that it has to be cut down. Of the specimens I have seen, some are fairly healthy looking, but the foliage is rather thin. Others are actually diseased. With so many disease-proof trees available, such as the ginkgo and the native elm, which are quick-growing and very attractive, I can see no need to experiment with the Chinese elm unless it proves to be of exceptional value.

16. In the mid-South where one may sit out of doors on mild days in winter, more use should be made of foliage plants. There are interesting contrasts in the fine, dark texture of the conifers, the shining leaves of the broad-leaved evergreens, and the grays and gray-greens of lavender, santolina, and rosemary. Beds edged with perennial candytuft have neat borders that are green all winter and burst into bloom on the first spring days. Ivy is especially attractive in winter. It is interesting to plant several kinds for the variety in their leaf patterns.

17. It is unfortunate that the most commonly planted summer-blooming shrub in the South should be seen most frequently in the hottest shades of magenta. Sometimes very old crape myrtles [*Lager-*

stroemia indica] are found in a soft shade of mauve that is lovely with the gray branches. Very old ones have thin foliage and beautiful bark. The salmon shades of crape myrtle are endurable if too many are not seen at once, but the white is safest. They must be planted in full sun if they are to bloom, and they need plenty of room to develop to their natural size and form.

18. The Banksia rose (*Rosa banksiae*), an evergreen climber used a great deal in the far South and hardier than is usually supposed, will grow luxuriantly in North Carolina. It drops its leaves there and is sometimes killed back in severe weather, but it will come out again. The flowers are small yellow rosettes born in clusters in April. Coming at the same time as most of the azaleas, their pale yellow is very desirable. *Rosa wichuraiana*, the memorial rose, is entirely evergreen. It has small, single, creamy-white flowers in June. The foliage is very fine and glossy.

19. Languid Southerners should fill their gardens with bulbs. All daffodils do well here, and there is an endless variety of tender bulbs that will thrive where the winters are not too severe. By planting the earliest varieties of snowdrops and crocuses and by making use of the many half-hardy fall-blooming bulbs, such as the British soldiers [or Guernsey lily] (*Nerine sarniensis*), a garden can have bloom from bulbs almost continuously from January until Thanksgiving. The various crinums bloom at different times from May until frost. There are many delightful summer-blooming alliums, and another member of the onion family, *Triteleia uniflora* [*Ipheion uniflorum*], blooms early in the spring.

20. Among the evergreen plants hardy in the mid-South are a number of useful vines. The common honeysuckle is evergreen here, but is also a strong grower and must not be used except in neglected corners. The yellow jessamine (*Gelsemium sempervirens*) is native, and may be gotten from the woods. It should be moved when it is in bloom, which is lucky, because it is inconspicuous enough when the fragrant, deep yellow flowers have faded. The southern smilax (*S. laurifolia*), also native, has black berries. *Elaeagnus pungens* var. 'Reflexa' [*E.* × *reflexa*] may also be used as a vine and is more attractive when it is climbing a tree than when it is used as a shrub. All evergreen vines will hold foliage better if fertilized.

21. In planning groups of plants to bloom together in the South, it must be remembered that our blooming dates are entirely different

from those in the North. Combinations worked out for the North can seldom be used here. As a rule, the Northern dates can be moved up a month for us, but that is not always so. In *House & Garden*'s gardening guide (November 1930), Mr. Rockwell gives April and May as the blooming season for doronicum. In my garden it blooms in March and April, but is at its best in March. The Iceland poppy, which he puts down as blooming from May to October, blooms here in the early spring and dries up when the first hot weather comes.

*The special charm
of a Southern spring is its
earliness; it is as long drawn
out as it is sweet.*
A Southern Garden

The Onset of Spring

In the South we go in quest of spring as soon as Christmas is past and the new year begins. The first days of January find us searching among the last fallen leaves for purple violets and white hyacinths and the yellow buds of winter aconite. And when we have found these frosty flowers close to the cold ground, we break off and carry into the house a few branches of Japanese quince [*Chaenomeles japonica*] with buds already swollen and ready to burst. By the time the quince buds have opened into flowers as pale as apple blossoms, their fellows in the garden may be in bloom too, if the days are warm.

Those who garden north of us wait longer for the end of winter and the delight of spring; but spring, when it comes, follows much the same pattern, and all eager gardeners will be in quest of it. Those who stay indoors until the golden flames of forsythias announce to all that spring is here will miss the first crocus (perhaps the silver and lavender of *Crocus sieberi*, perhaps the brown and gold of *C. susianus* [*C. angustifolius*]), the early blue of squills and chionodoxas, and the pleasure of being surprised by the snowdrops. No matter how closely you watch for the snowdrops, you never quite catch them on the way. One day the ground is bare, and the next time you look, the nodding buds are ready to open!

A tiny hyacinth that looks like a grape hyacinth blooms with the first little bulbs of the season. This is *Hyacinthus ciliatus* [*Bellevalia ciliata*] whose clear blue spikes repeat the blue of *Nemophila*—if I sow this lovely annual in the fall so that the first blossoms come early. At the same time (late February), there is a creamy white violet in bloom in Southern gardens. No one seems to know its name or provenience, but I advise all those interested in violets to search it out and make up to its possessors, for I know of no other sort so white or so early or so beautiful.

Late in February or early in March, the brilliant purple of *Iris reticulata* appears in the rock garden. It needs yellow for contrast, and I plant it with campernelles [*Narcissus × odorus*] and the best and earliest of the alyssums, *A. wulfenianum*, or with yellow pansies. To bloom early and close to the ground with the little bulbs, there are other precious rock plants. For blue there is blue-eyed Mary (*Omphalodes verna*); for pink, of course, the various tints of moss pink (*Phlox subulata*); and for white, *Arabis alpina*, which sometimes begins to flower with me as early as the end of January, but usually comes into bloom a month later.

Here the first daffodil to bloom is the short-stemmed pale yellow trumpet that grows in most old gardens. It comes with the crocuses and early shrubs, and has been in bloom the last days of January. But that was a season when the onset of spring ended before it seemed possible. As a rule, this little early trumpet is at its best in February, and is quickly followed by other early sorts. Mr. Wister says that it is the earliest daffodil with him, too, and that it blooms in Philadelphia late in March. With us, daffodils are in bloom by the middle of March. They bloom before the leaves are on the trees, and the shrubs that bloom with them are leafless too.

Very early in the spring, the purple-leaf plum is in flower with the saucer magnolia, Japanese quince, forsythia, and Thunberg's spirea. By this time, the common primrose is in bloom (late February or early March with us; late April in the vicinity of Boston) with perennial candytuft and black-purple pansies. Dutch hyacinths bloom with daffodils. I often wonder why they are not more generally planted. The soft tints are charming in combination with early spring flowers, and they are a welcome change from so much yellow. Late in March, the silvery blue of the hyacinth 'Electra' is delightful with pale yellow primroses of the Munstead strain and white candytuft.

When the daffodils are waning and the tulips coloring, dogwood and pearl bush, flowering almond, snowflakes, and the early white iris are at their best, and trees and trellises are dripping with purple wisteria. Then spring is in full flower with tulips, lilacs, and flowering crab-apples, followed closely by peony, iris, and mock orange.

2 : Trees & Shrubs

*Always in planting a garden
I would think first of the shrubs for it,
and my first choice in shrubs would be
the broad-leaved evergreens.*
A Southern Garden

Broad-Leaved Evergreens for the Mid-South

The chief beauty of Southern gardens is in the broad-leaved evergreens. Coming from southern Europe and the Orient, or native from Maryland and Virginia to Florida, many of them are tender. But plants considered tender are often hardier than is supposed. Some of the broad-leaved evergreens grown in the far South can be grown in the mid-South; many of those grown in the mid-South are hardy to New York or even New England.

I am always discovering to my surprise how hardy broad-leaved evergreens are; that *Mahonia japonica* [probably *M. bealei*] is grown in the Arnold Arboretum, gardenias in Williamsburg, and camellias in Norfolk, Virginia. A nurseryman in south Georgia says that *Azalea indica* [*Rhododendron indicum*] cannot be grown farther north than his nursery, but I find it doing well in a northern exposure in North Carolina and have read that it is perfectly hardy in Charlottesville, Virginia.

Again, I find the pineapple guava (*Feijoa sellowiana*) [*Acca sellowiana*], usually grown only in Florida or southern California, listed by a nurseryman in the Piedmont section of North Carolina. It is interesting to note that evergreens with narrow, thin leaves are more apt to be hardy than those with broad, thick leaves. The bayberry (*Myrica caroliniensis*) [*Myrica pennsylvanica*], for instance, is native from Nova Scotia to Florida, while *Magnolia grandiflora* is native only in the far South.

Although some of these broad-leaved evergreens can be grown in New England, many are hardy only to Washington. Often those that can be grown in the North do not reach their full height there or grow as luxuriantly as they do in sections where the winters are not so severe. Here in the mid-South, where they are at their best, they are not nearly so well known or so widely planted as they should be. We persist in planting such shrubs as arborvitae [*Thuja*], which do well in the North, but are not at their best in a climate where the summers are long and hot and dry. Broad-leaved evergreens are the most desirable of all ornamental plants. All of them are valuable for their persistent foliage, and many of them for brilliant flowers, or decorative fruits, or both.

In the mid-South where the weather is often mild enough to allow one to be out of doors most of the winter, evergreen foliage is especially important. Broad-leaved evergreens vary widely in size, form, and texture: from the slender leaves and drooping branches of the cotoneasters to the coarse foliage and imposing mass of photinia. There is variety, too, in the color of their foliage: the bronzed or silvered leaves of the elaeagnus, the yellow-green of ruscus, the scarlet-tipped branches of photinia, the dull, very dark foliage of the tea olive, and the high polish on the leaves of pittosporum.

The group of evergreens most commonly planted for their foliage is the Japanese privets. Easily grown and not overly particular as to soil so long as they are in the sun, they are desirable as specimen shrubs and for hedges. When they were first brought to this country, the labels of *Ligustrum lucidum* and *L. japonicum* were mixed. As the nurseries still list *L. lucidum* as *L. japonicum*, and vice versa, it is wise to order them from their descriptions rather than their names.

L. lucidum, so often used for foundation planting, is much too large and coarse for that purpose. It will grow to the second story, and two plants will entirely cover a small house. Usually it is allowed to do this, and then cut back so severely that its characteristic form is lost. Given room to grow to its full size, it is a very handsome shrub. It grows fast, and is the best evergreen to make a tall screen to shut out unattractive views. But it must have sunlight and be well fertilized to grow luxuriantly. In the shade its foliage is sparse and sickly.

I once saw *L. lucidum* used effectively to enclose a garden. Set about fifteen feet apart, they were close enough to come together to make a screen but not too close to spoil the shape of the individual shrubs. These privets were the pride of the man of the house, who told me that he kept them shapely and luxuriant by topping them once a year and fertilizing them with tobacco stems. In the summer they formed a proper background for the simple little garden; and in the winter, with their lustrous foliage and heavy bunches of large blue-black berries, they were beautiful in themselves.

Ligustrum japonicum is a round symmetrical shrub of medium height. Not so tall or spreading as *L. lucidum*, it has a finer texture and a much more compact form. It has glossy dark green foliage and bunches of dark blue berries in winter. *L. japonicum* var. *rotundifolium* [*L. japonicum* 'Rotundifolium'] (listed in some catalogues as *L. coriaceum*) is an angular shrub with stiff curly leaves. Too exotic for general use, it is desirable only in a place where a plant with striking individuality is needed. *L. lucidum* is hardy to Washington, and I have read that *L. japonicum* can be grown in Baltimore.

L. nepalense [*L. indicum*] has smaller leaves than those of the Japanese privets. *L. japonicum* may be used for foundation planting against a large building, or even against a small one if it is kept pruned from the time it is planted and never allowed to get too big. *L. nepalense* is better for planting around a small house. When buying evergreen privets, plants grown from cuttings should be selected, as the species do not come true from seed.

A more choice shrub than the Japanese privets is the beautiful *Pittosporum tobira* used so much in Charleston and hardier much farther north, at least along the coastal plain. Its characteristically square form and the way its dark leaves cluster at the ends of the stems give it marked individuality. Of very slow growth, it makes a most desirable specimen shrub for the discriminating and patient. It is also used for clipped hedges; I remember a very beautiful one in Charleston.

Another choice broad-leaved evergreen, desirable for its glossy foliage, is the Carolina cherry laurel (*Laurocerasus caroliniana*) [*Prunus caroliniana*], native from North Carolina southward. It is a slight, graceful shrub when grown in the shade and after many years becomes a slender tree. Grown in the open it is a well-rounded bush. It stands shearing well and can be had in standard form for formal planting. The small dark blue fruits are attractive but not very striking. The English laurel, *Laurocerasus officinalis* [*Prunus laurocerasus*], has a much coarser texture and is more spreading than the cherry laurel. It is recommended for planting in the South, but I have found it very apt to become diseased.

Butcher's-broom (*Ruscus aculeatus*), a curious spreading shrub from southern Europe known in the North by the dried, artificially colored branches used in funeral wreaths, is hardy in the mid-South. The foliage consists of leafless branches with spiny tips. It is a dull yellow-green, but the new growth in the spring is as shiny as if it were lacquered. The leaves are small bracts growing on the branches. The red berries are said to persist during the winter. I have never seen a plant with berries, probably because both sexes were not planted (the flowers are dioecious).

Low and sprawling in habit, butcher's-broom rarely grows to more than three feet. It is suitable for planting in front of taller shrubs and useful (because of its sharp spines) to discourage walking up a terrace or cutting across a lawn. It is suitable, also, for foundation planting.

The Japanese oleasters can be grown only in the South, although most of the deciduous species are hardy in the North. Of the two evergreen species, *Elaeagnus pungens* and *E. macrophylla*, only the first is common in trade. *Elaeagnus pungens* is not striking in form or texture. Its distinction lies in the foliage, the leaves being dark green and smooth on top and silvery with brown scales beneath. The inconspicuous creamy white flowers blooming in January are heavily and pervasively fragrant. The red fruits are edible. They are not as decorative as those of the deciduous species. *E. pungens* 'Fruitlandii' is considered one of the best varieties. *E. pungens* 'Reflexa' [*E.* × *reflexa*] is climbing. It will make a dense evergreen screen on a wire fence and is often grown on trees. Simon's oleaster (*E. pungens* 'Simonii') blooms in November and fruits in March. The oleasters are at their best in the sun, but they grow very well in shade and under trees.

The tea olives [*Osmanthus*] are among the largest and most imposing of the broad-leaved evergreens. Their small white flowers are inconspicuous, but very profuse and delightfully fragrant. They are cool and delicate against the dark coriaceous foliage. Tea olives will grow in the shade, but they need to be in an open sunny position to develop to their full beauty. Fortune's tea olive (*Osmanthus* × *fortunei*) makes a large round shrub, twenty feet or more in height, and with an equal spread. The dark holly-like foliage is very distinctive. It blooms both spring and fall.

O. aquifolium [*O. heterophyllus*] is similar to the tea olive. The sweet olive (*O. fragrans*) has large round glossy leaves, is more columnar in form than the other two, and taller, growing to thirty feet. It blooms in the fall and all winter. Devil-wood (*O. americanus*), native from North Carolina to Florida, is a graceful shrub, not very compact, and with foliage of a rather faded green.

Photinia serrulata [*P. serratifolia*] is another massive evergreen, much too large for foundation planting, for which it is most frequently used. It has a coarse texture, and its form is not interesting unless it is allowed to grow to its full size. Then it is a handsome shrub, especially in the spring when it is covered with large corymbs of white flowers. The scarlet leaves of the new growth make the foliage interesting.

In addition to the year-round effectiveness of their foliage, so many broad-leaved evergreens have exquisite flowers. Blooming at various times during the year, there are some for every season. By planting both *Camellia sasanqua*, which blooms before Christmas, and *C. japonica*, which blooms after Christmas, one may have their flowers until it is time for *Viburnum tinus* (*V. laurustinus*), one of the most charming of flowering evergreens. This evergreen viburnum from the Mediterranean is often used as a greenhouse plant in the North, but is hardy out of doors in the mid-South. Its delicate and fragrant arbutus-like flowers, bright pink in the bud and creamy white when open, appear in March in North Carolina and even earlier further south. It is a medium-sized shrub, suitable for small gardens in which the heavy tea olive and coarse photinia would be out of scale. It is suitable also for foundation planting.

Following *Viburnum tinus* [laurustinus], one may have *Zenobia*, which blooms in May. It is a semi-evergreen from the Southern shrub bogs hardy to Massachusetts. Closely allied to andromeda, it was named *Zenobia* for a queen who is supposed to have met the fate, similar to Andromeda's, of being chained up to await a monster. Because the beautiful clusters of nodding white flowers produce little nectar, its common name, honey-cup, is equally inappropriate.

There are two species, *Z. pulverulenta* and *Z. pulverulenta nuda* (*forma nitida*) [forms no longer recognized botanically], the former being more common in the Southern bogs. The foliage of *Z. pulverulenta* is distinguished by the white bloom on the underside of the leaf. Zenobia is a low shrub, from two to four feet, with arched branches. It is very desirable in cultivation, and easily grown if it is given partial shade and some moisture. Belonging to the *Ericaceae*, it has the same cultural requirements as andromeda and pieris.

Among the flowering broad-leaved evergreens, the one most frequently planted, *Abelia × grandiflora*, is entirely too common. It has little to recommend it in form and foliage, and all that can be said of the small, pale flowers is that they bloom profusely all summer. Abelias are hardy to Philadelphia, and even farther with protection.

There are several more desirable evergreen shrubs blooming in the summer. The cape jasmine (*Gardenia florida*) [*G. augusta*] is hardy along the coast, at least to Virginia. In North Carolina the foliage sometimes gets scalded in severe winters, but I always find baskets full of the fragrant, waxy white flowers at market in June.

Motoring late in the afternoon in midsummer, one comes to a dip in the road where there is a sudden coolness perfumed with the illusive fragrance of the sweet-bay (*Magnolia glauca*) [*M. virginiana*]. This graceful small tree, native to our swamps, should be seen more frequently in our gardens.

Another native evergreen flowering in midsummer is the loblolly bay (*Gordonia lasianthus*). It is native only along the coast, but I see it listed by a nursery in the North Carolina mountains, so I think it must be hardier than its habitat indicates. The flowers of the loblolly bay look like magnolias, but it is a member of the tea family. The globular white buds are as attractive as the open blossom. It is said to be hard to transplant from the woods, but I think nursery grown stock would grow in cultivation without difficulty.

The tea plant (*Thea bohea*) [*Camellia sinensis*] blooms in September and October. The lovely white flowers, cup-shaped with crinkled petals and numerous yellow stamens, resemble the improved varieties of mock orange. They come out a few at a time and make a charming pattern with the round buds, some nearly ready to burst into bloom and some still tight greenish balls. The tea plant is a graceful shrub if it is allowed to grow in its natural, rather open habit and not sheared back to a formless lump. It is especially valuable because it not only tolerates shade but likes it, and there are so few blooming plants for shady places.

Many of the shrubs most conspicuous for their berries are among the broad-leaved evergreens. The berries seem more brilliant against the lustrous green foliage. There is an interesting variation in the color of the berries of the different evergreens and in their characteristic habits of growth. Some are borne in heavy, terminal clusters, as those of the mahonias, others in corymbs as on the cotoneasters, and still others, as those of the yaupon, cover the entire branch.

The gay oranges and yellows and reds are in harmony with most of the fall colors, but the berries of many begin to show color in the late summer and should not be planted in groups of summer-blooming shrubs such as crape-myrtle or buddleia, whose flowers are on the magenta side. One must be cautious, too, in using them for foundation planting against any but white or gray buildings. The orange berries of the firethorns are disastrous with some shades of brick. Aucubas are fairly safe because their foliage is so heavy in proportion to the number of berries.

The firethorns [*Pyracantha*] are the most striking of the evergreen shrubs desirable for their berries. In the fall and winter, their great branches are entirely covered with brilliant orange or scarlet or yellow berries. There are two types of firethorns—the spreading ones that grow to a medium height and the tall erect forms that grow to twenty-five feet. *Pyracantha coccinea*, the hardiest of the tall forms, can be grown in Massachusetts in sheltered positions. *P. coccinea* 'Lalandei' is handsomer and more vigorous than the type.

The tall firethorns may be grown against walls. *P. crenulata* is tenderer than *P. coccinea*, and handsomer. *P. yunnanensis* [*P. crenatoserrata*] is the spreading type. Firethorns should be propagated from cuttings as the seedlings are sterile.

Although some of the evergreen cotoneasters can be grown in Massachusetts (*Cotoneaster horizontalis* is hardy at the Arnold Arboretum, but is semi-evergreen there), the tender varieties can be grown only in the South. Among these the handsomest of the taller varieties, *C. salicifolius* var. *floccosus*, is hardy at least as far north as Philadelphia. A graceful shrub with sweeping branches, it is one of the best cotoneasters for the South. It has corymbs of white flowers in the spring, followed in the fall by bunches of small red berries that are most attractive against the long narrow leaves that give this shrub its common name, the willow-leaved cotoneaster.

Aucuba is hardy as far north as Washington, and even farther with protection. Its wide coarsely-toothed leaves give it an exotic appearance. The enormous bright red berries are as shiny as patent leather. It is well to remember that Aucubas are dioecious, if they are grown for their berries. *Aucuba japonica*, an erect shrub to eight feet, has foliage of a very beautiful green. The popular variegated form looks as if it had had paint spilled on the leaves. When I see it in a foundation planting, I always look again to be sure that the painters haven't been careless. Aucubas need partial shade and some moisture. They are recommended for city planting as they are impervious to smoke and gas.

Euonymus patens [*E. kiautschovicus*], a luxuriant, spreading shrub loaded in the fall with fruits showing pendant orange seeds, is hardy to Massachusetts with protection. It will climb with support. *E. ja-*

ponicus, more erect and formal with very dark glossy foliage, is less desirable than *E. patens* because it is subject to scale. *E. radicans* 'Vegetus' [*E. fortunei* var. *vegetus*; *E. fortunei* 'Vegetus'], a useful dwarf evergreen, will also climb if given support and may be trained against a wall. The foliage of *E. fortunei* 'Coloratus' turns brilliantly scarlet in the fall.

Mahonia japonica [probably *M. bealei*], one of the handsomest of the broad-leaved evergreens, has interesting holly-like foliage. It is a tall shrub, and is particularly valuable for the panicles of bright yellow flowers in January, followed by dark blue berries. *Mahonia aquifolium* is more dwarf in habit.

According to Bailey, *Ilex opaca* and *I. glabra* are the only species of evergreen hollies hardy in the North. *I. glabra*, native from Massachusetts to Florida, is called inkberry in the North and gallberry in the South. Both names are appropriate, as the berries are very black and very bitter. The small white flowers are valuable for their honey. Another holly that should be seen more often in cultivation here is the yaupon (*I. vomitoria*), native from Virginia to Florida. The small, translucent red berries, clustered so thickly on the branches, are all the more conspicuous because they are not hidden by the narrow leaves.

These are only the more obvious of the broad-leaved evergreens that can be grown successfully in the mid-South. There are countless others, both foreign and native, for the gardens of those Southerners who are willing to experiment.

*In any season the flowering shrubs
make the garden, but they are particularly
important at the end of the year when they are
most necessary and least familiar.*
A Southern Garden

Here Are Blossoms for Southern Evergreens

Whenever I think of flowers for the South, whether shrubs or bulbs or perennials, I think in terms of continuous bloom, for the opportunity to have something flowering out-of-doors at all times is the great pleasure of gardening in a mild climate. The broad-leaved evergreens are beautiful throughout the year, even when they do not produce conspicuous flowers; furthermore, in addition to the perennial beauty of glossy foliage, there are species to bloom in every season.

Unless you have a very big place, there is a limit to the number of shrubs that can be cultivated; and it is all the more important, since evergreens should be an investment for a lifetime, to choose them with an eye to bloom in more than one season. In my own garden, I have always kept sequence of bloom in mind; and whenever I acquire a new shrub, I first consider whether it will bloom at the time when it is most needed. I also consider its eventual size because many of the broad-leaved evergreens are extremely slow growing but eventually grow to be massive plants fifteen or more feet high and as many through.

As you drive through Southern towns, you see any number of small houses completely overgrown by coarse, leggy Japanese privets. This is because the owners were not willing to buy from the nurseryman a small size of a low shrub but preferred a small size of a large shrub for the same price. When it was planted, the specimen was already the proper size for the place where it was to grow, and very soon it became far too big for it.

One of the delightful low-growing evergreens that could be used to advantage in situations that a large shrub would soon outgrow is the mountain andromeda [fetter bush], *Pieris floribunda*, a native of our own mountains but very seldom planted in this part of the country. In fact, I remember having seen it in cultivation only in the gardens at Duke University and in my own garden, although it is one of the favorite evergreens in the North and Miss Jekyll mentions it frequently in her descriptions of her English woodland. It makes a spreading plant of not more than two to five or six feet in height, and there are few dwarf evergreens that make such a dense, compact, well-rounded growth and are so little susceptible to insect pests and disease. The small, oval, dark green leaves are mottled beneath. The buds form in the fall and make a winter ornament as they wait through the cold weather for the first warm days to bring them into bloom.

In my garden, the first flowers open early in March, not so early as those of the Asiatic species, *P. japonica*, which comes in February—but still ahead of most of the spring-flowering shrubs. The flowers are nodding white urns that grow in upright panicles at the ends of the branches. The shrub will bloom better if the flowers are snipped as they fade. The mountain andromeda thrives in a light, well-drained soil in sun or partial shade. Like the other heaths, it requires an acid soil, humus, and moisture. It is very slow growing.

Later in the spring comes one of the most beautiful of the flowering evergreens, the banana-shrub, *Michelia fuscata* [*Michelia figo*], sometimes listed as *Magnolia fuscata*. It belongs to the magnolia family, and the small creamy flowers are like miniature magnolias, but they smell like ripe bananas. They measure an inch and a half across, and the edges of the petals are picoted in carmine. This shrub comes from China, and the only reference that I have found to its hardiness is Dr. Nehrling's statement that it will not survive farther north than North Carolina. All I know from experience is that it is hardy in Raleigh.

The most beautiful specimens that I have seen are a pair at Orton Plantation in Wilmington [North Carolina]. They are compact but spreading shrubs, branching from the ground and at least fifteen feet tall. In Florida, the banana-shrub blooms as early as February or March, but with me not until April or even May. The twelfth of April is the earliest date that I have for it. This evergreen does well even in fairly deep shade and flowers to a certain extent, but it blooms better in part shade or sun. It likes a rich well-drained soil and is not hard to grow.

When spring is over and the hot weather takes its toll of the borders, we will not be without flowering evergreens. Among the many that take summer for their season of bloom is our loblolly bay, *Gordonia lasianthus*. Although it grows only along the coast and ranges only from Virginia to Florida and Louisiana, it is plentiful in that section, making great trees in the swamps and small ones in the thickets along the roadsides. Its one drawback is the difficulty in getting it established in gardens (and I must admit to several failures myself), but it can be done. This is a discouraging trait of another fine summer-flowering tree, *Stewartia ovata*, the summer "dogwood" of our mountain districts, also a member of the tea family but not an evergreen.

In culture the loblolly bay is usually shrubby, though it sometimes attains tree-like proportions, especially in the far South. It is pyramidal in shape and branches from the ground. The leaves may be four or five inches long, dark and lustrous, and the old ones turn a brilliant red in winter. It blooms first in July with several sets of flowers during the summer, and I have known it to flower in Wilmington [North Carolina] as late as October. The round white buds like enormous pearls are as lovely as the wide, fragrant white flowers. The flowers are cupped. They measure three or four inches across and are similar to those of the other native gordonia, the deciduous *G. alatamaha* [*Franklinia alatamaha*]. Like other members of the tea family, the loblolly bay needs a moist acid soil mixed with leaf mold, and plenty of water and a deep mulch in summer.

The tea plant itself, *Thea sinensis* [*Camellia sinensis*], is one of the most satisfactory evergreens in that very exceptional family. It blooms early in September and continues until frost blackens the flowers. When the weather warms up again, more buds come out. Today, the fifth of December, as I was driving through the neighborhood, I saw a tea plant—a small one not over two feet high—blooming serenely in spite of two days of cold rain and wind; farther south it blooms all winter. The buds are round like gordonia buds, and the sweet-scented flowers are pleasantly cupped and filled with golden water-lily-like stamens.

The flowers of the tea plant are almost two-and-a-half inches across. In Georgia and South Carolina, it grows to twenty feet; and it may be that it would grow that tall here in time, but I have never seen one over four or five feet in North Carolina. One that I have had for ten years is not over four feet, but it is in dry, poor soil under an oak. It blooms there very well, but would bloom even better if I had a place for it in good soil where it would get some sun. The tea plant has a number of varieties, but the tea of commerce is made only from this species. I would have no idea how to go about preparing the leaves for brewing, but I always feel that it could be done and that having a tea plant in your garden would be something like growing your own herbs.

This brings us to winter. There are a number of fine evergreens that flower in the mid-South in winter, but the sweet olive, *Osmanthus fragrans*, is outstanding. This is a very large but slow-growing shrub that should be planted only where there is space for it to develop to its full size. It is an Asiatic species that grows to thirty feet in its own country, but here it is not more than fifteen; and it is not as widespread as the decorative holly-leaved tea olive, *Osmanthus × fortunei*, which is a hybrid between the sweet olive and sweet holly, *Osmanthus ilicifolius* [*O. heterophyllus*]. These three osmanthus all bloom in fall and winter and are often confused.

The leaves of the sweet olive are oval and entire, while those of the tea olive are large and holly-like, and those of the sweet holly are small, holly-like, and very spiny. The sweet olive begins to bloom in September, and from then on through the winter the small white flowers perfume the air on warm days. It is said to be hardy as far north as Washington, D.C.; and here in North Carolina, it will grow at least as far west as Statesville.

> *To those who do not like to make an effort in hot weather, a well-considered collection—with the addition of a flowering tree or so—would bring an abundance of bloom, and grateful shade, too, during these trying months.*
> A Southern Garden

Pinckneya pubens

Caroline Dormon said she wished I could be at Briarwood when the pinckneya bloomed by the pond. "No use to give you one," she said, "for it comes from swamps and would not grow in your dry garden." But it does grow in my dry garden and has grown there for ten years and has bloomed for eight of them. My pinckneya is one of two small plants that Mr. Crayton let me have when I happened to visit him after one of his collecting trips. The other plant died, but this cannot be a difficult thing to grow, for the roots were bare and after traveling from Florida to Biltmore, they came on down to Charlotte to be set out in the heat of early summer.

Several trunks are usual, but mine has only one, and it would be a shapely small tree by now if it had not met with an accident in early youth. The leader was cut off eighteen inches from the ground. The plant recovered slowly and has now reached a height of about ten feet. In the swamps it reaches twenty-five.

Pinckneya comes into bloom the last week in May or the first week in June, and is in its glory for a month or more. The clusters of tubular flowers that look as if they were cut from fine, cream-colored felt, are set off by an occasional enlargement of the calyx-lobe that looks like a leaf and turns a clear, bright pink that is a tint of spectrum red and very near the carmine 21/2 of the Royal Horticultural Society's color chart.

The flowers are followed by rather decorative green-gold fruits, to three quarters of an inch in diameter. These hang on for a year before they split and drop their winged seeds. The large oval, light green leaves take on warm apricot tones in October.

Mr. Hohman told me several years ago that at Kingsville, Maryland, he had one four-year-old pinckneya that had never bloomed. This, mine, and Caroline Dormon's are the only cultivated plants that I have known about. It seems to me too bad that we are not making use of one of our most beautiful native trees, especially as it seems to be easily propagated. Cuttings of mature wood are said to strike in sand under a hand glass. Seedlings need rich moist soil and shade, and the trees need some shade. Mine did much better before I lost a sheltering pine.

In spite of its restricted range, along the coast from southern South Carolina to Florida, pinckneya is well enough known to have several common names, such as maiden's blushes, calico bush, and Georgia bark. It is also called bitter-bark and fever tree because the bark has been used as a substitute for quinine.

> But the butcher's-broom is one of the most reliable
> shrubs for troublesome places. It will grow in the driest
> places, even under trees, and in all degrees of shade. It does
> need a good mulch of cow manure in the fall.
> A Southern Garden

Butcher's-Broom—*Ruscus aculeatus*

I suppose it is because it takes forever to grow to any size that the butcher's-broom, *Ruscus aculeatus*, is not in the trade. The only nursery that I know of that lists it is Monrovia in Azusa, California. There used to a be a lot of it in our Raleigh garden. It was there when the garden became ours in 1916, but the plants were so small that no one paid any attention to them until, suddenly, not long before we left Raleigh in 1948, we realized what nice clumps they had become and how very useful they were under the big oak trees that surrounded the garden. By that time, the clumps had reached a height of at least three feet, or it seems to me a little more, and were still increasing in width.

Butcher's-broom is a native of the Mediterranean region, but also it occurs in the south of England where it goes by a number of country names, though commonly called butcher's-broom. Parkinson says butchers used the stiff branches to sweep out their stalls, and I have read elsewhere that they tied them up with the meat to discourage rats and bats. Names such as knee holly and prickly box are derived from the needle pointed cladodes that serve as leaves, and the plant is called Jew's-myrtle because it is supposed to have provided material for the crown of thorns.

Butcher's-broom is not a true shrub because the stiff green stalks that shoot up from the roots are never truly woody. When young and tender they are even edible, which is not surprising because the genus belongs to the asparagus branch of the Lily family. The flowers on the cladodes are so tiny that no one not looking for them would know that the plant is in bloom; the berries are the size of small marbles and very conspicuous as they turn from shining green to shining red. The plants we had in Raleigh must have been all male, for they never fruited in all those years. *Ruscus* is mostly dioecious, but in his book *My Garden in Autumn and Winter*, E. A. Bowles describes a monoecious form of *R. aculeatus* with both male and female flowers on the same plant and a hermaphrodite form with perfect flowers [*R. aculeatus hermaphrodite*]. Seeds of the latter come true. Plants grown from seed sent from England by Clarence Elliott are now fruiting in my garden in Charlotte [North Carolina]. They were sown at least six years ago, maybe more, and now the plants are still less than a foot tall, but they have been bearing for three seasons. I even found two little seedlings under one of them.

Last fall I sent a slice of the biggest plant to Mr. Freeland for his garden in Columbia, South Carolina, and he sent me a slice of the variety 'Angustifolia' [*R. aculeatus* var. *angustifolus*], which had come to him from the U.S. Department of Agriculture. The linear cladodes, mostly less than an eighth of an inch across and less than three-quarters of an inch long, are well budded, and I hope—with the aid of Mr. Bowles, who goes into the matter thoroughly—that in the spring I can determine the sex of the flowers.[1] Whether it berries or not, the narrow-leaved form is a distinctive and utterly charming plant. I shall be interested to see whether it gets to be as big as the type—that is if I live long enough, which is doubtful if it grows as slowly as the others have done.

I am equally charmed with *Ruscus hypoglossum*, recently acquired from the Oakhurst Nursery. This is a much smaller plant than the butcher's-broom and new to me though known to English gardeners since the sixteenth century. Bean gives it a height of between eight and eighteen inches. The leaves are much larger, to an inch and a half wide, and more than four inches long, but the berries are smaller. Bean says it rarely fruits, but even so, it is one of the nicest low evergreens that I have found.

Both species are among the best groundcovers for growing under trees and in the densest shade. I have read that butcher's-broom will grow in full sun. It may, but I have a a feeling that in sun the stems and foliage would lack the quality that makes them so pleasing throughout the year—the myrtle green coloring.

---

1. The editors of *The American Horticultural Magazine* added the following note here when this article was published in 1963: "The variety 'Angustifolia' is male. The mother plant at the Chenault Nursery, Orleans, France, is about 3 feet tall and was procured from the neighboring forest."

*And still the rows of little trees on the North
Carolina mountainside must go to England to be appreciated,
for few people are moved by a written description to go out
and buy a plant and put it in their garden.*
A Southern Garden (*in reference to* Gordonia alatamaha)

Some Trees and Shrubs of the Southeast

For many years I have tried to grow all of the available flowering trees and shrubs native to our area, but not always with success, for some of the most beautiful kinds are difficult at best, especially in a small garden where conditions do not meet their needs.

A tree that I have never been able to establish is the mountain stewartia, *Stewartia ovata*, though I read of it in Northern gardens where it blooms in July and is hardy to Zone 5. (All references to hardiness are taken from Dr. Wyman.) *Stewartia malacodendron* of the coastal plain is hardy to Zone 7. Although it has a name for being difficult in cultivation, I have known of it in several Southern gardens near places where it grows naturally, and I have seen it in bloom in the woods in early May. The flowers are creamy white with wine-colored stamens. I measured flowers four inches across, and the tallest tree I saw was twelve feet. For a long time there was no source for this species, but it is in the recent catalogues of the Tingle Nursery Company in Pittsville, Maryland.

Yellowwood, *Cladrastis lutea*, is a large tree of the high mountains of North Carolina and Tennessee that is hardy to Zone 2. The only time I have ever seen a mature specimen in full flower was at the Brooklyn Botanic Garden late in May. The small pea-shaped flowers are pearly white with bright green calices. They are loosely strung in slender, delicate racemes—more beautiful even than white wisteria. Unfortunately, it is not a tree that blooms freely when young. I knew of one that bloomed a little after seven years, but I have read that they do not bloom well until fifteen or twenty years old. Mine has been growing in the garden for twelve years and has produced one small panicle so far. In the meantime, it has grown to a height of twenty-five feet, with an almost equal spread; and if it gets to fifty feet, as *Hortus Second* says it does, it will take up most of my garden. It is a graceful tree with a dark trunk (double from about three feet from the ground) and dark branches and large compound leaves that are bright green in spring and bright yellow in fall. The tree is called yellowwood because a yellow dye is extracted from the hard wood. It comes from limestone country and rich, moist mountain slopes, but seems to adapt itself to any soil, even a dry one.

The clammy locust, *Robinia viscosa*, is another member of the pea family that is endemic to the high mountains of the Carolinas and Tennessee, and hardy to Zone 3. It is a delightful little tree with fine leaves and short racemes to three inches long of mallow-pink flowers. In my garden it grew to twelve feet the first summer and must have been from fifteen to twenty feet tall when it was crowded out by some bamboo eight years later. It bloomed profusely the first of May and again very freely in July and August. If the suckering can be controlled, I cannot imagine a more pleasing tree. If left to itself, it makes a thicket.

Robinia kelseyi (hardy to Zone 5) is a formless short of shrub to something like twelve feet tall, but probably less. I planted it under a pine tree, and in April the phlox-pink flowers were so pretty that I left it until it had almost taken over, and then I had a time getting rid of it. I can't see that it is superior to *Robinia hispida*, and is equally invasive. Both bloom such a short time and are not at all attractive when out of bloom.

One of our best contributions to gardens is a pair of shrubby horse-chestnuts, *Aesculus parviflora*, the bottlebrush buckeye, and *A. pavia*, the red buckeye. Both have conspicuous flowers and deep green palmately divided leaves. *A. parviflora* is another shrub that suckers freely, but the suckers stay close to the plant instead of wandering over the garden. The shrub is usually not more than six feet tall, but it increases a little in girth each year and can spread to a width of 15 feet or more. It blooms in my garden about the middle of June and a month later in the North. Creamy sixteen-inch spikes of long-stamened flowers stand above the foliage like enormous candles, or like foxtail lilies. I don't know how hardy *A. pavia* is, but mine came from Kingsville, Maryland, and I see by the *Plant Buyer's Guide* that it is grown in nurseries on Long Island, in Connecticut, and in Cincinnati, Ohio. Mine was sent out as the variety 'Humulis', which is described as very low, almost prostrate at times, but in fourteen years it has grown to a height of ten feet and is more of a tree than a shrub. It blooms for about three weeks in late April and early May. The eugenia-red flowers are in erect panicles to ten inches long. Children and livestock are poisoned by eating buckeyes, but chipmunks carry mine off, and Indians are said to like them roasted.

Hydrangea quercifolia is another shrub handsome in flower and leaf. It is easily grown and will stand considerable shade, but it is native to the far South and is not dependable for flowering north of New York, though it is root hardy to New England. It blooms here in late May.

When I planted the silver-leaf hydrangea, *H. radiata* [*H. arborescens* ssp. *radiata*] of the Carolina mountains many years ago, it died without flowering, and I have not been able to try it again as it is not in the trade at present. Mrs. Lounsberry says the mountain people call it ninebark because the park peels off in layers.

One spring I happened to be in Asheville when Mr. Crayton, an old mountaineer who knows every leaf and blade from Virginia to Florida, had just come back from a collecting trip, and he let me have a small plant of *Pinckneya pubens* dug from the margin of a Georgia swamp. I did not suppose that it would live in my dry garden, but it did, and in three years it grew to five feet tall and began to bloom. For the next ten years it bloomed beautifully, but for the last two, whether it is suffering from the loss of a sheltering pine or from unusually severe winters, or both, the flowers and foliage have been sparse. The beauty of the tree is in the enlarged calyx lobes, which are sometimes three inches long, though usually less, and of a bright clear pink. They begin to color the last week in May or early in June while the small speckled flowers are still in bud, and they are effective to about six weeks. The leaves are large, to seven inches long, and of a bright calla green in summer and golden yellow in fall. I don't know how hardy pinckneya is, but Mr. Hohman told me some time ago that a small plant had wintered at Kingsville. Since it has grown so long in my garden under the least favorable conditions, I should think it would be worthwhile to try it in rich, moist soil and part shade at least as far north as Baltimore.

The foam-climber, *Decumaria barbara*, grows in swamps with pinckneya and tupelo and cypress, and it also grows on a wall in my garden in a very dry place, though it would appreciate a damp one. It is evergreen on the Gulf Coast, and might be here in a favorable situation, but mine loses its leaves in midwinter. The leaves are large and lustrous ovals to five inches long and of a bright yellow green. Small creamy flowers in frothy corymbs come into bloom the latter part of May. *Decumaria* is said to be hardy to Boston, but I should think, where it is at all doubtful, it would be better to plant its relative, *Hydrangea petiolaris*, instead. For the South it is a handsome vine, climbing up aerial rootlets to thirty feet on trees, but on the garden wall it has become shrubby.

Two more or less evergreen shrubs of the evergreen shrub bog will grow in drier places. Titi (or leatherwood), *Cyrilla racemiflora*, is a tree to thirty-five feet in the Pocosins, but in my very dry garden it has grown to little more than six feet. I thought it would be valuable because it blooms in July, but the narrow racemes of white flowers are rather dingy. They are something like those of the sweet pepperbush, only not fragrant and not so pretty—especially not so pretty as *Clethra acuminata*, a species of the Southern mountains, which also blooms in July. Titi leaves turn red in the fall, and sometimes in the garden they persist through the winter and are still pretty in January. Titi is said to be hardy to Zone 5. Mine came from Kingsville, and it is listed in the current catalogue of the Upper Bank Nurseries, Media, Pennsylvania.

In cultivation the loblolly bay, *Gordonia lasianthus*, does not grow to be a large tree as it does in swamps. Those I have seen in gardens are slender shrubs. I have learned that they need shade. One lived for some years in my garden and bloomed all through July and August and again in the fall; and in the winter there were always a few bright red leaves. The large round buds are as pretty as the silky white flowers, which are nearly four inches wide and very like those of the *Stewartias* (their relatives), but with more substance. *Gordonias* are extremely difficult to transplant, and I have been successful only with plants grown in containers.

Poison bay, *Illicium floridanum*, comes from the swamps of Florida and the Gulf States, but is hardy in Zone 7. It will grow in dry soil, but in my garden, it is the first plant to wilt in dry weather. As soon as I see its leaves dropping, I begin to water. The leaves are aromatic, but the many-petalled, oxblood-red flowers are fetid. Their scent gives it the name of wet-dog tree. In the *Mississippi Market Bulletin*, *Illicium floridanum* is advertised as "red magnolia."

Leucothoë populifolia, also from the Florida swamps, adapts itself perfectly to dry shady situations, and is one of the best evergreens in my garden, where it is a shrub to six or eight feet with an equal spread. In late May the slender arching branches are crowded with cylindrical flowers that look like tiny milk-glass bottles beneath the neat double rows of narrow acuminate leaves. The shrub is sometimes called pipewood because the hollow stems are used for pipestems. *Leucothoë populifolia* is less hardy than *L. fontanesiana*, but it must be satisfactory at least as far north as Pennsylvania as it is listed by the Upper Bank Nurseries.

I try so many native plants in my own garden without ever hearing what they do in other parts of the country. I should like very much to hear from anyone who grows these, or other Southern plants, or who knows what they do in other parts of the country.

3 : Bulbs

> *The spot where the bulbs are
> planted should be marked so that
> they will not be disturbed when
> nothing shows above the ground.*
>
> A Southern Garden (*in reference to* Lycoris squamigera)

Summer-Flowering Bulbs

Instead of agonizing over perennials that will never be at their best in our climate, we should use plant materials adapted to our hot, dry summers. With this in mind I have been experimenting for several years with summer-flowering bulbs. The amaryllis family alone is an almost inexhaustible source for Southern gardens. Among the low-growing ones are *Zephyranthes candida* and *Z. rosea*. *Z. candida* has shiny rush-like foliage that stays above the ground all year. Both are profuse bloomers, and persist and increase. They come in August.

The little yellow *Sternbergia lutea* (called the fall daffodil, though it looks more like a crocus) follows them at the end of August, and blooms on into September. The *Chlidanthus fragrans* is said to be very charming, but mine has never bloomed, although I have had it for several years. The choice member of this family is the *Amaryllis belladonna* (July and August) with its six or eight lavender-pink flowers in an umbel on a two-foot stem. It is perfectly hardy, and has bloomed for me in the poorest soil in both sun and shade. The charming *Lycoris squamigera* bloomed for two years and then disappeared. I have since learned that it was planted too deep. The fragrant white flowers of *Hymenocallis occidentalis* [*H. caroliniana*] are still found in old gardens. Why aren't they used in new ones?

The crinums are the showiest of the amaryllis family. Of the eight that I have tried only one, *C. erubescens*, was tender. To most people a crinum is the ugly *C. longifolium* [*C. bulbispermum*] (April), with its undistinguished white flowers on thick stems. But no lily is more exquisite than the pure white blooms of *C. powellii alba* [*C.* × *powellii* 'Album'] (July). *C. fimbriatulum* [hybrid of *C. americanum* and *C. scabrum*] (August–November), the milk-and-wine lily [or Nassau lily] of the old gardens, is the best bloomer. It has enormous umbels of creamy flowers with a wine-colored stripe on each petal. *C. kirkii* is similar to it, but not as attractive because the flowers droop. *C. moorei* has a small cup, but it is a delicate shade of pink. *C. asiaticum* has shiny, dark green foliage, but the fringe of delicate flowers is ludicrous at the end of a thick stem.

Among the other summer bulbs is a charming little gladiolus species that the country women bring to market in May. It has delicate magenta flowers on a slender stem, and it is nice with pyrethrum and columbine. I am not perfectly sure what it is, but the description of *Gladiolus byzantinus* [*G. communis* ssp. *byzantinus*] fits it.

Some of the commoner things, like montbretias and tritoma have been hybridized, and soft yellows replace the old reds and orange. The pale, dwarf hybrids of *Tritoma rufa* [*Kniphofia angustifolia* hybrid] make an accent in the flower border from May to August. And the gay watsonias with their wide range of color should be more used.

One of the things that I covet, but have had no success with, is the summer hyacinth, *Galtonia candicans*. I know that it does well here, so I think I must have put it in the wrong place.

Whatever it is, it is one of the most beautiful crinums and one of the most satisfactory garden plants to be had.
A Southern Garden
(*in reference to the milk-and-wine lily*)

Outdoor Hardy Crinums

Crinums are not looked upon with favor by most gardeners, I think because the only one well known is the common *C. longifolium* [*C. bulbispermum*], whose stem is so out of proportion to its flower, and because they take up so much space.[1] But there is nothing in the summer garden more showy than the sumptuous milk-and-wine lily that is grown in every dooryard in the coastal plain. I wonder that it is not more generally grown in the Piedmont. It blooms in August, and occasionally until frost. The enormous white flowers, with a red stripe in the center of the broad segments, are very heavily scented.

It is perfectly hardy in Raleigh, North Carolina, and I have read that it will endure the winters where the ground does not freeze hard. The milk-and-wine lily is a crinum hybrid of uncertain origin. Its ancestry probably includes *C. zeylanicum* and *C. fimbriatulum* [hybrid of *C. americanum* and *C. scabrum*], as it is listed under both names. It will endure drought, but it has never bloomed so freely as this year [1938] after a summer of unprecedented rain. The enormous milky-white flowers striped with wine-color are in umbels on thick three-foot scapes. Like most crinums, they open all at one time, and open very wide.

The bulbs are mammoth, and the foliage extremely luxuriant. The foliage does not appear until after that of spring-blooming species,

---

1. This material was originally published as two short articles—"Outdoor Hardy Crinums" and "Milk-and-Wine Lily"—in *Garden Gossip*, the newsletter of the Garden Club of Virginia. Elizabeth Lawrence continued her work with crinums and wrote more about them in 1943, 1946, and 1947, as subsequent pieces in this section reveal.

and does not get disfigured by the cold. The bright yellow-green leaves are fresh and shining at the end of the summer. Milk-and-wine lilies bloom from early August to November. There are often buds on them when they are cut down by frost.

I have tried six other crinums. *C. erubescens* is not so attractive as the milk-and-wine, to which it is similar. Its flowers are not so large, they don't open so wide, and they droop. *C. powellii alba* [*C.* × *powellii* 'Album'], and 'Roseum' are both exquisite, though not so showy. *C. asiaticum* has stringy little flowers on a thick stem. *C. kirkii* and *C. moorei* never bloomed.

Then the naked scapes of the
red lilies spring up from bare ground and
flower almost overnight, lighting all of the
dark corners and even the waste places.
A Southern Garden (*in reference to* Lycoris radiata)

Diverse Bulbs for the South

There are two ways of determining the best plant material for a given location. One is to study the native flora, and the other is to experiment with plants from similar climates. Gardeners on the Pacific Coast have already discovered that their hot suns and periods of drought supply the conditions necessary for maturing certain bulbs from tropical and subtropical countries, and we are beginning to learn that many of them can be grown with equal success in the Southeastern states. Some of the Eastern catalogues list a few tender bulbs, but most of them must be ordered from California growers.

Among the plants contributed to American gardens by the warm countries are representatives of the three great bulb families: the Amaryllidaceae, the Liliaceae, and the Iridaceae. Ranging in color from flaming orange and scarlet to clear pink and pure white, and in size from the magnificent crinum to the dainty *Brodiaea uniflora* [*Ipheion uniflorum*], they also offer a wide variety in form and foliage.

The Amaryllis family is a major source of bulbs for mild climates. Their grace and charm is suggested by the poetic and mythological names of some of the genera: Lycoris and Nerine for sea sprites; Amaryllis for the nymph celebrated by Theocritus and Virgil; Hyacinthus for the unfortunate shepherd, beloved of Apollo; and Zephyranthes, flower of the west wind. Amaryllis, the genus which gives its name to the family, has only one species, although many closely related forms are known as amaryllis. The common or garden amaryllis, a dull red lily with a white keel, is *Hippeastrum* × *johnsonii*. Hall's Amaryllis, sometimes called the hardy amaryllis because it can be grown farther north than most species, is *Lycoris squamigera*, and so on. The true amaryllis, *A. belladonna*, from the Cape of Good Hope, is common in gardens on the Pacific Coast, but is seldom grown out-of-doors in the East, although it is hardy to Washington. When I first saw its naked scapes, crowned with delicate pink flowers and growing right out of the bare, cracked earth of a dusty patio, I said to myself that my garden would be the perfect place for it. The flowers remain fresh for a long time under the hottest sun in spite of their apparently delicate texture. They are delightfully fragrant. *A. belladonna* blooms late in July or early in August and needs to be planted with some sort of a groundcover as its own foliage does not appear with the flowers. Annual ageratum does very well for this with the silvery foliage and soft lavender daisies of *Boltonia latisquama* [*B. asteroides* var. *latisquama*] for a background. The wide, narcissus-like leaves have a faint gray midrib. They come up in early spring and die down before the flowers appear. *A. belladonna* requires a warm, sheltered position. The bulbs should be planted six inches deep in soil that has been mixed with sand, leaf mold, and well-rotted manure. Good drainage is important. Once established, they should not be moved as long as they continue to bloom. They are said to prefer light shade, but I find that they do equally well in full sun. *A. belladonna*, unlike the capricious lycoris, is a dependable bloomer.

The nerines, commonly called spider lilies, are very much like *A. belladonna* and the lycoris in form and habit. Their flowers grow in umbels on bare scapes that push out of the ground and burst into bloom, as if by magic, in a few days. The lustrous dark green leaves follow the flowers and are valuable for a winter groundcover. *Nerine sarniensis* is common in Southern gardens. It is perfectly hardy in North Carolina and probably to Washington, but has not proved so in Maryland. It comes from the South African coast originally, but is called the Guernsey lily because some bulbs that washed ashore from a wrecked ship became naturalized on the island of Guernsey. The lacquer red flowers form a puff at the tip of the stiff stems; their long, bright red stamens curving up from the crisped petals suggest the name of spider lily. Nerines will bloom in sun or shade and flourish in any soil. Their only requirement is plenty of water before they bloom.

Nerines are extremely prolific. They should be divided in the spring when the scapes die down, and when replanted they should not be set very deep. As mine increased, I divided them and set them out wherever I could find a vacant spot in the borders or beside the pool, or under the hedge. For they bloom in September at that trying time when the phlox has gone to seed and the chrysanthemum buds are just showing color; at what would otherwise be a very dull time, the entire garden bursts into flame.

Spider lily is also the common name for hymenocallis, another genus of Amaryllidaceae, as well as for nerine, *Lycoris aurea*, and pancratium. For hymenocallis it is particularly inapt, as well as confusing, because it refers to the long, recurved perianth segments, which would suggest a spider's legs only to the liveliest imagination. Several species are native to the United States. The genus hymenocallis includes ismene (*H. calathina*) [*H. narcissiflora*], the Peruvian daffodil. This lovely summer-blooming bulb from the Andes rather resembles a large white daffodil with narrow petals curled back from a flaring, delicately fringed cup. There are several flowers to a stalk. The wide, linear leaves are dark and luxuriant.

Ismene is said to be hardy where the temperature does not go below fifteen degrees above zero, but I think it will stand even lower temperatures. Where there is any doubt of its hardiness, it should be taken up in the fall and set out again in the spring. It does very well this way as the bulbs bloom shortly after they are planted. It should be planted four inches deep in full sun, in a light, sandy soil.

The crinums, closely allied to the amaryllis, are striking garden plants with lily-like flowers and exotic foliage. Coming from warm and tropical regions, they are usually known as greenhouse plants in this country. But many of them can be grown out-of-doors in mild climates, and three are considered hardy. An enthusiasm for crinums is not always met with sympathy because the name usually calls to mind *Crinum longifolium* [*C. bulbispermum*], a hardy species and the one commonly seen in gardens. It is an awkward plant with yellowish white flowers on a thick stem.

The beautiful *C. sanderanum* from tropical Africa is a favorite in Florida, but it is not often grown in the mid-South although it is perfectly hardy here. It begins to bloom early in August, and I have had it in bloom in my garden as late as the ninth of November. Sometimes the last bulbs are killed by frost before they open. They are [one of the] milk-and-wine lilies because the pointed milky petals are streaked with wine. The flowers are in umbels, and all open at once. The broad leaves tapering to a long point are yellow-green and very luxuriant. Milk-and-wine lilies are of the easiest culture. They like a generous mulch of manure in the fall and plenty of water just before and during the blooming period. The bulbs increase rapidly.

The tuberose (*Polianthes tuberosa*)—an amaryllid[1] once popular but now associated with funerals—was a common bulb in old gardens in the South. It is seldom grown out-of-doors any more except in some dooryard gardens, where you may meet its intoxicating fragrance (intensified after dark) on a summer evening. A tall spike for midsummer is too valuable a form to be ignored; and tuberoses have the additional merit, being natives of Mexico, of having flowers with a texture strong enough to withstand the heat of the sun. They are rather leggy and should be put in the back of the border behind other plants. The double forms are stodgy, but the single Mexican everblooming variety has waxy white flowers that look and smell very much like orange blossoms.

The fairy lilies (*Zephyranthes*) are charming dwarf amaryllids. In April the low lying meadows from Virginia to Florida are white with our native atamasco lilies (*Z. atamasca*), but their possibilities for the garden have never been fully realized although they are easily transplanted and respond to cultivation. The atamasco lily is the lily type of zephyranthes. It has single white flowers and very narrow strap-like foliage. *Z. candida*, another white species—called the summer crocus although it blooms in the fall—is the crocus type. The small, cupped flowers tinged with pink on the outside when the nights get cooler appear in September and October, and the perennial leaves make a green edging for winter. It is native only to the marshes of the La Plata [in Argentina and Uruguay], which was named Silver River because its banks were covered with these small white flowers. There are several pink forms. The one in my garden came from south Georgia where it grows wild and is called the rain lily because it appears suddenly after a rain. It blooms all summer on the margin of a sunken border in combination with the velvety blue torenia, which (like the rain lily) likes plenty of moisture.

Among the summer-blooming bulbs of the Iris family, *Tritonia* (or *Montbretia*) [*Crocosmia*] and *Watsonia*, two half-hardy irids from South Africa, are particularly desirable for Southern gardens. Blooming in June when there is apt to be a gap between high spring and early

---

1. *Polianthes tuberosa* is now classified in the Agavaceae family.

summer, watsonias are brilliant in color and distinct in form. They are preferable to perennials such as the painted daisy or Canterbury bells to which our climate is not favorable. Growing from large corms, having sword-like foliage and spikes of wide-open flowers, watsonias are something like gladiolus; and for me their delicately formed flowers on thin, wiry, branched stems have more charm than the heavy, solid spikes of the gladiolus. There are crimson, rose, and white species, and the hybrids come in a number of delicate and brilliant shades from flesh pink and coral to orange and scarlet. Watsonias should be planted from four to five inches deep in well-drained soil in full sun; they should be left to establish a clump. Where they are not hardy, they may be taken up like gladiolus and planted again in the spring. But they do not keep as well as gladiolus, and it is better to leave them in the ground when that is possible. Already popular in California, they should certainly be better known in the East.

Tritonias, much like watsonias except that they are smaller, bloom gaily in the midsummer heat. I plant *T.* × *crocosmiiflora* [*Crocosmia* × *crocosmiiflora*], the common garden form (which multiplies very fast), as I do nerines, wherever there is a free spot in the borders so that they will be dominant when they are in bloom. The sprays of brilliant orange carry the borders through July and August. An old form with scarlet-edged petals is to be avoided. The hybrid tritonias are larger than the type and have a wide range of color, some with interesting markings. 'Fire King' is red, 'Star of the East' golden yellow with a paler eye, and 'Una' apricot with a carmine blotch. The small corms should be planted from four to six inches deep in sandy loam mixed with leaf mold. They should be carefully examined before planting, as it is very easy to mistake the top for the bottom and set them upside down. They will tolerate some shade, but do best in full sun. North of Philadelphia, tritonias should be stored over the winter.

Various half-hardy bulbs of the Lily family are adapted to garden conditions in the mid-South. The form to bloom in the spring is the spring starflower (*Brodiaea uniflora*) [*Ipheion uniflorum*],[2] a tiny bulb that smells like onions and has leaves like the leaves of garlic. The pale lavender flowers, starry and sweet scented, bloom in March with cowslips, violas, and grape hyacinths. The bulbs are said to be hardy in the North but not permanent. In the South they increase and are some-

---

2. Some authorities now consider *Ipheion* a member of the Alliaceae.

times used for a groundcover. *B. uniflora* is from Argentina and is entirely different from the Brodiaeas of western North America. The latter bloom in April and are more unusual than beautiful. The funnel-shaped, dull blue flowers of *B. laxa* [*Triteleia laxa*] are bunched at the ends of ridiculously long flexible stems that twine around each other or any other nearby plant. *B. crocea* [*Triteleia crocea*] is bright yellow, and *B. coccinea* [*Dichelostemma ida-maia*] crimson. Brodiaeas require a dry situation and should not be moved. They are hardy in the South although little known outside of California.

Ornithogalum arabicum, a tender bulb from the Mediterranean, is usually considered a greenhouse plant but is perfectly hardy in North Carolina. The fragrant white flowers are piquantly accented by shiny black pistils. They grow in many-flowered racemes on eighteen-inch scapes and bloom from the middle of April to the middle of May. The bulbs are almost as big and solid as Dutch hyacinths. They should be planted in the fall six inches deep in a warm sunny border. *O. thyrsoides* is not hardy in North Carolina.

Torch lilies (*Kniphofia*) are mostly of doubtful hardiness north of Philadelphia. They are not bulbs, but are usually classed as such. The tall red-hot poker plants (*K.* cv. 'Pfitzeri') with brilliant red spikes fading to yellow make a brilliant display in the fall. The dwarf hybrids are everblooming and very effective in front of the border. A pale yellow form that I have had for years blooms fitfully from the middle of May to late fall. The grassy foliage and solid flower-heads give character to a marginal planting of Alaska daisies and white petunias in front of a cluster of orange tritonias.

These are only the more obvious of the innumerable brilliant and extensive bulbs from tropical America, South Africa, Mexico, or the West Indies that are tolerant of—or even demanding—heat and lack of moisture in the resting period. They require a minimum of care, are not subject to disease, and—with the exception of a rare nerine or choice crinum—they are amazingly cheap. In a carefully planned garden, these bulbs will bloom almost continuously from early spring until frost.

*The hyacinths and
pale daffodils are a cool
blue and silver that reminds
one of things past.*
A Southern Garden

Narcissi for Next Spring's Garden

Those who grow daffodils to grace their gardens in the spring rather than with the hope of winning prizes may find varieties bought from lists made at last year's flower show disappointing out of doors.[1] Narcissi brought to a show are often protected from sun, wind, and rain, or picked in the bud stage and allowed to open in a cool, dark cellar. Without these attentions, delicate textures may be marred or grow limp in drying winds, and bright colors may fade under the hot sun. Moreover, daffodils that appeared of magnificent size in a vase or arrangement may look coarse and overgrown in a flower bed. With these facts kept in mind, flower show notes may be very helpful. So may the scale of points used by flower show judges, provided certain differences are considered.

The accepted scale divides fifty points between form and substance, and the other fifty between color, size, and length of stem. Form is as important outdoors as in—except where the bulbs are

---

1. In 1950, the Royal Horticultural Society revised its system for classifying narcissi. They discarded the leedsii, barrii, and incomparabilis groups and incorporated them into categories based on flower proportions, with further subdivision based on color combinations. *Hortus Third* listed eleven classifications in 1976. The Royal Horticultural Society now lists twelve divisions based on the current reclassification accomplished in 1989. Division XII was added in 1989 for miscellaneous narcissi, which includes all narcissi not falling into one of the above divisions. Although the classification information in this article is out of date, its advice about selecting daffodils for the garden is not, and it provides useful information on some varieties that are still commonly available. Regrettably, many of these old bulbs are no longer in the trade.

planted in great quantities for mass effect rather than for the beauty of the individual flower. Substance is more important out of doors, for a flower lacking it may make a good appearance in the showroom when it will not stand up in the changeable spring weather. A thin, flimsy perianth may look fine and delicate if the flower is kept in a vase and carefully protected from drafts, but it will not be proof against hot, drying winds. A good clear color is important in daffodils, whether grown to exhibit or for the garden; but harsh yellows become worse when seen in bright sunlight, whereas the delicate shades are more easily appreciated in cut flowers. Great size is not important in an out-of-door flower so long as it is graceful and nicely proportioned; nor is a very long stem as important as in a cut flower, so long as it is not disproportionately short. One quality not considered by show judges is good foliage; yet it is most important in the garden because daffodils bloom when the ground is more or less bare, and need their own foliage to set them off.

In a good collection of garden narcissi, all eleven divisions of the classification of the Royal Horticultural Society should be represented, with varieties chosen from each of them to give a long season of bloom and a wide range of form and color. This classification is based mainly on the length of the corona (or crown) in relation to the length of the perianth segments (or petals). In the trumpet daffodils (Division 1), the trumpet (or crown) is as long as or longer than the perianth segments or petals. In the other divisions, the crown (here called the cup) is less than the length of the perianth segments. As a result of much crossing of varieties in the different divisions, the lines cannot always be easily drawn between the divisions, and a variety may be classed differently by different growers. Thus, the famous pink daffodil, 'Mrs. R. O. Backhouse', is sometimes listed as a white trumpet and sometimes as a "giant leedsii" because it has the form of a trumpet and the color of leedsii. It is interesting to know that the choice of the Royal Horticultural Society of representative varieties picked from the several divisions for fine form and color, and without regard to price, is: 'Beersheba,' 'Beryl', 'Dawson City', 'Firetail', 'Fortune', 'Glorious', 'Havelock', 'King Alfred', 'Mitylene', 'Sarchedon', 'Trevithian', and 'Tunis'. Some were expensive when the list was first made, but most of them are now within the reach of the most modest pocketbook.

DIVISION I—TRUMPET DAFFODILS[2]

The daffodils in this division have trumpets as long as or longer than the petals and are in three sections: (a) yellow, (b) white, and (c) bicolor. Those in (a) may be a pale yellow like 'Serphine', which is a delightful small flower of a very pale canary with the trumpet slender and ruffled at the edge and short petals; or a deep yellow like the popular 'King Alfred', which, however, is often difficult to establish. To me the latter is a harsh yellow and in every way inferior in form and color to the older 'Emperor', which is certain to be permanent. With us in the South Atlantic region, the earliest variety is the common yellow trumpet; it is small but excellent for naturalizing. 'Golden Spur', also very early, is one of the oldest garden varieties. 'John Cairns' is a very late variety to be planted to lengthen the season. To me, 'Emperor' is the arch type and big enough for the garden. But for those who want even more size, 'Dawson City' and 'Robert Sydenham' are large and well-tried varieties, while 'Duke of York' and 'Olympia' are enormous. 'Olympia', a seedling of 'Emperor' and usually considered an improvement, is a uniform yellow of Olympian proportions, with a thick, deeply ruffled trumpet and a wide, heavy perianth.

The white trumpets are the most exciting of all daffodils. I have a very early one which begins to bloom soon after the first of the common trumpets. It came from an old garden and was called 'Silver Bells', but I think it is the swan's neck daffodil, 'William Goldring'.[3] The buds are bent down close to the stem, rising by degrees as they open, but always slightly drooping. The flowers open a very delicate primrose, pale out to ivory, and turn a purplish brown as they fade, somewhat like Indian pipes, which they delightfully resemble. 'Mrs. Robert Sydenham' and 'Sanctity' are small, the former being ivory-white and as smooth as ivory, with a narrow cylindrical trumpet that rolls back suddenly at the edge, giving it a very distinct form. Of the large white trumpets, 'Imperator' seems to me poor, the texture being coarse and the long, flaring trumpet too heavy for the perianth. 'Mrs.

---

2. Division I is now designated as trumpet narcissi of garden origin.

3. In her update to *A Southern Garden* (1967), Elizabeth Lawrence corrects the impression that 'Silver Bells' is 'William Goldring,' which she says has a dog-eared perianth. "If we could only be allowed to give them names, what a list we would have," she remarks.

E. H. Krelage', of a firm substance without being coarse, has a smooth rich texture and a good, distinct form, but I should call the trumpet yellowish rather than white. 'Beersheba' is uniformly pure white, and the best of its kind that I have seen. It is a large, fine flower, stands up well in the garden, and increases slowly but steadily.

The bicolor trumpets, their yellow crowns contrasting with the white perianths, make a gayer splash out of doors than the all-yellow daffodils. The small, old-fashioned 'Empress' shows good contrast and is fairly early. Mr. J. C. Wister suggests 'Herod' to lengthen the season. For large, showy varieties, 'Glory of Sassenheim' is, to my way of thinking, the most effective trumpet for the garden; it is a good color and in spite of its size and substance has a very fine texture. 'Vanilla' is good and to me very sweet, but Mr. Bowles say that it smells less like vanilla than like the fragrance of a box of chocolates after its contents have vanished.

DIVISION II—INCOMPARABILIS[4]

In the daffodils of this group, the crown or cup is less than the length of the petals, but not less than one third as long. There are two sections: (a) with yellow perianth and (b) with white perianth. The cups of the (a) varieties vary in color from the light yellow of 'Sir Watkin' through the orange of 'Fortune', to the red of 'Will Scarlet' and 'Gloria Mundi'. Or the cup may be thickened like that of the hideous 'President Viger'. The petals may be wide like those of the lovely lemon-colored 'Yellow Poppy', or curled and pointed like those of 'Frank Miles', which looks like a pinwheel. Of the large varieties, 'Loudspeaker' is as coarse and vulgar as its name; 'Fortune' has the merit of being earlier and having a more richly colored cup than is usual in a daffodil of its size; and 'Havelock' is fine in form and substance, though not a vigorous type in the garden.

The bicolors may have yellow, orange, or orange-rimmed cups. 'Holbein', to me one of the most beautiful and desirable of all daffodils, has a blazing yellow cup very lightly creased at the edges and wide, pointed ivory petals. It has a distinct form, good substance, and a very fine texture. 'Lucifer' has a glowing cup and a starry white

---

4. This division consists of large-cupped narcissi of garden origin and is botanically classified as *Narcissus × incomparabilis*. Plants in this division descend from various varieties and forms from hybrids between *N. poeticus* and *N. pseudonarcissus*.

perianth of very thin substance. 'R. M. Tobin' is an improved 'Lucifer' as to size, but with the same floppy petals. 'John Evelyn' is a fresh-looking flower with a sharp contrast between its snowy perianth and the deep yellow crown, which has a slightly thickened edge. 'Kennack' is particularly recommended for the garden in that it has an orange crown that doesn't burn.

DIVISION III — BARRII[5]

The barriis, in which the cup or crown is less than one-third the petal length, are light and graceful in form, but unfortunately not recommended without reservation for gardens, especially in exposed or hot locations. The typical red-rimmed cups burn in strong sunlight, and the petals are too thin to be very durable. When planted in the garden they should be in a shaded and sheltered position. There are two sections: (a) with yellow perianth and (b) with white perianth.

The typical yellow barriis have red-rimmed cups. The old *N.* × *barrii* 'Conspicuus' I have always thought thin, poor, and colorless. 'Bath's Flame' is large and delicately colored, with a graceful droop; it comes out nicely indoors, but a hot wind will ruin it. 'Brilliancy' is large and colorful, but also weak in substance. 'Glitter' is all yellow, with no red in the cup; it is very small, the stem being only eight inches.

The bicolors may have cups with or without red. 'Acida' is a fine example of the second type, with very broad overlapping petals of pure white and a yellow cup deepening in color at the margin. It is notable for being very late. 'Southern Star' is an early variety of this type. 'Firetail' and 'Bonfire' are considered good red-cupped varieties, but they are now as brilliant as 'Dragoon', which has a pale yellow, orange-rimmed cup against a dazzling white perianth. 'Pride of Virginia' is similar in color but inferior in form.

DIVISION IV — LEEDSII[6]

The leedsiis, which stand up particularly well in the garden and improve as they become established, are distinguished not by form but

---

5. The barrii group designation was discarded in 1989 by the Royal Horticultural Society. Division III now applies to small-cupped narcissi of garden origin; botanically these narcissi are forms and variants of the hybrid *N.* × *incomparabilis* × *N. poeticus*.

6. The leedsii division was discarded by the Royal Horticultural Society in 1989. Botanically *N.* × *leedsii* is now classified as *N.* × *incomparabilis*. Division IV now applies to double narcissi of garden origin.

by color; they have white perianths and white or very pale cups sometimes tinted with apricot or pink. There are two sections corresponding in shape to Divisions II and III, namely (a) giant leedsiis with cups from a third as long to equally as long as the petals and (b) small-crowned leedsiis with cups less than a third of the length of the petals. Of the giant group, 'Mermaid' is an old form still considered desirable: inexpensive, pure white, and early. The newer 'Tenedos' has been very high in price, but can now be bought for seventy-five cents a bulb. It has a handsome primrose cup approaching a trumpet in length. 'Mitylene' is another fine leedsii that has come down to more nearly everyday prices. 'White Pearl' is creamy white and magnificent. 'Tunis' is a distinct ivory-white, the crown frilled and deepening to buff at the edge. It is strong, tall, and very early, holds its head up well and increases rapidly. Though not found in all catalogues, it can be bought for about two dollars and a half. 'Cicely' is distinct in form and color, and very early.

The small-crowned leedsiis are light in color and form, and many are good for naturalizing. 'Southern Gem' is an early variety, and 'White City' a very late one. 'Evangeline', 'Albania', 'Queen of the North', and 'White Lady' are all old forms with very wide, very white petals and small yellowish cups. They all make a white drift when planted in quantities, and there is little to choose among them. 'Salmonetta', a small and dainty variety with a pale apricot cup, has the delicacy of form and color of the triandrus hybrids of the next division, but is rather uncertain. A very lovely leedsii of equal delicacy but a more durable substance is 'Beatrice'. The flowers, lightly poised on long, slim stems, have long pointed petals with slightly curled edges, while the cup is wide with shallow fluting and the foliage is pale green. 'Silver Salver', whose name comes from its very flat cup, is set apart from the others of this group by its green center. It is the purest white of any of the small leedsiis, and blooms late.

DIVISION V—TRIANDRUS HYBRIDS[7]

These lovely narcissi are not as fragile as they look. They prefer shade to sun, but are not particular as to soil. However, being delicate in color and texture, they show to better advantage in a rock garden or

---

7. This division is composed of forms and variants of *Narcissus triandrus* (angel's tears) of garden origin.

some place where they do not have to compete with larger forms. 'Thalia'—sometimes listed as a small leedsii—bears two or three pearly white flowers to a stem; it grows well and increases. The perianth is slightly ruffled, and the crown deep and bowl-shaped. 'Agnes Harvey' is similar to 'Thalia', but not as attractive. 'Silver Chimes' is a cross between triandrus and a tazetta (Division VIII) and is sometimes listed as one of the latter type. It has creamy petals, and "citron cups as clear as the light of an evening sky." There are also yellow flowers in this division, such as the little canary 'Queen of Spain' and 'Harvest Moon', which has a long, flaring trumpet.

DIVISION VI—CYCLAMINEUS HYBRIDS[8]

The daffodils of this group are prized for their early bloom. 'February Gold' is like its parent species in this respect only; in form it is a small trumpet, much less reflexed than in the typical cyclamineus perianth, with a long cylindrical trumpet. 'Orange Glory' is taller, a little later, and of a deeper color. It has not a good substance and is inclined to flop. 'Beryl' has broad, overlapping petals, paler than its short yellow cup. It is a hybrid of *N. cyclamineus* and *N. poeticus* and is especially lovely.

DIVISION VII—JONQUILLA HYBRIDS[9]

The jonquils are a distinct and lovely group, richly colored and with clusters of small, fragrant flowers and shining rush-like foliage. The hybrids are very desirable. 'Trevithian' is outstanding for its cool color, unusual in a jonquil. It has two flowers to a stem. 'Golden Scepter' I do not like because it looks like an insignificant trumpet. 'Buttercup', a rich yellow and almost a trumpet, is cheap. Both of these stay in bloom a long time and are good garden varieties. 'Orange Queen' is the deepest color. 'Primrose', outstanding but expensive, is unusual in having but one flower to a stem.

DIVISION VIII—TAZETTA OR POETAZ[10]

This division includes the tender *polyanthos* varieties that are very early in the South and forced for winter flowers in the North such as 'Soleil d'Or' and 'Grand Monarque', the paperwhite narcissus. These

---

8. *Narcissus cyclamineus* of garden origin.
9. *Narcissus jonquilla* forms of garden origin.
10. *Narcissus tazetta* of garden origin.

bunch-flowered narcissi are of medium height with stiff stems. The later-blooming tazetta hybrids are surprisingly varied as to color, form, and the number of flowers to a head. 'Laurens Koster' is an old variety with white perianth and deep yellow cup. 'Glorious' has a whiter, broader perianth and scarlet cup. 'Hameon' and 'Orange Cup' are yellow forms, the latter having more contrast between its cup (which is as orange as its name implies) and the petals, too much to my way of thinking. 'Elvira' and 'Aspasia' are forms with large flowers and fewer ones to a head. 'Aspasia' has four or five flowers to a head, the cup being citron and the perianth white and of a very fine substance. Similar but with two flowers to a head is *Narcissus biflorus* [*N.* × *medioluteus*], an old and very late variety that we in the South call "twin sisters" and of value because it blooms with tulips. 'Medusa' is a distinct and unusual form with two large flowers to a head and a bright red eye against a very white, broad perianth.

DIVISION IX — POETICUS[11]

The varieties of the poet's narcissus are well suited to the garden because of their good substance and the decorative value of their bright red and yellow eyes against the pure white perianths. But there is little variety in them. After one has had the early *N. ornatus* [*N. poeticus*] and the late [var.] *recurvus* (pheasant's eye), which is one of the last daffodils to bloom, some large varieties such as 'Dante' or 'Horace', and the small and exquisite 'Juliet', more would be duplication. Even so, I should like to have them for their names and that I might look forward every spring to the blossoming of 'Homer', 'Herrick', and 'Rupert Brooke'.

DIVISION X — DOUBLE VARIETIES[12]

Most of the types represented in the above mentioned division have double varieties. 'Holland's Glory' is a double trumpet. 'Sulphur Phoenix' and 'Orange Phoenix' are doubles of the incomparabilis division. 'Sulphur Phoenix' is creamy white and late-blooming, and 'Orange Phoenix' has white perianth segments and orange center segments. 'Red Huzzar' is a gay barrii—the center petals of yellow edged

---

11. *Narcissus poeticus* of garden origin.
12. Division X now consists of narcissi species, wild variants, and wild hybrids. Double varieties are now designated as Division IV.

with orange are in sharp contrast to the ivory-white petals. 'Snow Sprite' is a pure white leedsii. The jonquil group gives us the double *N. campernelle* [*N. × odorus*], called Queen Anne's jonquil. 'Cheerfulness' is a tazetta with several small double white flowers to a head, and *N. albus plenus odoratus* [*N. poeticus* 'Plenus'], the gardenia-flowered narcissus, is a double poeticus. It is an old form and a good one, but it is not always found easy to grow.

DIVISION XI—VARIOUS[13]

These, some of the smaller members of the triandrus and jonquilla divisions, and the small trumpets are usually considered rock garden material—not because they have any affinity for rocks, but because, being small and often of difficult culture, it is easier to see them, to attend to their special needs, and to keep track of them when they are segregated in separate spaces between rocks. *N. bulbocodium*, the hoop-petticoat daffodil, is not difficult if it is given a hot sunny situation and a gravelly soil. It has an enormously wide crown and the petals are reduced to mere strips. It is a deep yellow like the jonquils and has the same narrow foliage. The variety *citrinus* is very pale yellow, and the variety *monophyllus*, white. The crown of *N. cyclamineus* (whose hybrids form Division VI) is a long narrow cylinder, and the petals are bent back against the stem like those of a cyclamen. It requires a rather moist soil, and is difficult to grow. *N. triandrus albus* (angel's tears) [*N. triandrus triandrus*] is a similar and tiny form, very early and pure white. Like *N. cyclamineus*, it is difficult to establish, but is said to reseed if left undisturbed in a situation that is to its liking. One might go on indefinitely in this fascinating and varied division, which includes *N. juncifolius* [*N. assoanus*], the rush-leaved daffodil (from which the term jonquilla is said to be derived), and the rare autumnal daffodil, *N. viridiflorus*. However, anyone who has come thus far probably needs no further urging to try some of the many different kinds of daffodils that can bring so much loveliness to their gardens. And now, until frost shuts down upon us, is the time to get and plant them for spring bloom.

13. Division XI now consists of narcissi with split coronas. Various narcissi are now designated as Division X.

In my garden a month seldom goes
by without bloom from some member of the
amaryllis family, but it is in summer and fall
that they become the center of interest.
A Southern Garden

Amaryllids in a Southern Garden

It has been a little more than ten years since I began to collect amaryllids and to grow them in the garden—not that I thought, ten years ago, of growing amaryllids.[1] I thought only of seeing in bloom flowers new and strange. My mother had discovered Gordon Ainsley, and she and I would go through his little leaflet, especially the section headed "Miscellaneous Bulbs, Tubers and Rare Plants," and make a painful choice of the ones we most wanted to try. Before many seasons had passed, it became apparent that, on the whole, the bulbs most likely to grow and bloom for us belonged to the amaryllis family. It was then that Billy Hunt told me about the Amaryllis Society, and I poured over *Herbertia* and began to acquire as many members of the *Amaryllidaceae* as I could. Not having a greenhouse, I limited myself to those that would grow out of doors, and I tried to be systematic about keeping a record of them. In this tenth anniversary edition of *Herbertia*, it seems appropriate to review ten years of experiment in a North Carolina garden.

Because the provenance of many of the most beautiful amaryllids is tropical or subtropical, growing them out of doors this far north is largely experimental, and many that survive do not bloom when they are grown so near their northern limit of hardiness. Here, during an average winter, the lowest temperature is eight or ten degrees above zero. The weather bureau in Raleigh has recorded zero once in this century. That was in 1917.[2]

1. Since Miss Lawrence wrote this article, some classifications have changed as noted. Although some of the plants mentioned are no longer classified as Amaryllidaceae, their descriptions are still accurate and of interest to gardeners.

2. A temperature of −9°F was recorded in Raleigh in January 1985, according to the National Weather Service at North Carolina State University.

I sometimes read that amaryllids that have failed with me grow where the temperatures are much lower than these. Perhaps some factor other than temperature is involved, or perhaps the amaryllids were given more protection. Mine go unmulched, and I cannot bear to plant them very deep—I always feel that they will never find their way out of the dark earth into the spring sunlight. But it may be that with deep planting and a generous coat of manure, some of those that have died would have lived, and some of those that merely existed would have bloomed.

CRINUMS AND CRINODONNA [× AMARCRINUM]

The first record I have of an order from Mr. Ainsley (spring 1932) is for *Brunsvigia rosea* (syn. *Callicore rosea*; *Amaryllis belladonna*), *Chlidanthus fragrans*, *Lycoris squamigera*, *Sternbergia lutea*, and the crinum species *kirkii*, *C. × powellii* (both the white and pink forms), *C. erubescens*, *C. bulbispermum* (syn. *C. longifolium*), and *C. moorei*. The brunsvigia and the chlidanthus failed to bloom, though they sent up leaves each spring for a number of years, and the lycoris and sternbergia did not bloom for several seasons. But the crinums were an immediate success, and I wanted to grow as many sorts as I could.

The species that have proved garden worthy in North Carolina are *Crinum americanum*, *C. erubescens*, *C. kirkii*, *C. kunthianum*, *C. bulbispermum* (*C. longifolium*), and *C. moorei*. *C. americanum* grew for five years before blooming, but it has now bloomed for two seasons. The season is late August and early September when its narrow-petaled, pure white flowers are particularly striking in the ragged end-of-the-summer borders. In these parts, I think this may not be everyone's crinum, for it seems choice as to situation, growing well in heavy clay in a low bed that gets the morning sun, and not surviving when transplanted to a different place. But it increases rapidly when it is once established, and I can even imagine that it might increase too much. One could never have enough of the delightful flowers, but the foliage might take up more space than one wanted to give it. I was interested to hear from Mrs. Henry that she had bloomed this crinum in Pennsylvania, but that it had died the following winter. I imagine from its behavior here that it's not hardy very far north of us.

The species that have not survived our winters are *C. amabile* [perhaps *C. augustum*] and *C. zeylanicum* from the Royal Palm nurseries; and

C. giganteum (the Christopher lily)³ marked "species near giganteum"; *C. scabrum* [*C. zeylanicum*], a species from Burma; and one labeled "species near *amabile*" from Mr. Hayward. The species from Burma was always sickly and did not bloom and lived only a few months. *C. scabrum* [*C. zeylanicum*] bloomed in June and again in September, the fall bloom being especially large and handsome and long-lasting. The second spring it failed to put in an appearance. This is not such a loss, as there are many good crinums of the milk-and-wine type, but I was distressed when the rare and lovely "species near *amabile*" proved tender. Planted late in March with *C. scabrum* [*C. zeylanicum*], it did not bloom until mid-September, when the dark reddish purple buds opened into flowers striped amaranth purple and pure white. These flowers were comparatively small, and there were seven to an umbel. The second day all were open, and all were fresh. On the borderline of hardiness is a very small crinum sent to me by Mr. Hayward as *C. giganteum hybridum* [*C. jagus*], which has survived but has not bloomed.

Only one of the hybrids that I have tried has failed to be hardy. This is the most beautiful of all, the 'Empress of India'. The first time I had no better sense than to set out at once the magnificent bulb (sixteen inches in circumference) that Mr. Hayward sent me in the fall. A second time I asked his advice and kept the bulb in sand in the cellar until the end of March. After sunset on the fourth of September, the first long narrow bud began to open. We sat watching as if it were a night-blooming cereus. I do not think Balboa could have been more breathless when he first looked upon the Pacific than the Lawrences were when they first saw the fully expanded flowers (twelve inches across) of the 'Empress of India', milk-white, wine-striped, and heavily scented. This crinum blooms only at night. The flowers wilt as soon as the sun touches them in the morning and do not revive, as some crinums do, with the cool of the next evening. Both the bulb that flowered and the one planted in the fall died before spring. I do not think it worthwhile to try the 'Empress of India' again.

I think I might have better luck another time with the rose-colored form of *C.* × *powellii*, which lived through one or more winters and bloomed once. Probably it will not prove as robust and free-flowering

---

3. There is some confusion about which plant Elizabeth Lawrence meant when she used the name "Christopher Lily." 'St. Christopher' is a cultivar of *C. bulbispermum*. However, 'Christopher Lily' is a cultivar of *C. jagus*.

as the pink-flowered 'Cecil Houdyshel' or the dazzling white *C.* × *powellii*. 'White Queen', 'Ellen Bosanquet', and 'Virginia Lee' are satisfactory for the garden, though I have not had these long enough for them to become thoroughly established. The dark purple buds of 'Ellen Bosanquet' open in the afternoon into flowers of the brilliant deep rose that Ridgway[4] calls spinel red. They are shaped like the flowers of *C. moorei* and have the same vanilla fragrance. The plant is very large. 'Virginia Lee' is a small crinum with flowers like those of *C. moorei*, but paler.

Some of the most delightful crinums are those found in country gardens. The late-summer- and fall-blooming milk-and-wine lily of the dooryards of eastern North Carolina is one of the best of all crinums. From a garden in Atlanta, I brought home a very delicate and lovely one, pure white with pink filaments and a delicious and characteristic fragrance—something of vanilla and something of lemon. There are six flowers to the slender short scape. They open at night and last through the next day. This one multiplies very fast and blooms at intervals from the end of May to the end of October. From my great Aunt Rosalie's garden on Saint Simon's Island I brought the crinum—common in south Georgia—with fringe-like bunches of small white flowers on tall thick scapes, but this one did not live.

× *Crinodonna howardii*[5] seems to be as satisfactory in the garden as the crinums and has come through two winters during which the lowest temperature was ten degrees above zero. It blooms in August and September. The delicate pink flowers are much like those of its parent *Brunsvigia rosea* (syn. *Callicore rosea*) [*Amaryllis belladonna*].

The season for crinums is a very long one. From April to October there are few days when no crinum is in bloom in my garden. *C. bulbispermum* (*C. longifolium*) often begins to bloom in April, and our milk-and-wine lily sometime sends up a scape or two in November. The 'White Queen' follows *C. bulbispermum* and *C. kirkii*. *C. kunthianum* and the white × *powellii* bloom in June and July. The last three are the most profuse bloomers, with twenty or more blooms to a clump, but the scapes come all at once. However, each has repeated, on occasion,

---

4. The color chart referred to here is from *Color Standards and Color Nomenclature*, written and published by Robert Ridgway (Washington, D.C., 1912).

5. This is a bigeneric hybrid of *Crinum moorei* and *Amaryllis belladonna*. One cultivar is 'Fred Howard'.

in the late summer or fall. 'Cecil Houdyshel' sends up two or three scapes each summer month, and the milk-and-wine lily and *C. americanum* begin to bloom before its flowering is over.

LYCORIS AND NERINE

Except for the hurricane lily [*Lycoris aurea*], the species of *Lycoris* that I have grown have lived and bloomed, and bloomed regularly and freely. The only difficulty is that so few species are available. I long for *L. sanguinea*, *L. sprengeri* (which Colonel Grey says should be about as hardy as *L. squamigera*), and perhaps the white form of *L. radiata*. Colonel Grey describes *L. aurea* as perhaps the least hardy member of the genus. With me the bulbs are hardy, but the foliage is made in the fall and is injured by the cold. The bulbs live on indefinitely, but there is no bloom.

Lycoris radiata is a dooryard flower in the eastern part of North Carolina; and though it is not generally considered hardy in the mountains, I had a report last fall of bloom in Asheville. Long ago I sent bulbs to Mrs. Wilson in Anne Arundel County, Maryland, and she wrote me that they died. Years later, she went out one day in September and found them in bloom.

Bulbs which I had from Mr. Hayward as *L. squamigera* 'Purpurea', from Mr. Houdyshel as *L. incarnata*, and from Dreer (I think it was Dreer) years ago as *Lycoris squamigera* itself, bloom well most seasons and give increase. The flowers, to me, are the most delicate and lovely of all the amaryllids. They do not resemble the description that Colonel Grey quotes from the Gartenwalt of 1906 of "purple and carmine segments to Prussian Blue at the tips," but are white with a wine-colored keel. The leaves appear at the end of January, a week later than those of the typical *L. squamigera*. When they come up, they are edged with bright red.

Though I have tried a number of species over a period of years, no nerine has ever bloomed for me. Once I thought one was going to when a bulb sent from California as *Nerine undulata* produced a scape. As the days passed, the opening flowers looked suspiciously like *Lycoris radiata*, and when in bloom proved to be a form of it.

That the nerines do not bloom here saddens but does not surprise me. In the first volume of *Herbertia*, the Honorable Henry McLaren writes of them out of doors in England: "They want to grow in winter and rest in summer, and the climate forbids this." Our climate forbids it too, and I have found it forbidding to other amaryllids from South Africa and to South African plants in general. In a well-drained position in full sun, *N. bowdenii*, *N. coruscans* [horticultural name, perhaps for *N. sarniensis* variety], and *N. rosea crispa* (the last two are varieties of *N. sarniensis* according to Colonel Grey) have persisted for a number of years without bloom. Mr. Hayward sent me a fine bulb of *N. curvifolia* 'Fothergillii' [*N. fothergillii*], which, after a late summer planting, produced leaves in November but has made no sign of life since. *N. filifolia* refuses to grow too, though I have tried it more than once and in different soils and exposures.

BRUNSVIGIA ROSEA[6]

Another Cape bulb that wants to grow in the winter and rest in the summer and so does not accommodate itself to North Carolina is the delightful pink lily that we used to call *Amaryllis belladonna*, more recently *Callicore rosea*, but is now known as *Brunsvigia rosea*. It has bloomed in the garden only once though it has been tried a number of times. The bloom appeared in August from a bulb that had been planted in November. I have also tried the varieties *major* and *minor* and *rosea* and × *parkeri* [× *Amarygia parkeri*]. All persist. None bloom.

AMARYLLIS

The Barbados lily, which we now know to be *Amaryllis belladonna* [*Hippeastrum puniceum*], but that I planted as *Hippeastrum equestre*, fares no better. I think the bulbs Mr. Hayward sent to me have finally disappeared, though they survived several winters. *Amaryllis rutilum fulgidum* [*Hippeastrum striatum*] behaved in the same way. And *A.* × *johnsonii* [*Hippeastrum* × *johnsonii*], though it grew and flowered in old gardens in these parts, has always been a shy bloomer with me, if it bloomed at all.

One amaryllis which does flourish here is the little oxblood lily, *A. advena* [*Rhodophiala advena*]. It multiplies steadily and blooms profusely. The number of sharp-pointed bulbs that push up out of the ground from late August to late October is unbelievable. This lily seems to grow in any soil or situation, but it responds especially to barnyard manure.

---

6. The current nomenclature is *Amaryllis belladonna*. 'Major', 'Rosea', and 'Minor' are cultivars. *A. belladonna* is closely related to *Brunsvigia* and is sometimes included in that genus.

HYMENOCALLIS AND PANCRATIUM

There are reports of hymenocallis hardy as far north as Pennsylvania, and they should certainly be grown in the middle South. The difficulty is in the confusion of the names. Even when you find one that grows and blooms, you cannot be sure what it is.

Two species are native to North Carolina. I do not know how the small, spring-blooming *H. rotata* of the coastal plain behaves in cultivation. I saw the flower at a country flower show early in May. A farmer's wife brought it in, either from her garden or from the woods. The summer-blooming *H. occidentalis* [*H. caroliniana*] from the mountains grows in a damp part of the garden and blooms at the end of August.

H. galvestonensis, the Gulf Coast spider lily, is reported as failing to flower in cultivation, and I was about to confirm this report when I went out in the garden to cut iris and found the long bud of the spider lily almost ready to open. It opened on the sixth day of May, which is the earliest bloom on my records for hymenocallis. The wide flat cup and the narrow petals of the flower are very similar to those of *H. occidentalis* [*H. caroliniana*]. The bulb had come from Mr. Houdyshel three years ago and had been planted in full sun in poor but well-drained soil.

Spider lilies, like crinums, should be sought in gardens. Recently I found two delightful late summer hymenocallis in cultivation. Both were similar in general appearance to our summer-flowering native, *H. occidentalis* [*H. caroliniana*], but there were differences in length of tube, segments, and cup. Last September, Mrs. McMillan brought the flowers and leaves of one of these from an old garden in the southern part of the state [North Carolina]. The other came from Atlanta and bloomed with me in July.

My sister came across another summer-flowering hymenocallis in a garden in Alexandria, Louisiana. "Mrs. Peters has the most beautiful white flower that looks as if it belongs to that family you talk about so much," she wrote in August. When she came home this year in June, she brought me two of the bulbs. One of them bloomed after dark on July the sixteenth, and it seemed to me, as I looked at it in the moon light, more beautiful than any hymenocallis I had seen. The perfectly proportioned flowers seem larger than those of any other native species, though they are not very much so by measurement. The delicately fluted cup is an inch and a quarter deep, the dropping segments (incurved and revolute at the tips) are three and a half inches long, and the greenish tube is three inches long. There are five pleasantly but not heavily scented flowers to an umbel. They are of good substance and withstand the heat of the day better than most. One leaf came up with the stout glaucous scape.

When I wrote Mrs. Dormon, who lives in Shreveport, about Mrs. Peters's spider lily, she said that she thought it must be the same as an unidentified native species she had in her garden and which she designates as "fall blooming" to distinguish it from another native that blooms in the spring. I put two of the bulbs that she sent me in the ground at once, and wintered a third in a pot. One of those left outside put up one weak leaf late in the spring, but it soon died away. However, Mrs. Henry says she has found this spider lily to be hardy in Pennsylvania. "I have grown hymenocallis here for some years and enjoy them immensely," she wrote Mrs. Dormon. "I have them growing on a southern slope—in fact, the warmest spot on my place—and give them no protection whatever in winter. You sent me two kinds several years ago—one marked 'spring blooming' and one marked 'fall blooming.' Only one of these has bloomed so far, and it blooms in August. The leaves are a glaucous bluish. It is a tall vigorous species and very beautiful."

Some of the exotic hymenocallis species are hardy in North Carolina. One sent to me labeled *Pancratium maritimum* bloomed several successive years in late May or early June, occasionally repeating. I moved it to a damp shady place, and it has not bloomed again, though it always makes a good clump of dark green foliage. The leaves are narrow and strap-shaped and come before the flowers. The flowers are four to an umbel with very narrow segments, shallow cups, and very long green tubes. This hymenocallis is similar to a narrow-leaved species that came from Mr. Houdyshel as a "dwarf spider lily." It bloomed once in June, sending up a single scape, and did not bloom again for four years, though it increased and produced shining foliage each spring. Then, this year, the first of July, it suddenly bloomed again. Their erratic blooming habits are the only drawback I can discover to the use of spider lilies in the garden.

Mr. Houdyshel's "tropical spider lily" lived through three winters and bloomed two summers (in June and July), and then failed to come through when the thermometer dropped to six degrees above zero during the January that the weather bureau said was the coldest on record. I am trying it again, for the flowers are the most beautiful of any species that I have grown. There are twelve to an umbel, and they are very large and fragrant. The beautiful wide dark green leaves are like those of the ismene, and like them come up late in the spring and last until heavy frost. They are extremely decorative.

Ismene calathina [*Hymenocallis narcissiflora*] is hardy out of doors in North Carolina and blooms, but not well, for several years if left in the ground. However, it is not really satisfactory unless the bulbs are dug each year. The hybrid 'Sulphur Queen' is a better garden subject because the bulbs do not split up. I have wanted very much to try out the newer ismene hybrids, but they have been expensive. Now that the prices have come down, I have 'Advance'. I put it in the most protected spot in the garden, at the foot of a low wall facing south. If it succeeds, I shall try the others.

The bulb in the trade as *Hymenocallis caribaea* has not proved hardy here after many trials, though it is said to be hardy to North Carolina and perhaps even farther north. It may be that deeper planting would have got results.

In North Carolina, the sea daffodil, *Pancratium maritimum*, survives in well-drained soil, but I have had bloom only once, though I have planted it many times. The bloom was from a spring planted bulb; but, even with spring planting, it is not certain to flower. Because it is so very beautiful and the bulbs cost so little, I am still trying to prove it a satisfactory garden subject.

ZEPHYRANTHES, HABRANTHUS, AND CYRTANTHUS

In this part of the country, everyone is familiar from childhood with the milk-white atamasco lilies that bloom in April in low-lying meadows. Although this is the only species native to North Carolina, a number of zephyranthes flourish in my garden. The most prolific and floriferous of these are the handsome pink *Z. grandiflora* and the little white-flowered *Z. candida*. *Z. citrina* (from the Amaryllis Society) usually blooms once a month from July to October; the bulbs do not increase. This is the best yellow-flowered species. *Z. pulchella* (also from the Society) is similar to *Z. citrina*, but not so adaptable to garden conditions. It bloomed only once, early in September. The other yellow-flowered Texas species, *Z. longifolia* (from Mr. Ainsley), lived for several years but never bloomed. Afterward I learned from

Mr. Cory that it will bloom only in a highly calcareous soil, but I could not find it listed again. I doubt that the gardener would find the flower very different from that of *Habranthus texanus* [*H. tubispathus*], but once you have set your heart on seeing a little bulb in bloom, it haunts you until you have been able to secure it and at least proved that it will not bloom for you.

Z. simpsonii, another of the species that the Society sent to members, is similar to *Z. treatiae*, but neither as handsome nor as lasting. *Z. treatiae*, said to be difficult of culture, is well established with me. However, it does not increase.

The zephyr lilies that have not lived through a winter or bloomed even once are *Z. bifolia* and *Z. macrosiphon*. *Z. tubispatha* [*Habranthus tubispathus*] came up for one or two springs before disappearing for good. *Z. rosea*, which I have planted many times and which is my favorite, sometimes lives through the winter, but it does not persist many seasons. It bloomed once at the end of the summer, and the little deep rose-colored lilies are the most exquisite little flowers that ever appeared in a garden. I am still trying to find the sheltered place and the proper soil to allow it to become established.

The hybrid, *Z.* × 'Ajax' [a hybrid of uncertain parentage][7] is not very robust here. I have had it longer than I can remember, but it increases little and rarely produces more than one of its delicate pale flowers during a season. It blooms in the late summer or fall and is capricious, coming any time from August to October.

Of the three species of *Habranthus* available, *H. robustus* and *H. texanus* [*H. tubispathus*] have long bloomed in my garden, and *H. brachyandrus* bloomed there last summer for the first time. I have read that *H. texanus* is difficult in culture, but it is most amenable with me. It blooms freely at intervals from early June to late September and increases well. The flowers of *H. brachyandrus* are larger than those of any habranthus or zephyranthes that I have seen and of such tropical beauty that I could not believe they would endure any amount of cold. But the new leaves began to put out very early in the spring after a very trying winter. Whether it will bloom the second season is another question.

---

7. In a later article for *Plants and Garden* (Summer 1948), Elizabeth Lawrence stated her belief that *Z.* × 'Ajax' is a hybrid between *Z. candida* and *Z. citrina*. (See "Tender Bulbs for Summer Bloom" later in this section.)

Cyrtanthus is a genus that does not thrive in these parts, and I am not surprised, for the species come from South Africa. The bulbs seem to be fairly hardy, but they do not become established well enough to bloom with any satisfaction. *C. lutescens* [*C. mackenii* var. *cooperi*] was planted in April and bloomed in May and then lingered on for several seasons without blooming at all. *C. parviflorus* [*C. brachyscyphus*], planted in October, skipped a season but bloomed the second spring. That was the last of *C. parviflorus*, and *C. mackenii* and *C. angustifolius* never bloomed. These were all planted in a low place in clay soil with a mulch of cow manure. I put them there because that is the place where the zephyr lilies thrive, but it may be that in this climate they need more drainage.

SNOWDROPS AND SNOWFLAKES

I started growing snowdrops [*Galanthus*] on the theory that the species from Asia Minor would be better adapted than those from Europe to conditions in the South. But of those that I have grown, *Galanthus nivalis* 'Scharlokii' has been by far the most satisfactory over a period of years. *G. elwesii* persists, but does not bloom as well and does not bloom any earlier. *G. byzantinus* [*G. plicatus* ssp. *byzantinus*] bloomed in midwinter, but that effort was too much for it, I suppose, as it was never seen again. *G. latifolius* [*G. ikariae*, Latifolius group] did nothing.

As to snowflakes [*Leucojum*], as near as I can tell, all of those in the trade as *L. vernum* are *L. aestivum*. I have never got *L. vernum* under its own name or any other if it is, as described, a solitary flower. If this species is to be had in this country, I would like to know about it. Being particularly eager for fall flowers, I also tried *L. autumnale*. So far it has not bloomed in the fall, or at any other time. In general, I have not found bulbs from the Mediterranean satisfactory in North Carolina.

THE ALLIEAE[8]

In this tribe I have made attempts at growing many brodiaeas, many more alliums, *Milla biflora*, *Pharium elegans* (*Bessera elegans*), and *Leucocoryne ixiodes*, the last three without success.

Mr. James doubts (*Herbertia*, 1936) whether the two Mexican bulbs will stand many degrees of frost and thinks they should be dug,

---

8. The Allieae are now classified as Liliaceae (Alliaceae) rather than as Amaryllidaceae.

except in the milder climates. I suppose the climates in which they need not be dug are milder than this, for here they were not satisfactory even as summer bulbs. The milla was planted twice, once in the fall and again in the spring. The spring-planted bulb bloomed, but poorly. The pharium was planted in spring, but it did not bloom. Neither the milla nor the pharium lived through a winter, but I am trying them again this year in a more protected place.

Leucocoryne ixioides odorata [*L. ixioides*] fared no better, which was only to be expected as I set the bulb out in winter. I mean to give it another trial, though that is scarcely worthwhile, for it is said to require the same culture as freesias, and they are too tender for us.

The alliums are too numerous to take up in detail. Most of them do well (some only too well), but there are a few that I have not been able to grow. The beautiful azure *Allium caeruleum* did not persist. The somewhat tender *A. neapolitanum* seems to be hardy, but blooms so early that the flower buds are nearly always caught by the cold, and even when they are not caught, they are inferior to those of other species. *A. karataviense* lives, but that is all. *A. rosenbachianum* did nothing. *A. validum* was tried in vain a number of times. I cannot get enough moisture for it. *A. moly*, which is the most attractive one that I have seen, with large bunches of daffodil-yellow flowers, refuses to grow at all. This I cannot understand, and I mean to keep trying.

Brodiaeas in North Carolina are not what they are in the West. (Mrs. Rowntree says this is because I do not cultivate deep enough.) But they make charming and fragile bloom in the shady rock garden. *B. ixioides* [*Triteleia ixioides*], *B. coccinea* (*Brevoortia ida-maia*) [*Dichelostemma ida-maia*], and the white-flowered *B. eastwoodii* [*Triteleia peduncularis*] did not persist, but most of the species do. The blue dicks and a run-of-the-mill hybrid have bloomed in one place for more than ten years. The pale-lavender-flowered *B. bridgesii* [*Triteleia bridgesii*] is one of the prettiest, though the precocious flowers are often nipped by frost. *B. lactea* [*Triteleia hyacintha*] and *B. coronaria*, the harvest brodiaea, are the dependable sorts.

OTHER AMARYLLIDS AND ALSTROEMERIAS

After many years of trial, I have given up hope of establishing alstroemerias, especially after discovering that they are susceptible to the bacterial wilt that is the curse of Southern gardens. I have had *A. aurantiaca* [*A. aurea*] and its cultivar lutea and *A. chilensis*. Only *A. auran-*

tiaca bloomed. It bloomed in late June after having been planted in October, and when all of the gorgeous flowers were open, the whole plant turned yellow and died.

Ixiolirion tataricum, the one time I bloomed it, was a poor thing. Perhaps it should have been in a richer soil, or perhaps the bulbs were poor to begin with. At any rate, I was not sorry when they disappeared, but I should like to try again with bulbs from another source.

I have had the delicate lily, *Chlidanthus fragrans*, many times and from many sources and have planted it in various parts of the garden. Leaves appear season after season, but no blooms. It is said to be a satisfactory garden plant when taken up and dried off, but with me, even large spring-planted bulbs fail to flower.

Sternbergia lutea has been in Southern gardens since the days of the colonists. In mine, for some reason, it is chary of bloom, though I have had it for long years and the clumps are well established. Late in August or early in September there are always a few of the buttercup yellow flowers, but never many. I cannot help but think that the Amaryllis family as a whole is somewhat temperamental.

Agapanthus africanus 'Mooreanus'[9] grew in a low border for a number of years and bloomed once, at the end of June, but not before it was well established. Later it disappeared. The flowers were a dull blue, and I hope that when I try it again, I shall get a better form. *A. orientalis* (*A. umbellatus*) [*A. praecox* ssp. *orientalis*] has not bloomed, but has come back after its third winter. It is said to bloom out of doors in Raleigh. I have a root from Mr. Hayward and one from a garden in California.

Sprekelia formosissima is perfectly hardy with us, but capricious as to bloom. At least, it is capricious with me. But a friend who saw it one of the two times it did flower said, "Oh, those little red lilies used to bloom every spring in our old garden in Petersburg." I doubt whether she knew much about flowers, but I do not think that anyone could mistake the Jacobean lily.

Vallota speciosa (in the trade as *V. purpurea*) [*Cyrtanthus elatus*] was planted one September at the foot of a retaining wall and was never seen again. I should have planted it in the spring and on top of the wall and mixed sand with the heavy soil. If I can get hold of it again (it took me a number of years to procure the first bulb), I shall treat it better. Colonel Grey says that it is hardy with a little protection in the

---

9. Agapanthus is now classified as Liliaceae rather than as Amaryllidaceae.

south and west of Great Britain, so long as it is not water-logged in winter.

Daffodils (*Narcissus*) and daylilies (*Hemerocallis*)[10] flourish in the South, but these, of course, flourish everywhere. I would like to try more of the tender daffodils, particularly of the tazetta and triandrus groups. Of daylilies I have had mostly the standard sorts, but I have been interested in several of Mr. Hayward's, particularly one with a small dark red flower.

AMARYLLIDS IN ENGLAND AND THE UNITED STATES

It is interesting to compare one's own results in growing amaryllids with those of gardeners in other places. I noted particularly Major Pam's remarks in *Herbertia* (1940, p. 41) on the hardiness of amaryllids in his English garden where the winters are more severe than those in Piedmont, North Carolina:

> The past winter has been very cold indeed for this country, and record frosts have been recorded in many parts. In my gardens, the lowest temperature was 2 degrees below zero Fahrenheit in the open, and it hovered around zero for several weeks. Yet the amaryllids grown in the open did not suffer, and I have had but few losses. It seems as if established plants can stand very much more cold than we had expected, and I think it may be worth while for some lovers of this family who live in the more northern States of the U.S.A. to try to grow in their garden some species which were reputed to be tender. Among the plants which not only survived here but have flowered this year as freely as ever are: *Amaryllis* (*Hippeastrum*) *pratensis* [*Rhodophiala pratensis*], *Sprekelia formosissima*, *Amaryllis* (*Hippeastrum*) *ackermannii* [*Hippeastrum* × *acramannii*]; *Crinum* × *powellii*; *C. moorei*, and *C. longifolium* [*C. bulbispermum*]; *Alstroemeria ligtu*,[11] *A. aurantiaca* [*A. aurea*]; *A. chilensis*; *Pancratium illyricum*, in addition, of course, to all the species generally considered hardy. These flowers are untouched by frost and will certainly flower freely in their proper season: *Callicore rosea* (*Amaryllis belladonna*), *Nerine bowdenii major*, *Hymenocallis* × *festalis* (Mr. Worsley's hybrid), *Lycoris spp.*, and several other alstroemerias such as *A. brasiliensis*.

---

10. *Hemerocallis* is now considered a member of the Liliaceae family or Hemerocallidaceae.

11. Now classified as Liliaceae.

> *I think we have more beautiful weather in the fall than at any other time of year. In the garden this season should be the climax of bloom, rich in a new beauty of its own, and not just a period when there is some color left over from summer.*
> A Southern Garden

In Quest of Autumn-Blooming Bulbs

It is unfortunate that I have chosen this time out of a lifetime of gardening to collect the fall-flowering species of colchicum and crocus, for they have become increasingly difficult to obtain since I have been in search of them, and this year I could not add a single one to my collection. I have loved colchicums ever since, as a little girl, we used to bring the bulbs home from the "five-and-ten" and let them bloom on the parlor table. Afterward we planted them in a dank spot under the refrigerator drip, and they continued to bloom season after season. But it was much later in life that I learned that there are also crocuses that bloom in the fall. I acquired several kinds and planted them in the edges of the borders, where after a few years the tiny bulbs disappeared. I think they were pulled up along with the heavy roots of annuals. Anyway, the borders are no place for small bulbs, and now they are all in the rock garden along with the colchicums. The latter are practically indestructible, but they did not amount to anything in the borders either, so they are all in the rock garden with the crocuses, where they are grown under oak trees with plenty of leaf mold mixed into the stiff red clay and are fertilized only by an occasional dressing of sheep manure and bonemeal. Once established, they bloom faithfully and increase slowly, and it seemed to me this year that they have been lovelier than ever.

Here in North Carolina, the colchicums begin to bloom in the middle or at the end of August and continue—almost without a break—until the first fall crocuses thrust up their buds late in September. They do not always appear in the same order, so I shall describe them as they appeared in 1944, the year this article is being written.

Colchicum parkinsonii [*C. variegatum*] was the first. It bloomed on August fifteenth, five days earlier than last year. This is an odd little flower and not nearly so striking as some of the other species, but it was the favorite of Parkinson himself; and I like it because it blooms so freely and so brightly. The small, tessellated flowers are a glowing lilac and of a very individual form, being more open than the other species and with narrow twisted segments. This one is from southern Europe, and I imagine that it does best in a mild climate.

C. bornmuelleri, usually described as the earliest, came next. A single bulb planted years ago sends up a succession of pale buds that deepen to lilac as they open. When these have at last disappeared, the ground is bare again until the wide leaves appear in early spring. This Asiatic species is very tough. It blooms yearly in a poor, dry soil in deep shade. The flowers are comparatively large and very delicately colored. I expect they would be brighter in the sun, but in these parts, colchicums do not thrive in the sun.

'Premier' bloomed two days after *C. bornmuelleri*. It looks like a hybrid between that species and *C. parkinsonii*, having the form of the first and the checkered pattern of the latter. The checks are faint at first, but grow more intense as the flower matures until they are almost a Chinese lilac. The flowers are the largest I have had, three inches long. The only other [species] that I have tried is *C. giganteum*, which has not bloomed so far. It is supposed to be a late variety, and I am eager to see what it will do here.

Last year *C. speciosum* bloomed the first of all, coming on the tenth of August, but this year it did not open until the thirty-first. *C. speciosum* 'Album', which Mr. Craig says is the best white form, has not yet bloomed for me.

So far *C. autumnale* is the latest of the colchicums. This year it bloomed on the fifteenth of September. It is a small, delicately colored, crocus-like species, not spectacular but very desirable for winding up the season. The white form bloomed on September twenty-fifth and lasted into October. Last year it did not begin to bloom until early in October.

This fall the first crocus bloomed on the twenty-seventh of September. It was *C. speciosus*, which is usually later, seldom coming before the first week in October. This species is usually described as "blue," but I have never had one that was not red-violet. The type, as I have it, is a sort of wisteria-violet with dark feathering and red gold stigmas.

Then I have *C. speciosus* 'Globosus', which is similar but a little later to bloom. Both of these are good and permanent.

The lovely, pure white *C. niveus* bloomed on September twenty-eight. These white crocuses are large and free flowering, and so far have been more attractive than the white colchicums.

This season *Crocus zonatus* [*C. kotchyanus* ssp. *kotschyanus*] flowered on October first, but usually it is a week earlier and the first to appear. It is typically of a rosy color, but the form I have comes out almost white with a grayish tinge and becomes a delicate lavender with age. In the pale autumn sunshine, it looks too ethereal to be true. I keep thinking up excuses to go back in the garden when it is in bloom. The yellow zone in the throat and the delicate veining make such an intricate and lovely design that I can never look at it enough. But in spite of seeming so fragile, it is a robust sort, increasing rapidly and blooming over a long period—at least three weeks.

I used to have *C. sativus*, the saffron crocus, with its bright violet flowers blooming the second week in October. It bloomed for several years and increased, but it disappeared at last—lost, I am sure, in the roots of the weedy annual ageratum—and of course it cannot be replaced at this time.

The last and the least is *C. longiflorus*, with small mauve flowers darkly feathered and smelling of violets. These come with the leaves. The first one bloomed on the fourth of October, and now, at the end of the month, they are still coming.

Someday I hope to find still later kinds to extend the season into the late fall and perhaps even to stretch it out into the winter and until the early blossoms of *C. sieberi*, which in mild winters appear soon after the new year. It would be delightful to have colchicums and then crocuses from the middle of August until March, and the idea does not seem too fantastic.

A yellow species, Allium flavum, *also blooms in June, but it is not showy in the borders. In the rock garden the slight stalks and loose sprays of nodding lemon-colored flowers can be very charming.*
A Southern Garden

Ornamental Alliums in North Carolina

When I am asked to name the three best alliums in my garden, I must first inquire, "Best for what?" If we are choosing the most beautiful, I think I must say "None." For none of the outstandingly beautiful allium species has ever succeeded with me. *A. validum* blooms sparingly and does not persist, and *A. moly*—the loveliest of all of the alliums that I have seen—remains a failure after many trials. If we are considering distinction, I would mention *A. albopilosum* [*A. christophii*] first, for the broad heads of metallic lavender flowers are fascinating. For abundance of bloom, *A. senescens* would be one of the three, for it blooms from late May to late August, and blooms freely and continuously. But, I think that with me, the late-blooming alliums fill the greatest need; and, therefore, I choose *A. subroseum* [listed name of no botanical standing], *A. tanguticum*, and *A. ramosum* (or the plant that grows in my garden under that name).

A. subroseum is somewhat drab in color, but it is dainty enough to make a neat rock plant; and, in the South in midsummer, we do not ask too much. It does not appear in *Hortus Second*, so I all I know about it is that it takes to cultivation easily and braves the worst part of the season—late August and September. It is only five or six inches tall with spherical heads of pale lavender (not pink) flowers.

Years ago, Elizabeth Rawlinson gave me *A. tanguticum* as one of the best garden species, and I still think that it is. The pale opalescent flowers are showy only in mass, but the clumps increase rapidly and can be divided frequently. In a few years, mine have made a border that is very pretty in July and August, and blooms on into September. And this in a poor part of the garden where there is seldom bloom at any season. Colonel Grey describes the leaves of this species as four to six inches long, and the stems as rather longer. With me the stems are more than a foot tall.

The plant that came to me as *A. ramosum* is more like *A. tuberosum* as described by Colonel Grey and in *Hortus Second*. The flowers are not especially fragrant, and the segments are keeled with green, not red. Whatever it is, it is a good one. I did not think much of it the first season; but by the second summer, it made a very fine showing from late July to early September. The quantities of silvery flowers above the narrow gray foliage were refreshing in the scorched borders. It is the tallest allium I have had, with stems three feet long. From another source I have what seems to be the same plant as *A. odorum* [*A. ramosum*] and what seems to be the same, but blooms late in May, also as *A. odorum*.

*The tropical splendor of their
lush foliage and large flowers is unbelievable
in a garden where the temperature
sometimes approaches zero.*
A Southern Garden

Hybrid Crinums

The Piedmont region of North Carolina, where I live and garden, is in Zone 6, which is also the zone of Atlanta, Georgia; Birmingham, Alabama; Shreveport, Louisiana; and Wichita Falls, Texas. In all of these cities, I have friends who write to me about their gardens, and I find that we succeed and fail with very much the same things.

Among the half-hardy bulbs and plants that I have found hardy enough for this climate, I have been particularly impressed with the crinums, especially the named varieties. Of these, I have grown seven, and only one proved too tender. This was the 'Empress of India', a lovely and languid night-flowering variety that blooms only after sunset and fades before dawn.

It came from Winter Park, Florida, and I do not know whether it would be hardy above Zone 8, but I should think it would be worthwhile to try it in Zone 7. I am sure that it would be useless to try it here again, as the winter I left it out was a phenomenally mild one when the thermometer did not go below 21 degrees above [zero F]. I planted it in the garden late in March, and in September there were two dark red scapes with ten flowers to an umbel. Each night, two or three of the slender red-and-white-striped buds opened into wide delicate flowers with segments six inches long. The 'Empress of India' is a crinum of the milk-and-wine type with dark vinaceous midlines down the outside of the segments and showing through faintly on the inside.

Unlike the iris and the daylilies, of which there are so many similar named varieties that the lists are confusing, there are comparatively few crinum hybrids, and each is distinct. They are also very easy to grow, and practically immune to disease and pests. The only trouble that I have ever had is mustard seed rot on 'Virginia Lee', which was easily cleared up with semesan.

Most crinums like sun or light shade, but the variety 'Virginia Lee' needs shade. All are at their best in heavy soil that is deep and fertile, and plenty of water is essential to bloom. Sometimes crinums are slow to bloom, but once established, they are more floriferous every season. They should not be moved once they are planted, for it takes ten years for a clump to be at its best. Crinums are heavy feeders, and I give mine a mulch of dairy manure in the fall. That and water in dry weather is all of the attention that mine get, though. Cecil Houdyshel of LaVerne, California, recommends mulching with manure and humus several times a year.

In my garden, the first of the crinum hybrids to bloom is 'White Queen'. In an early season, its first flowers open before the middle of May, and the last come about the middle of June. It is said to be very free-flowering, but with me this is not so. It has no more than four or five scapes in a season, while *C. powelli* [*Crinum* × *powellii*] has between twenty and thirty. But I like it for its earliness, and for the vanilla-like perfume of the dropping white flowers and their curled tips.

Crinum 'Cecil Houdyshel' blooms steadily over a long period, sometimes with ten or more stalks in bloom at once. The twenty to thirty flowers of each scape open in pairs. It begins late in May with the Japanese iris; continues through June with loosestrife, larkspur, *Spiraea venusta*, *Stokesia*, the rosy shades of *Monarda didyma*; through July with 'Mallow Marvels' (pale pink ones), *Monarda fistulosa*, and *Phlox* 'Mrs. Millie Van Hoboken'; and on into August with pink *Boltonia* and *Physostegia* [*virginiana*] 'Vivid'. It is very tall (over three-and-a-half feet), and the deep pink, campanulate flowers stand high among the loosestrife and well above the phlox. It is wide-spreading too, and well-established clumps need from three to four feet.

The only real drawback to crinums is that they take up so much room. A border must be very deep and long to allow space for crinums and perennials too. In my garden there are four large clumps of 'Cecil Houdyshel' in a border that is thirty-four feet long and ten feet wide. It is a low border with heavy red clay soil. The bloom begins in April with spring-flowering white spider lilies from Louisiana, and a number of varieties of Louisiana iris. The bloom ends late in October with *Aster tartaricus* and the butterfly lily. In the margins of the border are several kinds of rain lilies, and the wonderful *Amarcrinum* [× *Amarcrinum*] that is low-growing and pink-flowered. In Florida, it is said to grow as tall as the crinums, but with me it is never over two feet. It blooms from early August to late October and carries on the lovely pink color when 'Cecil Houdyshel' has ceased to bloom.

C. powelli [*C.* × *powellii*], like 'Cecil Houdyshel', is a cross between *C. moorei* and *C. longifolium* [*C. bulbispermum*]. With me these two are the most prolific bloomers. *C. powelli* does not bloom for as long a time; it begins late in May or early in June and lasts well into July, but it has more scapes at a time. I cannot imagine anything in the garden that could be more beautiful than this pure white crinum in full bloom. This is one of the hardiest of all of the crinums. Its origin is unknown, but Colonel Grey thinks it probable that it was raised by Dean Herbert. It is nice to think it. There are several good color forms. *C. powelli roseum* [*C.* × *powellii* 'Roseum'] is a lovely pink one that I lost for some reason. I have wanted to try it again, but have never found it listed again. The flowers of *C. powelli* variety 'Krelagei' [*C.* × *powellii* 'Krelagii'] are of a more delicate pink than those of 'Cecil Houdyshel', but its constitution is less robust. The umbels are large, and the flowers of a very distinct character, open and flaring, and delightfully scented.

'Louis Bosanquet' is another hybrid of the *powelli* [*C.* × *powellii*] type. It is described as one of the best garden forms and one of the most floriferous, but with me it does not bloom well and is not a favorite. The pink buds and the smallish pink-tipped flowers are borne in a tight umbel on a very tall scape. They are more like *C. longifolium* [*C. bulbispermum*] than any of the other hybrids of this group, and I shall not give it space when I need room for new crinums. It begins to bloom late in May and continues into July.

'Ellen Bosanquet' is the most distinctive hybrid as to color. The dark buds open into spinel red flowers, a very rich and unusual shade, but difficult in a mixed border. Because it looked dull in the rather pastel group around 'Cecil Houdyshel', I moved it into another part of the garden where there are clumps of pink phlox like 'Rhinelander' and 'Jules Sandeau', with drifts of *Monarda didyma salmonea* ['Salmonea'] (which is not salmon at all, but a rosy red) and the darker wine color of *Allium sphaerocephalum*. With me, 'Ellen Bosanquet' is not so tall as the *powelli* [*C.* × *powellii*] types. The stout scapes are only two feet.

They appear late in June and into July, or sometimes earlier. So far it has made a good clump but has not bloomed very freely. The flowers open in the afternoon, and hold their vivid color the next day.

Mr. Houdyshel, who introduced 'Virginia Lee', a cross between 'Cecil Houdyshel' and 'J. C. Harvey', says that it is the first second-generation hybrid that he knows of. He describes it (in *Herbertia* 1935) as much like 'J. C. Harvey' in appearance, but finds it very free blooming, although its parent is (in California) a very shy bloomer. With me it has bloomed but once, in late June, though I have had it for five years. I think this is due to too much shade, and I am going to move it in the fall. It is said to resemble its ancestor *C. moorei* in requiring shade, but I have an idea that the degree differs in California and North Carolina. All of my garden has afternoon shade from oaks on the west, and I think that it would do better if planted in the open, instead of under trees. I want it to do well, for it is a small one, with leaves not over fourteen inches and a compact growth habit. With me the flowers (ten to an umbel) are very pale, really white, with a pink flush. This, also, is probably due to too much shade, for Mr. Houdyshel describes it as bright pink with a white throat.

'H. J. Elwes', the last hybrid added to my collection, has not bloomed yet, but seems to be hardy. This is another pink one.

Miss Willie May Kell, my Texas correspondent, has grown most of the hybrids that I have tried, and with much the same success. In addition, she reports 'Peachblow', a perfumed pinkish white variety, as hardy and one of the choice sorts. It bloomed for her in mid-June, and in Florida, it is said to bloom all year.

I always plant crinums in the spring, but I do not suppose that the planting time matters if you are sure that they are hardy. In warm climates they are planted with half of the bulbs above the ground. Here I plant them with just the neck above, and Mr. Houdyshel suggests that they be set with the base eight or ten inches deep where they are on the border line of hardiness.

The clumps bloom better every year that they are left alone, but they can be dug and divided when increase is preferable to bloom.
A Southern Garden

Further Notes on Hybrid Crinums

Very soon after the article on crinums (September 1946) had been sent off to *Home Gardening*, the variety 'J. C. Elwes' ['H. J. Elwes'] bloomed for me for the first time. That is always the way when you write about plants. This hybrid is such an unusual one that I would like to add a note about it, especially as I have never seen anything about it in garden literature (and I have searched and searched), and as the catalogue description tells you no more than that it is pink. No one had ever told me that it is late-flowering, which it is if this first season is characteristic. To me the summer- and fall-flowering varieties are far more desirable than the earlier sorts that bloom when most things bloom.

There was a single scape that produced an umbel of seven large fragrant flowers, which, unlike any other crinum I have known, came out one by one. Each flower lasted several days (which is unusual), and the scape was in bloom from the 31st of August to the 15th of September. The 25-inch stalk was dark wine color, and comparatively slender. The flowers were wide open, starry, a deep rose color that is near the tint called Spinel pink, and marked with a pure white throat. They were strongly vanilla scented. It is one of the most distinct varieties that I have had, and it is a very strong grower.

The spring I planted it was the spring that my springer was a young puppy. When I had at last got a deep enough hole in the damp heavy clay and worked in enough leaf mold and old manure, I turned wearily to pick up the bulb that I had laid beside me, and it was not there. It was a large, round, expensive bulb, very like a ball. When I found it, Mr. Cayce had eaten all but the heart. My mother said, "Let's plant it anyway." (She said lots more to Mr. Cayce.) I planted it, and it bloomed the second summer.

I have been thinking about the crinum 'Virginia Lee', and I do not believe it is ever going to do anything for me. The trouble is that it makes its growth in winter. The new leaves come from the dormant bulb in the fall, and they are very soon killed by frost. Even in a mild winter like this one, no new foliage is produced. Miss Willie May Kell wrote me that it has been very slow to grow in Texas, and that it has never bloomed. And the climate of Wichita Falls must be much milder than I thought (according to the zoning map), for she says she leaves her potted eucharis in the ground all year. She gives the same report of 'Sophie Nehrling', which makes me think I shall not try 'Sophie' as I was planning to do.

I had several interesting letters about the crinum article. Mrs. Slaughter wrote from Houston, "I think I may be able to help you in the identification of the white tulip-like crinum pictured at the top of page 436 of *Home Gardening*,[1] for I have a vase of the blooms in my room today. The photograph does not show the foliage of this crinum clearly—which is its unique feature. It is the only one I know whose wide upright leaves are totally different from the usual strap-like foliage of the others. I saw this crinum first with my husband when he was lecturing in China in 1927 and 1928. It is tender, a shade lover, and in central China was used in pots. But later, in southern China, I saw it growing in quantity in beds. Happily I was able to get one bulb in Florida, when I came back, and now have six large clumps. It is *Crinum giganteum* [*C. jagus*], and with us in Houston, is just beginning to bloom now (September 16th, 1946), and last season I cut the last blossom after the middle of December. As a rule, we do not have any serious cold weather here until after Christmas."

I had already identified the crinum in the picture (which I had not mentioned in the article as it is a species) to my own satisfaction as *Crinum giganteum* [*C. jagus*]. I had never seen this species in bloom, but it is so like one that I had once from Mr. Wyndham Hayward marked "Christopher lily, near *C. giganteum*" that I hadn't any doubt about it. It is interesting that this species is so widely grown in China, for it is not

---

1. When this article was originally published, the editors of *Home Gardening for the South* noted that the blooming time for the clump photographed for the September 1946 issue was always June.

native there. Its provenance is tropical Africa. I have a note that it was first pictured from a plant "received by her Ladyship, the Rt. Hon., the Marchioness of Rockingham about 1792 from Sierra Leone."

In the old botanies it was called the gigantic asphodel lily. I always wondered why "gigantic," for it is small like *C. moorei* and rather similar. I once planted the species in my garden, but I made the mistake of putting it out in the fall and it never bloomed though it lived through the winters. In Bailey's *Cyclopedia*, Dr. Nehrling describes *C. giganteum* as having leaves "as ornamental as an aspidistra or a dracaena." He says that (in Florida) it forms large clumps in a few years, and blooms even in winter when the weather is warm.

The "Christopher Lily" is one of the most beautiful flowers that I have had in my garden. It bloomed in July after a late spring planting (and never appeared again), and I remember the gray anthers "shaped exactly like a horse-shoe," described on the note to the picture. *C. giganteum*, like *C. asiaticum* and *C. amabile*, which also proved tender, is one of the evergreen species.

*Above the yellowing leaves of the
day-lilies, the wands of the blackberry-lilies,
Belamcanda chinensis, hold ephemeral flowers
of ochre spotted with carmine.*
A Southern Garden

A Review of the Iris Family

The Iris family, on the whole, has not taken to my garden as cheerfully as those other Southerners, the amaryllids, but the ones that thrive are among the most desirable garden flowers for this climate. Because the main centers of distribution are the Cape of Good Hope and subtropical America, only three genera are really hardy, and many find their northern limit in Zone 7. Through the years, I have tried out about half of the sixty odd genera in an effort to discover those that are hardy and garden worthy in Zone 6. A number have proved too tender for North Carolina—or for some other reason have failed to become established. But it will take many trials in many gardens before we can be sure just how far north they are hardy.

The hardy genera are *Belamcanda*, most irises, most crocuses, and the books say *Lapeirousia*. Lapeirousia is one of the Cape bulbs, a group that does not take to North Carolina. It is hard to acquire, unless you raise it from seed, and therefore I have tried it but once. It was planted in October, and that was the end.

Belamcanda chinensis is common in country gardens, and has even become naturalized in the North. The Japanese species, *B. flabellata*, is superior to it. This is supposed to be low-growing, but the thin, wiry flower stems reach two and a half feet with me. The wide, pale orange, rose-spotted flowers last but a day. It likes a light soil, rich and moist, and blooms late in summer.

The crocuses come from the Mediterranean region and southern Asia, so they would be expected to like warm climates, and it seems to me they should be made more of in Southern gardens. I started to collect them before the war, but had got only a few before they ceased to appear in the catalogues. Last fall when they reappeared, I began again. The fall- and spring-blooming groups overlap when the weather is propitious. This year they met for the first time in my garden—if you would call it meeting; they both looked so chilly. *Crocus asturicus* [*C. serotinus* ssp. *salzmannii*], which had begun to bloom early in December, still had a blossom when *C. tommasinianus* put forth buds (early, for it seldom blooms before February) in the middle of January. The first is a Spanish species, new this year. I don't know how it will behave as a permanent resident. The second is one of the best for settling down to grow and increase.

Another good species for these parts in December and January is *C. sieberi*, from Greece. *C. susianus* [*C. angustifolius*] of the Crimea can be counted upon for February. The first in the fall, and also a permanent species once it is established, is *C. zonatus* [*C. kotschyanus*], which blooms late in September and is followed by the blue-violet *C. speciosus* and the pure white flowers of *C. niveus* in October. *C. longiflorus* comes in November.

Of the tender members of the genus *Iris*, a few are hardy in Zone 6, and a few are on the borderline of hardiness. *Iris japonica*, sometimes listed as *I. fimbriata*, is a definitely tender member of the Evansia group that I could not resist trying again this fall though it has died repeatedly. I first saw it in bloom in April in Chapel Hill, a clump that Billy Hunt had set out the fall before. He dug a piece for me on the spot, and later I ordered it from California, but none of it lived.

Iris unguicularis, better known as *I. stylosa*, on the other hand, is one of our garden treasures. This is an Algerian species, said to be hardy to Washington. Here it is permanent and floriferous once it is established, and blooms in open winters from November to March. It is said to like lime, so I mix a little wood ashes with the bonemeal and sheep manure that I scratch around it in spring and fall. There are a number of color forms, which for me always turn out to be identical—a bright lilac; and then there is a pure white one that is the best of all. If I could have but one winter flower in the garden it would certainly be this lovely iris with its delicate and fragrant blossoms.

Iris dichotoma [*Pardanthopsis dichotoma*], the Vesper iris, is not tender, but it is naturally short-lived. This will not matter to those who are willing to raise it from seed, for it comes easily and sometimes blooms the first year. It blooms late in the summer and late in the day, the pale lavender flowers lasting but an afternoon.

Sisyrinchiums are counted with the hardy irids, but aside from the natives, only *S. bermudianum* has persisted with me. This is a delightful and satisfactory rock plant for shade and leaf mold. The blue-violet flowers appear among the grassy leaves in mid-April and bloom on into the summer. The showiest species, *S. douglasii* (*S. grandiflorum*) [*Olsynium douglasii*] from the Northwest, once produced brilliant magenta blossoms in my garden in February, but I have never been able to keep it for more than a season.

Hermodactylus tuberosus is like an iris of the reticulata section and is usually in the trade as *Iris tuberosa*. I am putting it between the hardy and the half-hardy iris because I am not sure how far north it will grow. Not far, I expect, though Violet Walker writes of it in her garden in Virginia. With me it is hardy but not permanent. I think the bulbs need lifting in summer wherever they are. I have had it several times from the California growers, and it blooms here in February or March. The shimmering flowers are dark green, the falls marked with gold and tipped with dark velvet.

The half-hardy irids, which can be lifted in winter in cold climates and set out again in spring for summer bloom, are the acidantheras, chasmanthes, crocosmias, cypellas, gladiolas, tigridias, tritonias, and watsonias. All but the *Cypella* and *Tigridia* are South African.

Acidanthera bicolor [*Gladiolus callinthus*] is usually classed with the South African bulbs, but it comes from the mountains of Abyssinia. I have had it but once, when it was planted in November and did not survive. In this zone it should certainly be set out in spring even if it is left in the ground for experiment. The white and purple flowers on eighteen-inch stems are supposed to bloom in late summer and fall.

Chasmanthe aethiopica (*C. antholyza*) had the same fate. It was planted in the fall and came up the following fall, but never bloomed. It is supposed to grow to three feet and to produce tangerine red flowers in June.

Crocosmia aurea [*C.* × *crocosmiiflora*] I am still looking for in vain. It should be hardy here as it is the parent of the garden montbretias (*Tritonia*).

The montbretia (*Tritonia crocosmiiflora*) [*Crocosmia* × *crocosmiiflora*], as everyone knows, is one of the best garden bulbs for the South. Here it is perfectly hardy, and the only problem is to keep it from taking the border. The named hybrids are less rampant. They lengthen the season of bloom and add to the range of colors. I used to have some lovely ones, but I had not kept records of them, so I started last summer on a new collection. The first to bloom was 'His Majesty' on July the twenty-sixth when the type had passed its height. The last to bloom was 'Hereward' on August thirty-first, a magnificent flower of spectrum red.

Watsonias live over the winter with me, and a few bloom the following spring in May or June, but they are not really satisfactory to leave in the ground this far north. This is because they make their foliage in the winter, and it is damaged by the cold. There are several types, but the hybrids I had were like enormous delicately colored montbretias. I remember particularly a beautiful salmon pink one. This year I am trying a new evergreen group. They bloom in late summer and fall, and I thought that might give them more time to recover from the frost.

I cannot remember ever having had *Tigridia pavonia*, though I have seen it in bloom in gardens in North Carolina, and I know that it sometimes endures the winter and blooms again. However, it is not permanent in these parts; and as it comes from the cool plateau region of southern Mexico, it really prefers to summer farther north.

Cypella herbertia [*C. herbertii*] is like a small tigridia. It comes from South America and takes much better than tigridias to our climate. I am very grateful to Mrs. Dormon for giving me this delightful little irid that blooms and blooms all summer. The flowers are golden yellow, on wiry stems more than a foot tall. *Cypella* is not particular, but it seems to like a well-drained place in full sun.

The tender iris are for gardens in warm countries that are free from frost, or nearly so. None of the group from South Africa has been successful with me. Aristeas, babianas, freesias, dietes, *Schizostylis*, and moraeas are not garden worthy north of Southern California, the Gulf Coast, and Florida. In a charming walled garden in Shreveport, I saw some stiff iris-like foliage that I could not identify, and when I inquired about it, all that I could learn was that it "had a flower as blue as your pencil." I wrote to ask Mrs. Dormon if she knew of a low-growing irid as blue as my pencil, and she replied on a post card: "It is *Aristea ecklonii*, eighteen inches tall, well branched, bright blue flowers. It is a little grown in Shreveport, a great deal in New Orleans, will stand only twenty degrees of cold. I had it, but a surprise drop to three above killed it. There is a more robust one, *A. capitata* [*A. major*], but I have never seen it here. It grows and spreads well by seed, but is a little thing too tender for me."

Most things that are hardy with Mrs. Dormon in Shreveport are hardy with me, so that will give an idea of the northern limit of these tender bulbs.

Moraeas are sometimes grown out of doors in Shreveport, but Mr. Giridlian classes them with freesias as to culture, which does not sound very hardy. With me they have never been a success, though one or two have bloomed. I had had *Moraea glaucopis* [*M. aristata*], *M. ramosa* [*M. ramosissima*], and *M. ramosissima*. In *Hortus Second*, the dietes are not separated from the moraeas, but the California growers list them separately.[1] They have rhizomatous roots and require the same culture as irises. Mr. Giridlian says they are hardy where the fig grows and, as figs are hardy with us, I have decided to take a try at them although Mr. Houdyshel says they will not do where the temperature goes below fifteen degrees. They are evergreen.

Dieramas, sparaxis, and ixias are hardier Cape bulbs that are on the borderline in Zone 6. All three have lived through the winter with me, but not to bloom thereafter. Ixias are supposed to be hardy to Washington, but they have not proved so here, though they have wintered and bloomed at least once in the neighborhood. I am trying them again this year, planting them deeper than before and in a sheltered corner. I put them out very late in the fall as they are said to do better if they are not allowed to come up during the cold weather.

Three delightful irids from our own Southwest and the countries south of us are not so tender or so difficult in gardens. I am very grateful to Mrs. Dormon for an introduction to them. *Herbertia drummondiana* (if you follow *Hortus Second*—otherwise *H. caerulea*) [*Alophia drummondii*] is an exquisite little thing as you can see by its portrait in Miss Caroline Dormon's *Wild Flowers of Louisiana*. It blooms with me from late April into June. The short-stemmed flowers are rather like small fugitive moraeas, but the scant foliage is like crab grass. *Eustylis purpurea* [*Alophia drummondii*] is another Louisiana wildflower. It has dark blue-violet flowers very like those of cypella and as fleeting. With me it blooms in early June. I am trying it in the open and in shade, and it seems to have no preference, but it does like moisture. *Nemastylis acuta* [*N. geminiflora*] is native from Tennessee to Texas and Louisiana. I really believe it is the loveliest irid of them all. Also the

---

1. *Dietes* is listed separately from *Moraea* in the Royal Horticultural Society's *Dictionary of Garden Plants*.

most fragile. The flower is something like a large pale blue clematis. I have it planted in a soil rich in leaf mold in a woodsy part of the rock garden where it has bloomed but once, in April.

The maricas [*Neomarica*] are plants from tropical America that I know only in pots, but I shall mention them for the benefit of those south of me. Mrs. Dormon wrote me that she had grown one species for several years, but that hard winter carried it off. *Marica gracilis* [*Neomarica gracilis*], the walking iris, is from Central America. The flowers are very like those of the cypella except that they are blue. Cypellas are sometimes included with maricas.

*To me summer is a season for taking delight
in a garden. For there is no time when it is more inviting than
in the early freshness that precedes the heat of the day, or the
cool twilight and fragrant darkness that follow it.*
A Southern Garden

Tender Bulbs for Summer Bloom

Two members of the Lily family that come from the mountains of Mexico and are grown in California can also be grown in the East if the bulbs are lifted in the fall and stored like gladiolus. One is Mexican star (*Milla biflora*), the other coral-drops (*Bessera elegans*). The bulbs should be planted in the spring up to six inches deep in a light rich soil. Good drainage is essential, but water must not be lacking from the time growth starts until just before the flowers bloom. They bloom from July to September.

The fragrant white blossoms of *Milla biflora* are six-pointed stars, striped on the outside with pale green. There may be several flowers to a stalk, but, as the name *biflora* indicates, there are usually two. The leafless wiry stalks are twelve to eighteen inches long. The basal foliage is blue-green and grass-like. Millas can be grown indoors for winter and spring bloom—treated the same as freesias.

The flowers of coral-drops are in sprays of five to ten, dangling like little bells from the tip of a two-foot leafless stalk. The bells are scarlet outside; and within they are cream-colored with orange strips; the stamens are blue. The few inconspicuous leaves are about the length of the stalk. Bulbs sold as *Bessera elegans* often turn out to be *Milla biflora*.

Among the easiest and most rewarding of the smaller members of the Amaryllis family for summer bloom are the zephyr lilies (*Zephyranthes*) and their hardier relative, *Sternbergia lutea*. *Zephyranthes candida*, probably the hardiest of the zephyr lilies, is said to survive the winters of New York when planted in a sheltered place. The others should be lifted in the winter and stored in sand.

Zephyranthes grandiflora, best known as a pot plant, is native from southern Mexico to Guatemala. When the bulbs are planted out in the spring, they bloom in the garden throughout the summer. The large flat flowers are Spinel pink, on stalks about eight inches tall. This species is commonly known as *Zephyranthes carinata* [*Z. grandiflora*], and is often sold as *Z. rosea*.

Zephyranthes robusta (now called *Habranthus robustus*) from Argentina is one of the very best summer bulbs for the garden. The white flowers are flushed with pink. They are large and lily-like; and where the ground is moist and rich, they bloom at intervals during the summer. Apparently they can be planted at any time, for bulbs planted in October have bloomed very soon after they were put out. *Zephyranthes candida*, another South American species, produces quantities of small white crocus-like flowers in late summer and fall. They are crowded among the shiny green rat-tail leaves. Similar, but even lovelier, is *Zephyranthes* × *ajax* [*Z.* 'Ajax'], a hybrid between *Zephyranthes candida* and *Z. citrina*. The lemon-colored flowers come in August and September.

These, I think, are the best kinds for the summer garden. I have many more in my garden in North Carolina, but I am not sure how well they would do if they were planted where they had to be lifted in the fall. The zephyr lilies are sometimes called rain lilies because they bloom after showers. They bloom better in a moist soil than in a dry one. They need a soil that is on the acid side; and mine do well with a yearly mulch of cow manure. They will bloom in some shade, but full sun is more desirable.

The zephyr lilies are American plants, but sternbergia comes from the Mediterranean region. *Sternbergia lutea*, the only kind common in cultivation, is sometimes called the winter daffodil or fall daffodil, or the fall crocus. The crocus-like flowers are the color of a daffodil. Sternbergias are said to be hardy as far north as Boston; but they bloom better in my garden when they are lifted and replanted. They can be put out at any time during the summer; and even if planted late in August, they will bloom in the fall of the same year. They bloom in September and October. The narrow strap-shaped leaves come up with the flowers and mature during the winter. Both flowers and leaves are very resistant to frost. *Sternbergia* grows in any good, well-drained soil; with me they bloom in sun and in shade, but they are said to do better in a warm position in full sun.

*Whatever the difficulty with the names, there is
none in procuring the bulbs under one or another of them,
or of getting them to grow. In any part of the garden
they grow, increase, and bloom unfailingly.*
A Southern Garden

Habranthus

I was interested in what Mr. Morrison wrote about habranthus. He said that *Habranthus brachyandrus* does not like his soil or climate (in Mississippi); yet it comes from southern Brazil, and you might think it would prefer the Gulf Coast to my garden and Canon Ellacombe's. "I have rather a nice thing in flower now—*Hippeastrum brachyandrum* [*Habranthus brachyandrus*]. Do you know it?" the Canon asked Mr. Bartholomew in a letter dated November 14th. "I advise you to get it. Mine came from some out-of-the-way garden in Berkshire, so you will have no difficulty."

I have no clue as to the year this letter was written, but it must have been about the turn of the century, as *Habranthus brachyandrus* was not in culture in England before 1890, and the Canon died in 1916. I would dearly love to know more about the performance of this still rather uncommon amaryllid in the garden at Bitton Vicarage, but there is no comment on it in either of the Canon's books.

In North Carolina *H. brachyandrus* has never bloomed in November, but recently it has taken up flowering in October. These late blooms are much the loveliest, as they open wider and last longer than those that bloom in the hot weather. I have grown it in Raleigh and in Charlotte for twenty years or more, and have found it the most steadfast of its family, though it is slow of increase. Occasionally it blooms in June, and usually there are flushes in July, August, and September. Yet it is recommended only for the far South.

Habranthus robustus, which is considered much hardier, bloomed faithfully in Raleigh, but suddenly disappeared from my Charlotte garden after it had become well established. Once it bloomed in May, and at times there were no flowers before July but more in September. Usually there were flushes in June, July, and August.

Plants from Chile are not apt to take to North Carolina, but the oxblood lily, which came to me as *Habranthus miniatus* and is now (by some) called *Rhodophiala bifida*, blooms profusely and multiplies almost alarmingly. Dr. Traub suggested that I try *Habranthus bagnoldii* [*Rhodophiala bagnoldii*], which I did without success. Another bulb was planted a year ago last March, and now there are some slender leaves, twelve inches long and an eighth of an inch wide, lying flat on the ground beside the label. But they look suspiciously like those of a nearby *Nothoscordum* that Miss Willie May Kell sent me from Texas.

I have a theory that amaryllids in general don't care much whether they are wet or dry (within reason) or in sun or shadow, but that they have some private reason for blooming or not blooming. This fall Mrs. Sheets wrote that she had in bloom in her garden in Reidsville, North Carolina, a bulb with a flower like those of *Lycoris radiata*, but smaller, daintier, and pinkish lavender. It came into bloom on the nineteenth of November, and on the twenty-eighth she wrote that it was still fresh though there had been temperatures down to 25 degrees F. for four nights and the sasanquas had been nipped. She said I had sent the bulb to her, but without a label. *Nerine undulata* is the only bulb of that description that I know of that blooms in November, but I have no recollection of having sent it, and certainly wouldn't have expected it to survive, much less to bloom, in Mrs. Sheets's garden, which is much colder than mine, for it is uncertain and short-lived here. But it is just like a member of the Amaryllis family to hop up and bloom when you least expect it.

The zephyr lilies are small, solitary flowers that appear and disappear as suddenly as spring snow. Because they often follow summer rain, they are sometimes called rain lilies.
A Southern Garden

Zephyranthes smallii in North Carolina

Mr. Morrison wants to know how many flushes of bloom there are on *Zephyranthes* (or *Cooperia*) *smallii* in one season. I am sorry to say that I have not made a note of them, in spite of the fact that my two little bulbs are planted right outside my studio window. Whenever I look up from my work and see that scrap of yellow, all I would have to do would be to draw their card from my file and make a note. I know there are three flushes, and I rather think there are four or maybe five. The first two flowers (they are usually in pairs) generally appear about the middle of August, but once they came in mid-July. There is one in bloom today, the fifth of October.

I read about this amaryllid in *Herbertia* in 1953. Fred Jones wrote that he was driving along in southern Texas one afternoon in July about 2:30 in the afternoon, and saw some rain lilies just opening, and one of them proved to be *Z. smallii*. The next spring I found it on Wyndham Hayward's list, and it has bloomed in my garden ever since, delighting me by its habit of beginning to open punctually at 2:30. You can almost tell time by it. The color of the flowers is near Ridgway's amber yellow with a reddish flush on the back of the petals. They are practically scentless, and their stems are tall, eight to twelve inches, for their diameter, about an inch and one-half. The lax, rat-tail leaves are a little longer than the stems. Though there are lots of seed, I have never had any seedlings; the original bulbs do not seem to have multiplied much.

4 : Perennials & Annuals

> *To be out of the way when out
> of bloom is one of the most desirable
> traits a perennial can have.*
> A Southern Garden
> (*in reference to* Ratibida pinnata)

Perennials Suitable for the Mid-South

In the mid-South, bloom in the perennial borders is spread out over more than eight months instead of bursting forth all at once in a brilliant display as it does in colder climates. To keep a garden in bloom for so long a time requires thought and labor. It is an exciting and a complicated undertaking. Many plants and many varieties are needed to make a showing over such a long period. My beds are so full that I cannot thrust the trowel into the soil to make a hole for some new treasure without cutting into the white flesh of a dormant bulb or digging up a plant whose top has died down.

The first perennials to bloom in my garden early in March are hardy candytuft and English cowslip (*Primula veris*). They are permanent possessions, edging a bed of campernelles and early daffodils with yellow and white year after year. *Vinca major*, used as a groundcover for the bulbs, blooms at the same time. Its scattered blue flowers are pleasing with the yellow and white and the deeper shade of single blue hyacinths. *Vinca minor* grows closer to the ground and can be planted over small bulbs. The rare white form brought from an old garden in Virginia has an exquisite flower worthy of being planted with the most choice of the little daffodils. *Verbena venosa* [*V. rigida*] also comes very early, but it must be used with care, for its purple flowers are apt to verge on the magenta. Even so, it is a relief from the overpowering yellow of so many of the early shrubs and daffodils and is useful for filling in spots where more difficult plants fail.

In the South, perennial borders begin to be effective by the middle of March. Doronicum, bleeding-heart, camassia, *Alyssum saxatile* [*Aurinia saxatilis*], arabis, Iceland poppies, Siberian wallflowers and *Phlox divaricata* make a brilliant showing—too brilliant if one is not careful with the colors. The lavender blue of *Phlox divaricata* is best combined with pinks and very pale yellow tulips, such as 'Moonlight', with a few of some dark variety, such as 'La Tulipe Noire', for accent; but the clear blue of *Camassia leichtlinii* may be used with the brilliant yellow of doronicum. *Alyssum saxatile* [*Aurinia saxatilis*] with solid orange wallflowers, yellow violas, and crinkled orange and lemon poppies on slender stems make a gay group for the margin of any border. Bleeding-heart (*Dicentra spectabilis*), a plant of great distinction, should be planted by itself instead of being lost in a mass of color. The rows of pink and white hearts on graceful stems rising from fern-like foliage are like an old-fashioned valentine.

None of these gay spring perennials are very permanent in the South, but they are worth raising (or buying) every year. Doronicum may last two or three years, and the alyssum will sometimes live over. Blue phlox can be kept in a neat border if it is divided every spring and set back in the same place. Bleeding-heart is difficult here but would be permanent, I think, if once established.

Iris germanica and several other species of bearded iris begin to bloom by the middle of March. I like the dark purple of *I.* × *kochii* with the fresh yellow of cowslips. Sometimes when *I. florentina* [*Iris pallida* var. *dalmatica*] and *I.* × *albicans* bloom with snowflakes and white wisteria, the garden is all in white for a few days after the early-blooming daffodils have faded and before the tulips and early perennials appear. *I. pumila* and the intermediates bloom late in March and early in April, and are more satisfactory than the tall bearded iris for combining with tulips. I have the delicate iris, 'Bluette', planted with 'Clara Butt' tulips and English daisies.

The tall bearded iris blooms from the middle of April to the middle of May. Several of the early hemerocallis come at the same time. The lemon lily (*H. flava*) [*H. lilio-asphodelus*] begins to bloom the first of May. Its pale yellow can be used in pastel combinations with light blue iris, such as 'Souvenir de L. Michaud', and delicate pinks, such as 'Frieda Mohr'; or in striking contrast to the rich purple of 'Mme. Gaudichua'. The deeper yellow of hemerocallis 'Apricot' and 'Dr. Regel' is effective with the more brilliant coloring of iris 'Ambassadeur' or 'Prosper Laugier'. The orange brick-red geums bloom at this time and prove very satisfactory for the South.

Another valuable May-blooming perennial that persists here is baptisia. It has dark blue pea-shaped flowers [*Baptisia australis*] and graceful gray-green foliage. The blue flax (*Linum perenne*) is the perfect perennial for planting with iris because its light foliage contrasts so prettily with the iris swords and does not keep the sun off their rhizomes. One must enjoy breakfast in the garden, however, to enjoy the pale blue flowers that fade by the middle of the morning. The early varieties of peonies (which are the satisfactory ones for the South) also bloom with iris. The silvery pink ones are lovely planted in masses with *I. pallida* 'Dalmatica' [*I. pallida pallida*].

The early edging plants, the alyssum, phlox and wallflowers, are past their best by May, and some new perennials are needed to take their places. Two attractive low-growing veronicas will provide blue at this time. The deep azure spikes of *Veronica incana* [*V. spicata* ssp. *incana*] are very striking against the silver leaves that cluster at their base. It is a plant that persists and can be divided and increased. *V.* 'True Blue' is more like a taller form of the prostrate veronicas. It has numerous clear, light blue flowers. Another low-growing perennial for May is *Salvia pratensis*. It is a brilliant dark blue. *Alyssum rostratum*, blooming after *A. saxatile*, is a rather garish yellow, but it is one of the perennials that persist and has the additional merit of enduring drought. It is pleasing in a group with the early-blooming elder daisies and *Salvia pratensis*.

Pyrethrum, Oriental poppies, columbine, heuchera—the perennials most frequently used to make up the May floral borders in the North—are not adapted to our climate. Except in the mountainous parts of the South they will never reach the perfection of those grown in the North. And even if they bloom fairly well the first season, they will not persist. A much better effect can be achieved by using perennials that are adapted to our climate. An interesting little gladiolus species that can be bought from the country women in market is delightful in a border of *Achillea rosea* [*A. millefolium* 'Rosea'] and pale pink annual larkspur (which is at its best in the South), with a touch of the glowing crimson flowers and silver foliage of the mullein pink (*Lychnis coronaria*) and for accent the heavy stalks of yellow flowers and the enormous wooly leaves of the giant mullein (*Verbascum olympicum*).

The beardless iris bloom at this time in an endless variety of form and color. They are eminently suited to cultivation in the South. No one who can have the brilliant iris 'Mme. Dorothea K. Williamson' need regret anything that he cannot grow. The wide purple flowers marked with yellow are characteristically arranged on tall stems rising from the vigorous clumps of swordlike foliage. 'Mme. Dorothea K. Williamson' is a hybrid of those Mississippi iris [Louisiana hybrids] that are becoming better known in gardens and are well adapted to the South.

Iris ochroleuca [*I. orientalis*] is the most distinguished of the spurias, another group with which we are successful. The delicately formed white flowers look as if they had lighted upon the stiff stems. It is a very shy bloomer with me. The Siberian iris with smaller flowers and narrow leaves are also good subjects for a perennial border, especially the vivid blue variety 'Emperor'.

By the last of May the Japanese iris are in bloom. They make a splendid display in my garden if they are watered during the growing season and after they have bloomed. Masses of the single white varieties with heavy drooping petals are imposing with the flat, mustard-yellow heads of *Achillea filipendulina* and the shorter-stemmed light blue iris in the foreground. The gorgeous purple forms are planted with branching, double-flowered white larkspur. At the end of June when the Japanese iris are gone, tiger lilies dominate the border. Their pinkish orange flowers are lovely with the drooping, creamy sprays of *Artemisia lactiflora*, their uncompromising stiffness softened by its graceful, finely cut foliage. It smells like waterlilies.

After the first of June, the borders begin to have a look of summer rather than spring. Hardy phlox, the veronicas, and *Salvia farinacea* will be in bloom from then on making a background for the more transitory flowers. The veronicas keep the border supplied with blue from May until October. *V. longifolia subsessilis* [*Veronica subsessilis*] has enormous spikes of bright blue flowers, but its growth habit is not as good as that of the bushy and erect *V. spicata* or *V. amethystina* [*V. spuria*]. The white form of *V. spicata* is one of the loveliest things in the summer border.

The Chinese bellflowers supplement the blue of the veronicas. I have very little luck with them, but I see them blooming in other people's gardens all summer long and late into the fall, especially the dwarf variety, *Platycodon grandiflorus mariesii*. Blooming in June in the front of the border with the veronicas and *Hemerocallis* 'Florham' is the Alaska daisy. A form of *Chrysanthemum maximum* [*Leucanthemum maximum*], it is much more satisfactory than the shasta daisy.

The idea prevalent in the South that it is futile for us to try to have flowers during our hot summer months is fostered by those who go away for the summer and do not like to think that they are missing anything and by those who do not want to garden in the heat. Last summer I stayed at home and labored, and my garden was so beautiful that I made up my mind never to leave it again. In order to keep the garden fresh and gay in spite of the relentless heat of midsummer, we must strive for brilliant effects instead of delicacy of form and color. The coarser flowers, skillfully grouped, can be as interesting as some of the more choice varieties whose delicate colors fade and whose petals droop when the sun is on them. The flamboyant pink and red mallows with their thick leaves and fleshy roots are ideal hot weather plants. Too large for the border, they are stylish planted in clumps for background or with the pink and crimson shades of the early-blooming cosmos.

Hemerocallis are the center of interest in July. *H. thunbergii* produces pale yellow lilies in profusion in all weathers and in all soils. This year I am trying out some of the newer varieties, among them 'J. A. Crawford' and 'By State', with larger flowers and in richer colors. I am not sure that they will stand the glaring sun as well as *H. thunbergii*, but they may prove to be valuable in the shade.

Liriope graminifolia [*L. muscari*], a tender perennial from China and Japan, is hardy in the mid-South, and is unaffected by heat or dry weather. I have it planted in hard clay soil by the pool. The stock spikes (about a foot high) are covered with lavender flowers in August, followed by shining black berries that persist well into the winter. The tufts of lustrous grass-like leaves do not die down until the new foliage appears in the spring.

Sunflowers are indispensable to borders that must make a brave showing in the face of midsummer heat. *Heliopsis pitcherana* [*H. helianthoides* 'Pitcherana'] is an attractive dwarf variety that is not too coarse to be effective in a border with veronica and phlox, but of a texture firm enough to withstand the hot sun without wilting. Hardy phlox blooms all summer when it is watered, but it is best not to depend on it for the dominant plant because the petals droop in the middle of the day. I find the white varieties, especially 'Mrs. Jenkins' and 'Flora Reedy', the most satisfactory. The salmon and crimson shades fade in the strong sunlight. *Plumbago larpentiae* [*Ceratostigma plumbaginoides*], a useful border plant with heat and drought enduring qualities, blooms profusely from June to September. It is an intense blue and may be substituted for lobelias, which are sadly lacking in the qualities so necessary for plants grown in Southern gardens in summer.

Another coarse perennial that will hold up its head on the hottest day is the gaillardia. The Portola hybrids [*Gaillardia* × *grandiflora*] and the richly colored 'Burgundy' are a great improvement on the old form of the blanket flower. And the odd little straw-colored gaillardia, 'The Bride', is a flower of much more refinement and will endure the heat equally well.

Campanulas, on the whole, are for cool climates, but *C. elegans*, with its short sturdy spikes of deep blue, blooms from the middle of June until late in October and is both drought- and heat-resistant. During the last of August, the heleniums begin to bloom gaily even under the most adverse conditions. Very tall and erect, they do not have to be staked, nor do they take up more than their allotted space. The large flower-heads of bright daisies are attractive in the border, and very useful for cutting. 'Riverton Gem' has pale yellow daisies with dark centers. 'Riverton Jewel' is brick-red.

Most people discard *Boltonia asteroides* as too rapacious for the flower border, but it can be easily kept in bounds if it's divided (as it should be) every two or three years. The large flower-heads of white delicacies with gray-green foliage are fresh and cool to bring into the house on humid days in August. The more uncommon *Boltonia latisquama* [*Boltonia asteroides* var. *latisquama*] is the daintiest of summer perennials, bearing quantities of fringed aster-like flowers of a delicate orchid shade. There is no danger of its taking the border as it is one of the plants that has to be coaxed.

In September, borders in which there is still a scattered bloom from the summer perennials are revised by the glowing lavenders and purples of the Michaelmas daisies and *Physostegia virginiana* 'Vivid'. The latter alone can bring a bedraggled garden to life. *Aster novae-angliae* and its cultivar 'Roseus' do especially well here, proving much better than the paler kinds. I am also pleased with the new dwarf varieties that I had last year for the first time.

I find many perennials such as boltonia, plumbago, or *Artemsia lactiflora* on fall lists, but they bloom for me in the summer and cannot be depended upon for any real effect later on. Others such as aconite are not successful here. The Japanese anemones are among the fall flowers that do well for us and do bloom at the proper time, which is in October. The silvery pink 'Queen Charlotte' [*Anemone* × *hybrida* 'Kønigin Charlotte'] is lovely with the remontant iris 'Autumn King' and the pale blue *Scabiosa japonica*, which begins to bloom two months ahead of time but is still making a show when the anemones appear.

Because our schedule is moved up, we must depend more on the very late varieties. A brilliant sunflower comes into bloom early in October. I think I have identified it as *Helianthus angustifolius*, called autumn glory. It grows to four feet, has many large heads of deep yellow daisies, and makes a gorgeous display with the gaillardias, which are still in bloom, and annuals such as zinnias and marigolds planted late enough for a fall effect.

Another treasure for October is the rough-leaved aster, *A. macrophyllus*. It is very tall (sometimes to nearly seven feet), and produces clouds of lavender blue flowers for over a month. Last year, early in November, I saw it still in bloom with annual ageratum, pink petunias, pink zinnias, *Salvia farinacea*, yellow chrysanthemums, and some flaring single dahlias of a soft canary yellow. *Salvia farinacea* is one of our standbys. Its thin, silvered blue spikes are produced in abundance throughout the summer and in the fall. Another salvia resplendent in the late summer and fall is *S. pitcheri* [*S. azurea* var. *pitcheri*]. It grows to four feet and is a mass of intense blue.

Chrysanthemums are at their best with us late in October. The early varieties are not so satisfactory here, as they come too early and are affected by the heat. But we can have the late kinds (such as 'Christmas Gold') usually caught by the frost when they are grown out-of-doors farther north.

Even in November there are still perennials in bloom. This year the first killing frost came later than usual, and gaillardias, *Physostegia* 'Vivid', the lacy white verbena, white veronica, *Potentilla warrensii* [*P. recta* 'Warrenii'] and Chinese and 'Tom Thumb' delphinium were still in bloom with a number of annuals and some late chrysanthemums on November fifteenth.

Most of the common annuals are spring-planted and summer-blooming. Those that are fall-planted and spring-blooming add a great deal to Southern gardens in March and April and May.
A Southern Garden

Annuals Down South

In considering annuals for the mid-South, it is important to find out where they come from, as those from climates similar to ours are most likely to do well for us. Because heat and drought are our two main problems, we should look for plants that have been conditioned to these difficulties in their native habitats.

Among the California wildflowers, California poppies, phacelia, and nemophila have proved to be good annuals for the mid-South. *Godetia* [*Clarkia*] is unsatisfactory. Coming nearer home, we have success with the Texas bluebonnet and Drummond phlox from Texas and from the Southeastern states with calliopsis [*Coreopsis*] and the annual rudbeckias.

Most of the annuals from southern Europe do well for us. For soft colors we look to larkspur, snapdragon, scabiosa, calendula, nigella, silene, statice, and matthiola. Mexico provides us with our brilliant marigolds, zinnias, tithonias, ageratums, cosmos, nasturtiums, and hunnemanias. South American annuals are good material for Southern gardens, with the exception of those from the mountainous countries. Salpiglossis, a native of Chile, is very beautiful in Northern gardens but is a failure in the South. And we do not have much success with heliotrope, which is a native of Peru. Nicotiana, one of our best annuals, is from Brazil, as is portulaca (indispensable for blooming in spite of heat and drought). Our dependable petunia is from southern South America. Browallia (from Colombia) and cleome (from Tropical America) will also endure our summers.

South Africa would seem to be a likely source for annuals for the mid-South, but it has not proved so. With the exception of *Anchusa capensis*, South African annuals do very poorly for us. Nemesias are poor, and lobelias to be successful at all must be planted very early, and even then will not do well unless we have an unusually wet season. One would expect the African daisies [*Arctotis* and *Gerbera*] to revel in our summers, but, for the most part, they are disappointing. I planted 'Ursinia', the 'Jewel of the Veldt', and 'Venidium, the Monarch of the Veldt', with high hopes, but with the first dry weather, they curled up. I was told that this was what they did on the Veldt, that they were merely conserving their energies and would burst into bloom with the next rain; but they never revived.

I saw agathaea [*Felicia amelloides*] at the florists and was so charmed with the little French-blue daisies that I bought some plants for the garden. But they never amounted to anything out-of-doors. *Brachycome*, the Swan River daisy (from Australia), never does much for us either, nor does the Cape marigold. But I think the trouble with the latter is due to the type of soil rather than to the climate, for we used to have them when we lived near the coast where the soil was light and sandy. I remember planting them when I was a little girl, spelling out the long name *Dimorphotheca aurantiaca* [*D. sinuata*] and muttering it over the seeds as I put them in the ground. And, like some grown-up gardeners, I was much prouder of knowing the name than of my success with the flowers. The only one of this group of daisies that we can count on is arctotis, which usually does very well and is valuable for its gray foliage as well as the fresh blue and white daisies.

The best thing that has happened to Southern gardens in many years is the introduction of crotalaria, a green manure crop from the tropics. Two varieties can be bought at the local seed stores.[1] *C. spectabilis* is a tall plant, growing to five or six feet, much branched, and with fresh gray-green foliage and long erect racemes of yellow papilionaceous flowers. Striking in form and foliage, it is interesting in the border even before it blooms. *C. retusa* is similar, but smaller, and the flowers are marked with a dark red-brown. There is also a white form. Crotalaria is an especially good hot weather plant because its leaves stay fresh and crisp all summer.

To keep a garden continually in bloom over a long period, it is necessary to plant lavishly some of the common and easily grown annuals such as larkspur, ageratum, coreopsis, and cleome. If they are

---

1. Since Miss Lawrence wrote this article in 1936, crotalaria has been banned from seed stores because the plant is toxic to livestock.

allowed to seed themselves, they become pests; but pests are sometimes of value. Ageratum comes up so thickly that it chokes out everything else unless it is continually weeded out, but there are always little plants to transplant to bare spots in the flower beds.

Every year when calliopsis[2] comes up in all of the beds, I leave a few plants in each place. I like a flower that is all over the garden when it blooms. I like the monotony for a short time, and in a carefully planned color scheme it is delightful to find an accidental harmony where a dark red calliopsis has come of its own accord beside *Lilium umbellatum* [*Lilium* × *hollandicum*], or the unexpected discord of red and yellow with the coral spikes of *Penstemon barbatus*. Calliopsis grows so quickly that it does not hurt the permanent plants if its pulled up as soon as its brief period of bloom is over.

Cleome, which flourishes in every farmyard, can be used effectively in a more sophisticated setting. With the pink phlox 'Millie Hoboken' and zinnias—some frankly magenta and a few of a very dark purple—it will bloom all summer and still be blooming in the fall with *Physostegia virginiana* 'Vivid' and a fresh supply of zinnias. The exquisite white form is very desirable but difficult to obtain, as the variety usually sold as white is not a pure white. Cleome is a good foliage plant. Its large, dark green, five-lobed leaves make an interesting pattern. The flowers fade in the middle of the day, but no one can go into the garden at noon in midsummer without getting a sun stroke, so this is not a drawback. In the late afternoon, as soon as the sun is off them, they are fresh again. The name "cleome," which means uncertain, is the only thing uncertain about the plant, for it blooms steadily over a long period unaffected by weather, insects, or disease.

Another common annual which should be used in Southern gardens is the rose campion, *Silene armeria*. It is of the color politely called "rosy pink," but it can be used to good effect with a pale blue, such as the Caucasian scabiosa [*Scabiosa caucasica*]; and its smooth, gray-green foliage is very pretty.

A number of annuals are proof against midsummer drought. Some, such as *Phacelia campanularia*, which comes from the dry or desert regions of southern California, will not grow where there is too much moisture. Arctotis, dimorphotheca, portulaca, and statice also need a fairly dry, well-drained soil. Sanvitalia, rudbeckia, petunias,

2. Most authorities now consider *Calliopsis* to be *Coreopsis*.

ageratum, cosmos 'Orange Flare', and dwarf zinnias are definitely drought-resistant. Last summer when there was no rain for over a month, the group of plants least affected was a border of salmon-colored 'Lilliput' zinnias, annual ageratum, and sweet alyssum. Mexican zinnias are also invaluable for undiminished bloom in dry weather. They are extremely floriferous, and the little yellow or red and yellow flowers are most attractive. I do not know why they are not used more often. Cosmos 'Orange Flare' has proved a splendid annual for our climate. It blooms over a long period, and its vivid color does not fade in the sun.

Narrow-leaved plants such as calliopsis [*Coreopsis*], Mexican zinnias, and cosmos 'Orange Flare', having less leaf surface exposed for evaporation, adapt themselves very well to an insufficient water supply. Other plants such as *Statice sinuata* [*Limonium sinuatum*] are able to endure drought because water is stored in the thickened parts of their stems. This annual statice is absolutely drought-proof. It has crepe paper flowers of lavender, yellow, or market-grower's blue above rosettes of basal leaves. It is a low plant suitable for edging.

Two other drought-resistant edging plants are browallia and miniature marigolds. Sweet alyssum is not only drought-proof, but is one of the last annuals to be killed by frost in the fall, sometimes blooming until Christmas. Petunias are good for dry places, and with the many new fluted and frilled varieties, they are no longer commonplace. The dwarf fluted petunia, 'Martha Washington', has proven especially desirable for the South.

Nemophila, nemesia, hunnemannia, browallia, torenia, and the annual pinks are for the edge of the border. The Chinese pinks are valuable because they bloom early and late, and even a little in winter. Grown as annuals, they are really short-lived perennials, and sometimes live over for a year or two. Torenia is a good hot weather plant, and it will endure extreme drought, but it must have moisture to do well. *T. fournieri*, from China, is light blue with a velvety royal purple lip and a bright yellow throat. *T. flava* (usually listed as *T. baillonii*) from India is yellow with a brown throat. There is also a white form, 'The Bride'. Torenias bloom profusely all summer and late into the fall, the leaves turning red with the cold weather.

The large-flowered browallias, *B. speciosa* and *B. speciosa* 'Major', are greenhouse plants, and are not satisfactory in the garden. But *Browallia elata* [*B. americana*] is a delightful little plant with intensely blue, white-throated flowers, or all-white flowers—the latter being less attractive. Nemophila is particularly desirable because it is one of the few annuals to bloom in the early spring. If sown in the fall or allowed to seed itself, it will bloom in April. The pale blue form, which is the best, may be planted to bloom with *Myosotis alpestris*, cowslips, arabis, violas, the pastel tulips, and intermediate iris. California poppies will also bloom in April if sown early in the fall.

In the fall a Southern garden is rejuvenated after the long summer, and it should be ablaze with late-blooming annuals. Those susceptible to frost, such as tithonia and the Klondyke cosmos, planted farther north with the hope of "a fairer Summer and a later Fall than in these parts a man is apt to see," will bloom two or three months for us before they are caught. Last year, the vermilion, orange, pale yellow, and light blue of tithonia, marigolds, crotalaria, and ageratum made a striking combination in a long border. But tithonia grows to twelve or fifteen feet here, and it is out of scale in a border eight or ten feet deep. This year I am going to put it at the foot of the garden where it will have the protection of the fence. It needs to be planted against a wall or fence because the shallow roots are not adequate for its height and spread, and it is apt to be blown over in the autumn storms even if it is well staked. Thunbergia is a gay annual vine for late summer and fall bloom in the rock garden or on a low wall. The flowers are a rich yellow with dark brown throats.[3] They will seed themselves and come up again year after year.

When and how to plant the seed is an important consideration in dealing with annuals. Seedlings of some sorts can be bought from nurserymen, but for the most part they are better sown where they are to grow; and some, such as poppies of all kinds, hunnemannia, phacelia, crotalaria, lupine, and nemophilia *must* be sown where they are to grow.

The best time to sow annuals out-of-doors is a debatable question in the South. We cannot go by a rule such as sowing poppies on the last snow when we are likely to have no snow. Most gardeners are coming around to the idea of fall sowing for all hardy annuals, although there are some who still think that the winter losses are too heavy to make it practical. Because plants from fall sowing, when they

---

3. The yellow species mentioned here is *Thunbergia alata*. There are also nonyellow species.

do come through the winter, are much larger and finer than those from spring sowing, I think it is much better to take a chance on it and to sow again in the spring if necessary. Nigella, nemophila, larkspur, Shirley and California poppies, matthiola, arctotis, hunnemannia, cleome, and silene can be sown in the fall; Texas bluebonnet (*Lupinus subcarnosus*) and *Anchusa capensis* must be sown in the fall to be successful in this climate.

If hardy annuals are sown in the spring, it is safer to follow the old rule of doing it when the first trees are coming into leaf than to go by the dates on the seed packets, which are usually meant for use farther north. The important factor in growing annuals in the South is to start them early so that the plants will be big enough to withstand the heat when it comes. It is better to plant early and replant if the seedlings are killed than to wait until later when they are sure to be affected by the heat. There are exceptions to this. Calendulas should be planted late as they are cool weather plants, and will not do well with us when they are planted to bloom in July and August. It is useless to sow torenia or thunbergia early as the seeds will not germinate until the weather is very warm. Phacelia should be planted in March or April. Phacelia and nemophila will bloom within six weeks of the time they come up. They must be sown where they are to bloom, but they need to be sown in fine soil. The seeds of hunnemannia and crotalaria have a thick coat and should be scarified before planting; otherwise they will not germinate. Tithonia should be planted the last of April so that it will begin to bloom in August.

Certain cultural points must be kept in mind if one is to succeed with annuals. As a whole, they are sun lovers, but torenia, nemesia, nemophila, and nicotiana prefer light shade. As a whole, annuals like a slightly acid soil, but dianthus and hunnemannia need lime. Nemophila, calendulas, cosmos, larkspur, nigella, and African marigolds must have moisture. Nasturtiums, portulaca, browalia, and sanvitalia thrive in poor soil. Nemesia and tithonia prefer light soil. Torenia likes a rich light soil. Because we have such a long blooming season, I usually sow alyssum, Drummond phlox, browallia, zinnias, and marigolds three times so that there will be a fresh supply when the first batch dries up or blooms out. I sow them in April, June, and again in July. Crotalaria should be sown in April and early in June. Torenia keeps reseeding itself all summer. Numberless little plants come up around the big plants whenever it rains.

It is a common fallacy that annuals are a great deal of trouble and hence to be avoided, while perennials practically take care of themselves, and should almost entirely fill the borders. It is true that the border should be planted around perennials, but annuals must be relied upon for delicate color schemes and for quick effects. All gardens are subject to the uncertainties of the weather, but Southern gardens are particularly so, and annuals are necessary to repair the damages. When garden phlox is ruined by a month of dry weather in the early spring, nothing can be done about it for that season. But Drummond phlox can be resown if drought kills the first seedlings. And annuals, important to all gardens, are indispensable to those in the mid-South where we expect to find bloom for nine or ten months.

*Garden phlox is the
foundation of perennial borders
in June and July, and its scent is
the scent of summer.*
A Southern Garden

Garden Phlox

I found an article in my garden scrapbook whose author, a man, says that he has rooted up all his garden phlox and planted in its place black-eyed Susans, which he knows will flourish in a hot, dry climate. I have just gone out into my own garden and cut back the gaunt stalks of tall phlox that was to have been at this time the glory of a long border. But the failure of the phlox in that border is not to its being unsuitable to a Southern garden but to my negligence in allowing the roses on the fence to grow out over it, encouraging mildew and rust, and to my neglecting to spray or dust with sulphur against those diseases. Even without the preventive spray, the phlox that is in a bed where it gets plenty of sun and air has good foliage and no disease. No amount of black-eyed Susans could make up to me for that tall white phlox.

Phlox is the backbone of the summer garden, and it should dominate the borders. Other flowers will come and go, but the phlox should be there all along to fill in. You will read in articles written by over-enthusiastic gardeners that phlox, if kept cut back, will bloom from "June until frost." I hope you will not take this too literally and will not be as disappointed as I was when, having read in the catalogue that some plant could be "a riot of color from June until frost," I found it without a bloom in midsummer—and in spite of my having conscientiously snipped off all of the dead flowers. There will be such lapses, but phlox, if you do your duty by the dead flowers, will bloom a second time and even more, almost as abundantly as at first. In the North perhaps it will bloom until frost; here I think it will peter out after August. But, of course, it begins earlier for us.

Being very thorough, when I read that phlox should be cut back after blooming, I took it to mean that the stalks should be lopped off near the ground. I did this and wondered why my phlox bloomed no more. The strength of the plant was going into forming new stalks and foliage, and none was left for flowers. In time I thought of this and pinched back the flower heads at the base (not letting them linger when they began to bloom sparsely). To be kept blooming, phlox must also be free from disease and must have a mixture of bonemeal, wood ashes, and sheep manure in July and again in August, and must be watered. So, perhaps if you are one of those who say that watering is useless and that it is impossible to have a mid-summer garden in the South, you had better stick to black-eyed Susans.

In order to have a long season of bloom, the varieties of phlox must be very carefully chosen. There are two species of tall phlox: *P. glaberrima* var. *suffruticosa* [*Phlox carolina*] and *P. paniculata* (sometimes called *decussata*). *P. suffruticosa* blooms earlier and does not grow as tall. The best known phlox of this type is 'Miss Lingard'. It blooms from the middle of May until the middle of June (and again in July if it is cut back); its white flowers have a pale pink eye, but the effect is pure white. 'Miss Lingard' has dark green, shiny, disease-resistant foliage, and is said to grow to three feet. It is at least four for me, so I think it must like the South. Other varieties of *P. suffruticosa* are 'Perfection', a white phlox with a pink eye; 'Magnificence', which is purple carmine; and two others blooming later in the summer. I have never had any of them except 'Miss Lingard', but I want to try 'The Queen', which I found listed in a catalogue as "an ideal companion for foxglove." I find 'Miss Lingard' an "ideal companion" for Japanese iris; also for Madonna lilies and white foxglove. I am going to try some of the other varieties of *P. suffruticosa* and also some of the ever-blooming Ardensii hybrids [*P.* × *ardensii*], which are all named for girls, 'Louise', 'Kathy', 'Hilda', and 'Marianne'—I have 'Louise' on my list for next year.

The varieties of *Phlox paniculata* begin to bloom in the middle of June. I find the white one by far the most satisfactory. 'Mrs. Jenkins', an early bloomer and pure white with good foliage and of medium height, is the best midsummer phlox in my garden. I find it the one most frequently listed in Southern nurseries. 'Flora Reedy' is another good pure white. The bright reds, 'Beacon' and 'Firebrand', are poor. I find the bright pinks rather unsatisfactory too. All of the bright colors fade in the hot sun. But the pinks are so lovely that it is hard to do without them in spite of the fact that it is difficult to find anything to go with them except blue. The best varieties are 'Jules Sandeau', 'Rheinländer' (has a red eye), 'Thor', and 'R. P. Struthers' (one of the last to bloom).

It is essential to prevent phlox from going to seed and to divide them every three or four years to keep them from running out. The clumps should not be allowed to become more than six inches across before dividing. Divide in the fall (using a sharp saw to prevent injury to tissues), cut away the woody core, and don't cut the old clumps into too small pieces if you expect them to bloom much the next summer. Phlox should be planted in the sun in a moist, well-drained soil that has plenty of organic matter in it. Thoroughly decayed leaves, peat, manure, and humus should be spaded into the upper twelve inches. Phlox should be planted in the fall. Plants coming from a nursery should be soaked before they are set out. Lime should be dug around the roots of colored phlox every year to make them keep their color. Begin early to dust with sulphur to prevent mildew, red spider mites, and rust. Be sure to get the sulphur under the leaves and put it on when the plants are wet so that it will stick.

And one thing more—be firm about pulling up all magenta phlox. Do it at once, as soon as you see a magenta flower. Don't wait until fall; you will forget it in the fall. The magenta is the strongest growing kind and will soon be all over the garden and will cover up all of your choice plants. Don't allow it to stay because nothing else is in bloom or because it will grow when more attractive things won't. Pull it right up and pull up every particle of the root. If you leave a single snip in the ground, it will be back before you know it.

> *Torenias are as fresh in fall
> as in summer if the old plants
> are pulled up and late seedlings
> allowed to take their places.*
> A Southern Garden

Torenia bailloni

Ever since I saw *Torenia bailloni* (listed as *T. flava* in *Hortus*) in the DuPont Gardens years ago, I have wanted to have it in mine. After a long search, I found it listed in Thompson and Morgan's catalogue, but the seed were too fine to be expected to survive my desultory sowing, and no torenias appeared. Later I discovered an American seedsman who listed it, and this time I gave the seeds to a careful nurseryman who raised five little plants for me. More trailing than the blue species, they covered a surprising amount of ground in a surprisingly short time, but I thought they would never bloom. At last, early in August—when *T. fournieri* had been in bloom for a month, the quaint yellow flowers began to open. *Quaint* is a word that I dislike to hear in descriptions of flowers, but this yellow torenia is quaint. The small flowers are tubular with dark maroon throats in sharp contrast with the bright cadmium yellow lips. The way the stems lie on the ground and root at the nodes makes it an excellent groundcover. The leaves as well as the flowers of this species are smaller than those of the blue torenias, but otherwise similar.

This desirable annual comes to us from Asia, and is not subdued by heat. Torenias are among the most drought-resistant plants, but they are at their best with plenty of moisture. The crisp leaves and stems show the lack of it very quickly, even though they can survive being dried out for a very long time. Although they are very hard to get from seeds the first time, once they have bloomed, they reseed freely, and there are always plenty of the little plants when the warm weather makes the seed germinate.

As yet I have found no source for this species,
but it blooms in the garden of my imagination,
where the flowers are rare and unobtainable.
A Southern Garden
(*in reference to* Crotalaria laburnifolia)

Some Crotalarias for the Mid-South

Brought from the tropics for use as green manure crops, two annual crotalarias, *C. retusa* and *C. spectabilis*, have found their way into Southern gardens.[1] The success of these species, whose yellow flowers and crisp gray-green leaves bring the color and freshness of spring to the end of summer, led me to wonder whether there were not other crotalarias adapted to cultivation in the South.

A search brought to light *C. argyrea* and *C. juncea*. If the catalogue mentioned their height, I did not heed it. By fall the garden was a forest, with ten-foot *Crotalaria argyrea* and eight-foot *C. juncea* flaunting bright flowers just out of reach. Properly used, they would have had great value. *C. argyrea*, with the silvery foliage its name implies, is a more graceful plant than the coarse-leafed *C. spectabilis*, although its bunches of small lemon-colored flowers are not so showy as the great golden candelabra of the latter. Its habit of branching from the ground and its shapely contour make it a desirable plant for a temporary screen. The tree-like *C. juncea* is too open for this purpose and too leggy to be used without some sort of low planting in front of it. Its value is in the large deep yellow flowers, the largest of any species I know. They are very like those of *C. retusa*, except that they are not bronzed and have a curious fruity odor. *C. retusa* is scentless. Planted in mid-April, *C. juncea* began to bloom early in July. *C. argyrea*, planted at the same time, did not bloom until September. Both were in full bloom when they were blackened by late November frosts.

The story of these giant crotalarias is a sad one: the seedsman from whom I bought them has never listed them again. And I, thinking that

---

1. Crotalaria has been banned from seed stores because it is toxic to livestock.

I could buy seeds in the spring for five cents, neglected to save any. I hope I shall be able to find them again because I want them in my garden.

These exhaust the catalogue possibilities as far as I know. From the Department of Agriculture, I had several more. The best of these, perhaps the best species of all for garden use, proved to be *C. usaramoensis* [*C. zanzibarica*]. It has a long period of bloom (from July 23 to November 25 in my garden last summer), grows to a reasonable height (four-and-a-half feet), is graceful in habit, and has foliage of an interesting texture, and flowers in long slender racemes of a distinct and unusual form. It has such wide spreading branches that a few plants make a good showing. One of its best points is that the flowers at the top of the spike do not begin to fade until nearly all of the buds on that spike are out. As they fade, they turn from a clear lemon-chrome to an unfortunate terra-cotta, making the plant look very unattractive if they are not clipped off.

Crotalaria verrucosa, described in Bailey's *Cyclopedia* as making a "magnificent show in early spring," bloomed out a dirty blue in mid-summer. The color deepened toward fall, and we became somewhat attached to it, but I noticed that it wasn't admired outside the family.

Others tried and found wanting were *C. intermedia* [*C. brevidens* var. *intermedia*], *C. incana*, and *C. lanceolata*. All have decorative foliage, but their flowers are inconspicuous.

All of the crotalarias mentioned so far are annuals. In the Brookgreen Gardens in South Carolina, I found a rare and charming native species that is perennial. Its specific name, *C. rotundifolia*, shows that its foliage differs from the long oval leaves of the other species. It also differs from them in that the flowers are borne singly or in pairs, not in racemes. It is a small prostrate plant, suitable for light soil in a sunny rock garden and blooming in late spring. It is known by the enchanting name of rabbit-bells.

Crotalarias bloom in their own good time, and an early start will not hurry them. It is useless to plant too early, for the seed will not germinate until the ground warms up. In my garden they seldom reseed themselves. In harvesting the seed, one remembers that crotalaria are called rattle boxes, for the seeds are not ripe until they are dry enough to rattle in the pod. They are troublesome to get above ground because their coats are tough, and they do not germinate readily. It is well to scarify the seed and to plant lavishly, for they will not all come up.

Certain perennials are almost everblooming in these parts, but they are not the ones usually described in the catalogues as "covered with flowers from spring to frost."
A Southern Garden

Permanent Perennials

Every spring and fall, when I check the borders, I look with dismay upon the number of discarded labels that record the many so-called perennials that have died after blooming once or without having bloomed at all. A perennial, according to Bailey's *Hortus*, is "an enduring herbaceous plant, one that remains year after year." But this definition is modified by the statement that "A perennial may not endure forever; many of them are at their best in about the third year, and then gradually fail; but tansy and bouncing-bet may remain after the house falls down."

I am not recommending that the borders be planted with tansy and bouncing-bet, but I do think that, at all times (and especially when most of us are expending our energies on Victory Gardens), it is wise to choose perennials that endure and grow in beauty rather than those that require constant attention and frequent renewal. If we choose perennials that endure, that are free from insect pests and disease, that do not overrun neighboring plants, and that do not require resetting in a few years, we save valuable time for war activities and also preserve the beauty of the garden, which is more than ever precious.

Plants like phlox that need to be divided in order to remain at their best and plants like bearded iris that are maintained only by a constant fight against borer and rot may demand more time than we have to give them, and permanence is not always desirable in perennials such as boltonia and plume poppy. But the hemerocallis has all of the virtues. It is free from disease and, except in a few sorts like the old orange daylily and the hybrid 'Margaret Perry', it is not invasive. An occasional resetting is recommended, but a clump of the variety 'Ophir' that has been in my border for seven years is more beautiful than ever this season, and the only attention it has ever had is a mulch of cow manure each fall.

I think if I were choosing a single daylily it would be 'Ophir'. It blooms freely and at length, and the large, medium yellow flowers do not fade in the sunlight. To those who prefer even larger flowers to a wealth of bloom, 'George Yeld' will be a satisfaction. Among the standard varieties are a number that are both free-flowering and large. The flowers of 'Gaiety' are even bigger than those of 'Hyperion', the general favorite among the pale yellows. 'Golden West' is a tall medium yellow of large size and one of the best for form and substance. 'Golden Sceptre' is a deeper yellow, also tall, and has been known to have as many as 47 flowers to a stalk. I have not seen a large-flowered daylily of pure orange, but two almost-orange, small-flowered sorts are among those I would choose for myself. These are 'Golden Dream' and the gay and pretty little 'Goldeni'. 'Golden Dream' is long in bloom. From the first flower to the last, I have counted six weeks. 'Mikado' is still my favorite among the patterned sorts. It begins to bloom early and lasts for a long time, and frequently repeats later in the season. For further contrast with the yellows, I like the Morocco-red marking of 'Daylily Wolof', the brilliant copper of 'Bagdad', and the dark mahogany-red of 'Theron'.

The Siberian iris is the least demanding and the most unappreciated of hardy perennials. Like the daylily, it blooms abundantly for many years without resetting and thrives wherever it is planted, though it grows best in a rich moist soil. The charming old varieties, the dainty early-blooming 'Snow Queen', the mulberry purple 'Emperor', and the grayish blue-violet 'Perry's Blue', are common in gardens, but I never see the newer ones. These come in a wide range of color. There is lavender in 'Mrs. Rowe', light purple in 'Periwinkle', dark pansy-purple in the tall and late-blooming and very handsome 'Caesar's Brother', lilac in 'Morning Magic', and deep soft blue-violet in the large-flowered 'Florrie Ridler'.

Japanese iris also flourish in one spot for a long time, but it is useless to try to grow them without rich soil and sufficient moisture. The old white variety 'Gold Bound' and a number of the older purples have bloomed for me without care for many years.

One of the most permanent and satisfactory plants in my garden is false indigo (*Baptisia australis*). It blooms with the hemerocallis and Siberian iris, and later in the summer its graceful gray-green foliage spreads over them. Why it is called *Baptisia australis* I have often wondered, for it is native from Pennsylvania southward. It grows naturally in dry places, but the handsomest plant I have is in heavy wet soil. It does well in sun or shade. In a favorable situation it will grow to four feet, producing 18-inch, lupine-like racemes. The rich violet flowers are loosely arranged on apple-green stems. The lower ones do not fade until the tips are fully out. The plant is in bloom for over a month. False indigo improves with age and makes a large clump. Plenty of room should be allowed for when it is set out.

Another perennial that improves with age is the plantain-lily [*Hosta*]. I had always thought that it had no diseases, but I see in Cynthia Westcott's book, *Plant Doctor*, that it is susceptible to crown rot. Fortunately, that is not prevalent enough to bar it from a list of permanent perennials. Like most of the plants under discussion, it grows best in good soil with sufficient moisture, but will stand drought and neglect. Plantain-lilies are sometimes found in catalogues as hostas and sometimes as funkias. The most commonly planted variety, the blue plantain-lily (*H. caerulea*) [*H. ventricosa*], has dull blue flowers that bloom in the early summer. The August plantain-lily (*H. plantaginea*, usually advertised as *H. subcordata grandiflora*) blooms in the late summer and is one of the indispensable perennials for shady places. The large, pure white flowers are exceedingly fragrant, and the broad, light green leaves make a bold accent. The neat low foliage of the narrow-leaved plantain-lily (*H. japonica*, usually advertised as *H. lancifolia*) makes it useful as an edging plant, and the blue, campanula-like flowers are very acceptable for late summer and fall bloom.

Rose mallows (*Hibiscus moscheutos*) are out of scale in a small garden, but they are permanent and desirable where there is space for them—too permanent when it is necessary to move them, as anyone who has tried to excavate their fleshy roots knows. It is well to be sure that they are in their permanent places when they are set out. The plants are coarse, but rather striking with their pale foliage and bright red stems. The enormous flowers open only in the morning, which is a decided drawback; they are unsightly in the afternoon when they hang limp and faded on tall stalks. But the morning freshness and tropical brilliance of the splendid hybrids, the 'Mallow Marvels', make up for this defect. The wide, dark-centered flowers in shades of clear pink or rich rose are worthwhile wherever there is space and moisture, but they are worthwhile only under these conditions. Natives of swampy places, their foliage droops and their flowers are small when they are allowed to dry out.

Peonies found blooming steadily in old gardens bear witness to their permanence. I have read that they should not be moved for seven or ten years. That should not tax even the laziest or busiest of us. For their striking and characteristic foliage as well as their handsome flowers, peonies are among the plants to be considered as the backbone of the herbaceous border.

Certain plants often found difficult to establish are extremely permanent once they become settled in a situation suited to their needs. Of such are madonna lilies and bleeding-heart. I see frequent complaints—particularly in the English horticultural papers—that madonna lilies are so difficult to establish on estates, although they are found blooming in profusion in cottage gardens. This is probably due to over-fertilization, which increases their susceptibility to the botrytis blight. Failure to establish them may be due to too deep planting or lack of proper drainage. Like all other lilies, they must have perfect drainage; and unlike most other lilies, they require very shallow planting with only an inch or two of soil over their crowns. Sound bulbs properly planted with plenty of leaf mold should become permanently established in sun or shade.

Bleeding-heart (*Dicentra spectabilis*), with its drooping pink flowers on long arching stems and its fine foliage, is so picturesque a plant that it has been a favorite in England and America ever since it was discovered in Chinese gardens by Robert Fortune. I do not know why it is so difficult. Its preferences are a deep soil, partial shade, and protection from wind. A northern exposure is most favorable. If it does not settle down under these conditions, the only hope is another trial—and probably another.

With so much more to be done in even the smallest garden than can ever be got through with, the sweetest sound to the gardener's ears is the direction, "Do not disturb thereafter!" Two delightful perennials not only tolerating but demanding a permanent position are the gas plant and meadow rue.

It is particularly important to know the requirements of plants that are to remain in the same spot the rest of their lives, and yours. The first time I tried the gas plant (*Dictamnus*) in my garden, I was thinking more of its relation to the color scheme than of its adaptability to the soil and situation. I planted it in a low damp bed where it soon rotted. One of the essentials for growing it is a well-drained soil. It is slow to become established in a new place, and it took me a long time to make up for my mistake, for the newly transplanted plants will not bloom the first year or so. Once it is established in sun or partial shade and in a rich, heavy soil, the flowers are finer and more numerous every year. On a well-grown plant, the racemes are a foot long and stand well above the glossy, fragrant foliage. The flowers are typically white, but the pink form is more often planted. The striking dark foliage and showy flowers of the gas plant are more effective if it is used as a specimen than when it is planted in groups. It gets its name from the volatile oil it gives off, which will burn with a blue flame if a lighted match is held to it on a still hot night. This old-fashioned plant has been neglected for a long time, and is now coming into favor again.

Meadow rue (*Thalictrum*), dependable, permanent, and easy to grow, is a godsend to shady borders. *Thalictrum aquilegiifolium*, with its columbine foliage, will outlast the uncertain columbine. Its characteristic, fuzzy inflorescence, in which the prominence of the enlarged stamens makes up the absent petals, almost equals the range of color found in columbines. There are varieties with white, purple, and yellow stamens. Other species offer varied and delicate leaf patterns. Meadow rue requires a well-drained soil in which there is sufficient humus to keep the roots from drying out. In dry, thin soil and in full sun, the foliage turns yellow.

Camassias, although they are bulbous plants, have a place in the herbaceous border and deserve mention here for that same desirable trait—resenting disturbance. Native to wet meadows, they thrive in low moist situations, but will also tolerate drier ones if they have sufficient moisture in the spring. They should be planted four inches deep in heavy soil in which there is not too much manure. They seem to bloom equally well in sun or shade. *Camassia leichtlinii* is the most desirable species with the largest flowers. They are wide and starry with narrow petals of mauve flushed with pink or, in the variety 'Alba', pure glistening white. After the bulbs are established, the flower stalks are often three feet or more. Camassias have one bad fault. The lower flowers come out first and fade before those at the tip are open, giving the racemes a ragged appearance after the first few days.

When a plant is not to be reset for a long time, it is more than ever important to see that it is in a situation suited to it and that there is good fertile soil beneath is roots. Fall planting for perennials is coming more and more into favor in the North, and in the South it is essential. Somewhat tender plants like rose mallows should not be planted in the fall in climates where the winter is severe; but if you're raising rose mallows from seed, the seed will germinate better after a winter in the ground.

*Among the really fine daylilies
it is difficult to make a choice,
but most of us will want a variety
in form, color, and height.*
A Southern Garden

My Best Twenty-Five Daylilies

Daylilies are at their best in cool (not too cold, however) damp weather.[1] They are said to stand heat and drought better than other perennials, and this is true; but they are at their best only when they have an abundance of moisture. I was amazed this summer to find how much larger and taller 'Hyperion' was in the damp borders of the garden at Longview in Northampton County [in eastern North Carolina] than in my garden [in Raleigh] where it is in a very dry place.

I keep daylilies that are on trial in a part of the garden that is usually moist, but I keep them watered in dry weather and mulch them with cow manure and leaf mold after their bloom is over. They are in afternoon shade, and some of them are subject to the gambols of my springer pup [Mr. Cayce], who loves to plunge through a clump of daylilies when the dew is on them.

It takes about three seasons to evaluate a daylily. At first you consider the individual flower, its size, form, substance, pattern, and color. Later you take into account the mass effect of the clump, the season and length of bloom, and the general garden value. When you consider the effect of the clone in the garden, the size and pattern of the individual flower are no longer important. 'Dr. Stout', a clone that

---

1. This article is a composite of three daylily reports that were originally published separately in *Herbertia*, the journal of the American Plant Life Society (now the International Bulb Society). The reports included details on daylily seedlings that Elizabeth received from Dr. Hamilton Traub in March 1944. She evaluated and described each plant based on records that she kept over a three-year period. Only a few of the clones that she evaluated were included in her final report on her favorite daylilies. Although the varieties described are no longer available in the trade, their descriptions should be of interest to garden historians and to daylily breeders.

I did not fully appreciate at first, has grown in its third year to such fine, strong, floriferous clumps and has bloomed so gaily for so long, that I now rate it with 'Carnival' as one of the finest. It is tall with large tawny flowers on stiff, well-branched stems. The flowers are covered with a fulvous dust. The season is about three weeks.

When you consider bloom in the border over a long period, the early and late varieties become more important, in spite of their faults, than fine midseason varieties, of which there are so many. Daylilies take up a lot of space. To have a long season of bloom in a fairly small garden, one must eliminate fine midseason clones and choose instead less beautiful ones that bloom early and late in the season. The earliest in my garden bloom in April. In this season, I have been able to find no greater variety than the pale yellow of *Hemerocallis dumortieri* and the deep orange yellow of 'Dr. Regel'.

For the late ones, there is more variety, but still not enough. There is continuous bloom from early April to the end of July, but the July bloomers are comparatively few; and in August, in my garden, only 'Boutonniere' is left. It is not really a very good daylily. The stems are weak and the flowers small and a poor color, and yet I would not be without it because of its late bloom.

A few plants, like a few people, have all of the dependable qualities and beauty besides. 'Carnival' is one of these. I know of no plant in the garden that has made a better show. This year [1947] it produced seventeen fine stiff stalks that remained in bloom from mid-June until the end of July. It happened to be against a background of cosmos 'Orange Flare', which seemed to bring out the brilliance of the glowing red flowers with their golden throats. The flowers are large—the segments four-and-a-half inches long—and bright. As with most of these lovely shimmering daylilies that change in every light, and from day to day according to the amount of heat and sunlight, the color cannot be found in Ridgway nor can it be accurately described. It is somewhere between Nopal red and Pompeian red with a quivering iridescent sheen. This is an outstanding daylily on all counts—size, brilliance, and number of blooms.

'Victory Taierhchwang' is one of my favorites, for I am very partial to the bright dark colors and much prefer a mass of color to a few large flowers. There were five stalks this year with thirty or more flowers to a stalk. It began to bloom the first day of June, and bloomed until the end of the month. The stalks are forty-two inches tall. The flowers are dark—a mixture of Brazil and Morocco reds with a bright chrome throat and distinct yellow midribs. They are comparatively small with narrow fluted and recurved petals.

'Victory Montevideo' is not outstanding except for its season. It comes when daylilies, especially reds, are scarce and are much needed. It begins blooming early, in mid-May, the time when spring flowers are on the wane or faded and summer flowers have not come.

'Berwyn' is one of the clearest and most sparkling reds that I have seen in any daylily, a color a little deeper than scarlet. The flowers open wide (which always seems to me more effective), are of medium size, and there are up to eighteen on a stalk. In its second season, it produced four stalks and was in bloom for thirty days.

Here are my twenty-five best daylilies, listed according to their season of bloom and in the order of my preference:

MY BEST 25 DAYLILIES

Early (April)	Early Mid-Season (May)	Mid-Season (June)	Late (late June and July)
		I. My 15 Best Daylilies	
'Dumortieri'	'Mikado'	'Carnival'	'Dorothy McDade'
	'Queen of May'	'Iowa'	'Boutonniere'
	'Lidice'	'Fire Red'	
		'Mrs. B. F. Bonner'	
		'Ophir'	
		'Golden Dream'	
		'J. A. Crawford'	
		'Dr. Stout'	
		'Victory Taierhchwang'	
		II. My Next 10 Best Daylilies	
'Dr. Regel'	'Victory Montevideo'	'Berwyn'	'Potentate'
	'Mayor Starzynski'	'Goldeni'	'Chandra'
	'Queen Wilhelmina'	'Starlight'	
		'Tejas'	

I always try to remember to buy a pot of
Thunbergia alata from the florist in spring to put in the
garden for fall, picking out from those already in bloom the creamy
ones in preference to the bright yellow.
A Southern Garden

The Curtain in Your Garden

Some years ago I looked for annual vines to make a temporary screen, or a curtain in my garden, while slower shrubs and perennial vines established themselves. I found a number in catalogues that grow like the beanstalk overnight, but learned when I grew them that they often wait until midsummer to get started, and then speed their energies climbing to the top of the support, leaving the lower part bare. Then happily I came upon the energetic balloon vine (*Cardiospermum halicacabum*).

Here in Charlotte, North Carolina, gardening begins early. I sowed the round, black balloon vine seeds, each imprinted with a white heart, in the open early in April. You must plant them about an inch apart if you want a heavy screen because the vines are slender, and the foliage is thin and lacy. By July the seedlings had reached the top of a seven-foot fence, and were sprinkled with a fine mist of white flowers that became apple-green balloons. Given a higher fence, they would have climbed higher, ten, twelve feet or more. I have never had to plant seeds again. If they come up in the wrong place, I have no trouble transplanting or uprooting them.

Farther north (where balloon vine does not self-sow), you plant seeds outdoors after danger of frost is over, or use the native wild-cucumber vine (*Echinocystis lobata*), which does self-sow in colder climates. Its seeds germinate slowly, so plant them in fall, or soak them overnight before planting. Both these vines are annual and shade-tolerant. For really deep shade, though, Japanese hop (*Humulus japonicus*), which also makes a heavy screen quickly, is more satisfactory.

Clock vine (*Thunbergia alata*), the best annual I know for a curtain of bloom, covers a fence neatly and quickly with overlapping heart-shaped leaves and golden, dark-centered flowers. It grows well even outside after frost. But you gain by starting them earlier inside, or by getting potted plants from your florist.

Perennial vines need a year or more to become established. Once started, they are effective for a long season. In my garden, the first to cover its allotted space was the native virgin's bower, *Clematis virginiana*. This, not handsome in leaf or flower, and seeding so freely as to be a nuisance, makes a high, thick curtain of green. Until better things are ready to take its place, I shall to continue to use it.

Woody *Akebia quinata* grows as rapidly as any perennial vine, holds its fine, five-fingered foliage late, and makes a dense mantle if you cut dead wood out. Here its quaint purple flowers often come at the end of March. In the North, they come in May. Akebia is not particular about soil and grows and blooms even in shade. I have heard that it suckers, that it does not keep to itself, but I have grown it many years without finding this habit a problem.

Dutchman's pipe (*Aristolochia durior*) [*A. macrophylla*] takes a year or so to settle, then grows fast. It is luxuriant even in shade, and in city gardens, which are so hard on plants. It grows to 30 feet, has bold leaves, and for a dense canopy, it cannot be surpassed.

Certain vines can climb on anything; you do not have to provide supports for them or train their runners. Hardy ones are Boston ivy, Virginia creeper, trumpet vine, climbing hydrangea, and euonymus.

Plant the native trumpet vine (*Campsis radicans*) only where you do not care if it gets out of control for its tuberous roots go so deep that it is difficult to get them out. Smallest pieces send up new shoots, and suckers travel rapidly in all directions. The only trumpet vine that seems to stay put is the beautiful hybrid 'Mme. Galen'. I have grown it four years, and so far it has given me no trouble and is worth much trouble for its coral flowers that come in June here, and in July in New England. It blooms on new wood and very freely if you prune it thoroughly each spring.

I think I know why *Hydrangea petiolaris* is not seen more often. It takes forever to bloom. I know of one vine that bloomed for the first time after fifteen years, and of one we had in our old garden in Raleigh that never bloomed. However, it is a handsome, hardy vine for covering a wall, and when in bloom, it is magnificent.

As to evergreens, *Euonymus fortunei*, and its forms, is the only really hardy climber. It is a good vine for the South. It may take longer to cover a fence than ivy, but once it does, it is easier to control.

*In the crevices of stone walls
and steps, and between flagstones,
thyme and the evergreen sedums
have an all-season charm.*
A Southern Garden

Groundcovers

My garden was designed for quiet and leisure. No power mower comes into it, for there is no grass to cut. It is carpeted by a collection of groundcovers.

Quiet is there, and at last I am beginning to achieve some leisure, although leisure is not so easily gained as I had been led to believe. Groundcovers do *not* put an end to all labor, for their very virtue—their will to cover the ground quickly—makes extra work when they go where they are not wanted.

The ideal groundcover is one that takes over rapidly but is easily restrained; that grows too thickly for weeds to come through; that needs no clipping; that stays green throughout the year. I think bugle weed comes as near as any to answering all these requirements. Perfectly evergreen in the South and practically so in the North, it does well in any soil and in sun or shade—though better in shade. *Ajuga reptans*, one of the bugle weeds, has light green leaves and gentian blue flowers that start in April in the South, in May or June in New England. One in the trade as *Ajuga brockbanki* also has blue flowers and beautiful curled leaves of a dark, burnished wine. Bugle weeds make a close, flat mat in a short time. A variety called 'Pink Spire' is a little taller, equally quick, or quicker, at covering the ground, and produces spikes of rose flowers all summer.

Sedums accomplish much the same thing as ajugas. They make neat and even covers and, being shallow-rooted, are easily pulled out when they travel too far. In shade *Sedum ternatum*, with its rosettes of rounded pale green leaves and its lacy white flowers in late spring, makes a splendid carpet. It is called common stonecrop, but with all its good qualities it is most uncommon in gardens. In sun the mossy stonecrops take over. *Sedum acre* is invasive, but *S. sexangulare*, which is similar, makes tidy clumps. Both have yellow flowers in summer, and in winter their linear leaves turn a warm russet. White-flowered *S. lydium* is considered superior to either, but I have not grown it, and have an idea that, like most superior things, it is more difficult to establish.

The fragrant thymes cover the ground quickly—in sun and in poor, dry soil—but are not altogether reliable. They have a way of turning brown in spots just when you want the garden to be at its best. With me the most dependable is *Thymus herba-barona*, but I am not sure of the extent of its hardiness since it comes from the hills of Corsica.

Epimedium pinnatum sulphureum [*E.* × *versicolor* 'Sulphureum'], the Persian barrenwort, is one of the most satisfactory cover plants I have ever grown. It is not really evergreen; the leaves become bronzed in the fall and then turn brown, but they persist until after the new ones come out. This means you have to clip them with hedge shears in late winter to keep the old leaves from hiding the flowers and spoiling the freshness of the new leaves.

Pachysandra and periwinkle are the most prosperous of all evergreen groundcovers. Never mind their being commonplace. So is grass. In wide spaces, under trees and shrubs where there are no small plants for it to smother, there is no better green than pachysandra. A good stand is practically weed-free. But it takes time (yours) to restrain it for its underground runners are very determined.

Periwinkle (*Vinca minor*) is equally hard to keep in bounds, and a good deal of weeding is required until it is well established. It is recommended as a cover for bulbs by some gardeners. Very stalwart ones will come through it, but their flowers have a choked look and their decaying foliage makes the planting hideous. Then, when the bulbs must be separated, getting them out of the thick periwinkle mats is a miserable job. For economy of labor and for peaceful green, groundcovers are best left to themselves.

Used as groundcover, the best form of ivy is *Hedera helix gracilis* [*H. helix* 'Gracilis']. It is neat and small-leaved, slower-growing, and hardier than the type that is good as a groundcover only in spots where nothing else will grow. No vines make satisfactory groundcovers for their nature is to climb, and wherever they come in contact with a tree or shrub, up they go.

In sun or in shade, lily turf (*Liriope spicata*) makes the quickest and cheapest covering for banks. It is evergreen in the South. In sections of the country where it turns brown in winter, you can replace it with *Juniperus chinensis sargenti* [*J. sargentii*] in sunny places, pachysandra in shade.

Where greenery in winter is not important, you can consider flowers. In spring, in deep shade, a large bed of lilies of the valley is fragrant as well as beautiful; and in the open or under trees, *Ceratostigma plumbaginoides* is a sheet of gentian blue from the middle of July until September. I have never heard of anyone who had more lilies of the valley than he wanted, but the plumbago increases only too well—though it has been with me many years without causing serious trouble.

Leaves, dappled white or cream, play an important part in the garden pattern. *Pachysandra* 'Silver Edge', the variegated form of English ivy, and (where scale is not prevalent) *Euonymus fortunei* are nicely splashed with white or cream. In the South and on the West Coast, *Saxifraga sarmentosa* [*S. stolonifera*] is often seen. Being almost hardy, it should be tried in Northern gardens. Its round, scalloped leaves and frail white flowers are very dressy in a shady place where nothing else will grow. It is well named "mother of thousands."

*Most of us have not room for an acre, but as Bacon—
also a lover of color in the landscape on grey days—suggests, we can
have a few "such things as are green all winter: holly; ivy; bays;
juniper; cypress trees; eugh; pine-apple trees; fir trees."*
A Southern Garden

Ivy: Cool Green in Summer, Warm Green in Winter

Ivy is good for covering barren ground, for decorating a wall, or for covering a wire fence, but it is bad when it climbs trees, gets under the eaves of a house, departs from the border to choke the path. I don't believe the English gardeners when they say that ivy will not harm a healthy tree or a sound structure, but this never prevents me from planting ivy. It is such a comforting green, both winter and summer, and it is so easy to control with the shears.

The strong-growing forms of English ivy make the best ground-covers for a large area. In some places they are the only plants that will grow at all, and they will cover banks too steep for grass. The Baltic ivy, which is much hardier than common English ivy, is good for Southern gardens.

The strong-growing forms of English ivy make the best ground-covers for a large area. In some places, they are the only plants that will grow at all, and they will cover banks too steep for grass. The Baltic ivy, which is hardier than common ivy, is good for Southern gardens.

On a masonry wall, ivy is a good servant if it has a good master. It is at its best when you clip it to a definite pattern or keep it trimmed to a light tracery. I have seen an ivy lattice growing on a south wall. I have never seen it at any season when it was not fresh and green, but, in general, a north wall is preferable. As a pleasing incidental on a garden wall or house the small-leaved variety *H. helix meagheri* [*H. helix* 'Meagheri'] makes a delicate design. It is sometimes listed as 'Green Feather', a name that describes it well. The bird's-foot ivy, *Hedera helix*

'Pedata', is sometimes listed as *H. helix* 'Caenwoodiana'. The small, dark green claw-like leaves have white veins.

I don't know how far north ivy can grow successfully on a wire fence, but I should think that the Baltic ivy might be given a trial for this purpose at least as far north as where the temperatures do no fall below zero. In my garden in Charlotte, North Carolina, I grow a number of forms this way. None of them were touched during our last severe winter when the temperature was not much above zero. The variety *meagheri* [cultivar] proved to be equally hardy. It has been grown outdoors without difficulty as far north as Ithaca, New York.

Where it is hardy, the Irish ivy covers a wire fence quickly. When it gets to the top, long trailers begin to hang down attractively. But they must be cut off regularly so that they do not shade the leaves on the fence or reach the ground where they will root and form a tangle. It is better, I think, to be patient and wait for the slow-growing varieties to cover a fence. They require little attention beyond weaving the new shoots into the wire. I have found *meagheri* ['Meagheri'] one of the best of the slow-growers. It makes a fine-textured and very dense screen.

The strong-growing ivies are often used for edging paths and flower beds, but eternal vigilance is the price of keeping them trim. Slow-growing shrubby or many-branched varieties with dense habit look better as edgings and need much less clipping. The variety that I have found most satisfying is 'Albany', a stiff, shrubby grower with smooth bright green leaves about 3 inches long. 'Maple Queen' with small light green leaves; 'Pittsburgh' with larger leaves; and 'Hahn's Self-Branching' with the largest leaves of the three make good plants in the South. They may be enjoyed as house plants in the North and may be grown outdoors at least as far north as southern New England.

So far I have never found any trailing or climbing ivies suitable for a rock garden, but the slow-growing and upright varieties, *H. helix* 'Conglomerata' and *H. helix* 'Erecta' are good for they are easy to confine to a small area. The first, which is called the clustered ivy, is to me an awkward thing, but the second is one of the most charming of all ivies. Both have ruffled, dark, crowded leaves. On the whole the variegated forms of English ivy are more tender than those with green leaves, but 'Star', a variant of the Baltic ivy, is advertised as a groundcover. The light green and white marbling of the variety "Marmorata" is much prettier, and the small gray-green leaves of 'Glacier', daintily outlined in white, are utterly charming. There is a handsome variant of Algerian ivy, *H. canariensis*, which nurseries list as 'Gloire de Marengo'. It has leaves from one to six inches long, some entirely white, some with deep cream and white margins, and some with a deep glossy sheen except for a few white flecks in the margin. The stems are the color of burgundy. This is a tender ivy, and even in my Southern garden looks shabby by the end of the winter. Sometimes new growth is curled back. For those who cannot grow it outdoors, it is an excellent pot plant as are many of the varieties, including 'Fleur-de-lis', which is the most adorable of all and well worth investigating.

5 : Native Plants

The big blue flag grows with a clump of wild indigo, Baptisia australis, *that flourishes in the heavy moist soil of the iris border. It is a beautiful blue, much deeper than the iris.*
A Southern Garden

Handsome Wild Indigos

For some years I have been working on a collection of wild indigo. I suppose it is because they are sometimes difficult and always slow to become established that these lovely natives of the Eastern states are so little appreciated, for they are valuable and durable perennials requiring no care once they are settled. Most of the species in *Hortus* can be had from dealers in rare and native plants, although *Baptisia alba* was not forthcoming when ordered, and I have never seen *B. perfoliata* offered.[1] Those that I have been able to find and bring to bloom have been delightful.

B. australis is the first to bloom. With me it comes along with Delta irises and lemon daylilies and larkspur the last week in April or early in May. In the North, it blooms from late May into June. The flowers are sometimes a pale, dull blue, but in good form they are a deep, intense violet on long apple-green racemes. This tall and lupine-like perennial, to about four feet, is the best known of the wild indigos, but it is met more frequently in books than in gardens.

B. bracteata blooms next, with me in early May; in the North in May and June. This is a slow-growing species of rock garden proportions. The height is given as 18 to 25 inches, but with me it is not more than a foot tall. It did not bloom until it had been in the garden for three years, but the beautiful ivory flowers were worth waiting for.

B. leucantha [*B. lactea*], like *B. australis*, is a tall spreading perennial grown to four feet tall. It blooms here in late May or early June, and in the North it blooms in July. The small flowers are a pure dazzling

---

1. Most baptisias are now readily available in the trade.

white, the clover-like leaves are pale green, and the stalks are silver-colored.

The yellow-flowered *B. tinctoria* blooms in August. Every time I see it flowering in the mountains, I bring plants home to try; but I have never succeeded with the collected plants nor with plants from nurseries. This is not as beautiful as the other species, but is none the less valuable for summer bloom. Perhaps it should be grown from seed.

I once planted seed of another low-growing, yellow-flowered species—*B. villosa* [*B. cinerea*]. This is described as very short, and I was disappointed not to get any plants from my sowing, especially as it is a southern species growing in the sandhills of North and South Carolina.

The wild indigos, according to *Hortus*, are all dry soil plants. Moisture is recommended for *B. leucantha*, but it does well for me in a very dry border. On the other hand, *B. australis* is satisfactory in heavy, damp clay. *B. tinctoria* and *B. villosa* need an acid soil. All of the species prefer an open, sunny situation. All can be grown in ordinary soil and, so far as I know, they have no pests or diseases.

I am writing, then, not for those who want to grow rare and difficult plants, but for those who want to grow a variety of plants in an average garden, giving them a reasonable amount of care and spending a reasonable amount of intelligence upon them.
A Southern Garden

Native Plants for the Country Doctor's Garden

I hope everyone will go to Bailey [North Carolina] to see the garden of medicinal herbs at the Country Doctor Museum. The herbs in it, at present, are mostly the ones that came from England in colonial times, but we are working on a collection of the American plants that the colonists learned about from the Indians.

People speak of medicinal plants as if their use is a thing of the past, but barks and roots and leaves are advertised in every issue of the Georgia *Farmers and Consumers Bulletin*, the old names are on the price lists of the wholesale drug dealers, and teas and tonics are still household remedies all over the South.

Because the herb gatherers, the dealers, and the country people use English names, and seldom resort to Latin, I have had to match the common names by sending for the plants advertised in the market bulletins and by consulting the *Illustrated Flora* of Britton and Brown. The *Flora* has the most complete listing of common names that I have come across. In *Southern Wild Flowers and Trees*, Alice Lounsberry tells about the folklore and uses of the flora of the North Carolina mountains at the turn of the century; and Mrs. M. Grieve, in *A Modern Herbal*, gives the medicinal virtues of American as well as European herbs. Hannah Withers sent me a *United States Dispensatory* published in Philadelphia in 1881. It belonged to a country doctor in Monroe, North Carolina, and throws more light on the use of herbs in horse and buggy days.

I think I have identified most of the native herbs that I have found in the bulletins and on the dealers' lists, but I should like very much to hear from anyone who knows local names or who uses home remedies.

We already have calamus root [*Acorus calamus*], and it is flourishing, although I have planted it in my garden a number of times and have never gotten it to grow.

Gordon Butler brought us pipsissewa (*Chimaphila maculata*), which is in the market bulletin as ratsbane; it is also called spotted wintergreen. The Indians used it for rheumatism and scrofula.

He brought us a Saint John's wort, too, *Hypericum stans* [*H. crux-andreae*]. *H. perforatum* is the species of the dispensary, but I think they are all medicinal.

Mr. Shinn has promised to give us rattle root (*Cimicifuga racemosa*), one of the most frequent offerings of the *Georgia Bulletin*. The specific name was formerly *serpentaria*, and it is called rattlesnake root, or sometimes black snakeroot (and, in the bulletins, black snake root), being one of the many plants the Indians called rattlesnake masters, guaranteed to cure snakebite. In the mountains, it is taken in whiskey for rheumatism, Mrs. Lounsberry says, and helps the sufferer to bear it even if the cure is not complete.

We should, I think, have Jamestown weed (Jimson), *Datura stramonium*, in the garden. In the *History and Present State of Virginia* (1705), Robert Beverley describes its effect upon some soldiers sent out to Jamestown to "pacifie the troubles of Bacon." They gathered young shoots for greens. A "very pleasant comedy followed," and lasted 11 days; one soldier blew feathers in the air, and another shot darts at them; one sat in a corner like a monkey grinning and making "Moos" at the others, and one "would fondly kiss and pay his Companions." In retelling the tale, Anne Pratt says, "The love of the marvellous, so prevalent in those days, doubtless led to an exaggerated statement of those effects; but the plant is now well known to be a powerful narcotic." She says it is called thorn-apple because it belongs to "The Prince of Darkness, the origin of all evil."

Dr. Wood, in the *Dispensatory*, says that *Datura* was first introduced into regular practice by Baron Storck of Vienna who used it in treating mania and epilepsy. Other uses are for neuralgia and rheumatism; and, in 1846, Dr. J. Y. Dortch of North Carolina reported its being very useful for ringworm.

At the dedication of the garden [the Country Doctor's Garden], Paul Green spoke of poke-root (*Phytolacca americana*) as a home remedy; but, handsome as it is with its wine-colored stems and wine-dark berries, I don't think its virtues sufficient to warrant our having it in the garden. We would soon have nothing else. "Poke" is an Indian word for smoke, and was first given to some plant that the Indians used for tobacco. I have been unable to discover its connection with *Phytolacca*.

Pokeberries are said to have poisoned children and perhaps adults, but birds, especially thrushes and mockingbirds, love them.

Robert Beverley said, "The planters pretend to have a Swamp-Root which infallibly cures all Fevers and Agues." I asked Paul if this is what they dosed him with when he was little. He said no; the swamp root he took was a patent medicine. I hope someone can tell me what the planters pretended to have.

*Where winters are mild, all
sorts of flowering plants burst into
bloom in "unseasonable" weather, particularly
in warm and sheltered situations.*
A Southern Garden

Pennyroyal

There are two kinds of pennyroyal: the American native *Hedeoma pulegioides* and the English *Mentha pulegium*. The specific names come from the Latin *pulegium* for "fleabane," meaning that it will do away with vermin. In our mountains [of North Carolina] the henhouses, the sleeping places of the hounds, and the walls and floors of the cabins are washed with a strong solution of pennyroyal and homemade soap.

It was once called *Pulegiecem regium* (I don't know why) and therefore "royal," and also "pudding grass" from its flavor of "hakt meat or Haggas-pudding." Parkinson says it is good and wholesome for the lungs, to expel cold and thin phlegm, and afterward to warm and dry it up; and it is also of the "like propertie as Mintes to comfort the stomach, and stay vomiting. It is also used in womens baths and washing, and in mens also to comfort the sinews."

As far back as the days of Apuleius it was known as a remedy for seasickness and on a long voyage to put in the drinking water. "If you have one when you are at sea," Gerard says, take "Penny Royall in great quantity, and cast it into the corrupt water, it helpeth it much, neither will it hurt them that drinks thereof." It "groweth naturally wild in moist and overflown places, such as the Common neere London called Miles End, about the holes and ponds thereof in sundry places, from hence poore women bring plenty to sell in London markets. . . . A Garland of Pennie Royal made and worne about the head is of great force against the swimming in the head, and the pain and the giddiness thereof."

Italians find it useful for and against sorcery, and hang it on fig bushes to keep the fruit from falling before it is ripe. Husbands and wives drink pennyroyal tea and live in harmony. And it has its place in the language of flowers:

> Peniriall is to print your love
> So deep within my heart,
> That when you look this nosegay on
> My pain you may impart.
>
> In Sicily, as I was told,
> The children take Pannyroyal,
> The same that lurks on hill and wold
> In Cotsall soil.
>
> The Pennyroyal of grace divine
> In little cradles they do weave—
> Little cradles therewith they line
> On Christmas Eve.
>
> And there, as midnight bells awake
> The Day of Birth, as they do tell,
> All into bud the blossoms break
> With sweetest smell.
>
> (Quoted by Mrs. Grieve from *Punch* magazine)

*Even a small garden can afford raised borders
for plants from arid regions, some low spots for moisture
lovers, shade and leaf soil for flowers from the woods,
and a sunny place for those from the fields.*
A Southern Garden

Southern Endemics

My correspondent, Weesie Smith, sends me all sorts of interesting plants and notes from Birmingham, Alabama. She sent me *Croton alabamensis*, an endemic evergreen (six to nine feet tall) belonging to the spurge family and growing on limestone hills in mid-Alabama. I didn't even know there was such a genus as *Croton*, never having heard of any but the florist's plant, which is *Codiaeum variegatum*, a tropical shrub. But when I looked in Dr. Small's *Flora*, I found twenty-one species of the genus *Croton* in the Southeast, and five of these are native to North Carolina.

The Alabama croton looks very like an elaeagnus. It has the oval leaves (to six inches long) that are rough on top with a silver sheen at first, and then a smooth dark green. The underside is covered with silvery scales. So far my shrub hasn't bloomed but, from the drawing in Bailey's *Cyclopedia of American Horticulture*, the flowers must be small and inconspicuous. The species are said to be of no horticultural value, but I think this one is worth keeping for the sake of its foliage, especially as it looked better than most evergreens after the severe spells last winter. The generic name comes from the Greek *kronos*, a name given to *Ricinus*, which belongs to the same family.

Weesie sent me what Dr. Wherry calls *Phlox pulchra*, an endemic of northern Alabama. It is not in our manual, or the *Flora*, or Dr. Wherry's wildflower book, but it is in *Standardized Plant Names* as a variety of *Phlox ovata*, though Dr. Wherry refers to it as a species in *Gardener's Chronicle* (March 1942) in an article entitled "The Pick of the Phloxes." He calls it the pastel mountain phlox, "for its large flowers tend to have unique and altogether charming pastel pink coloring." It was worth pulling down the steps and facing the heat of the attic to look up Dr. Wherry's choice of ten phloxes for the wild garden and to find his quotation from Reginald Farrer's *English Rock Garden*: "The day that saw the introduction, more than a century since, of *Phlox subulata*, ought to be kept as a horticultural festival."

I often wonder where writers get the things they quote. In my two-volume edition of *The English Rock Garden*, Farrer says no such thing. He says "That we should sit contented with even 'Vivid' and 'G. F. Wilson' among the Phloxes makes one ashamed, as one goes through the long list of exquisite and longed-for alpines that are still vainly offering themselves to us on the desert mountains of America.... Now for the complete perennial roll-call of this race, incomparably the most important that America has yet evolved for the benefit of the rock garden, and one of which it has an almost undisputed monopoly."

As this was written in 1919, the roll-call is no longer complete; Dr. Wherry says Farrer would have sung the praises of the newer species as well, if he could have known of them.

Phlox pulchra is one that he did not know, and he says of *P. ovata* that it is not among the most attractive of its race. He didn't know about the Ozark phlox either. This is in *Standardized Plant Names* as *P. pilosa* ssp. *ozarkana*. Caroline Dormon sent it to me years ago as 'Peach Blossom', and not long before she died she sent it again. "I call it the Caddo phlox," she wrote, "because it grows in the old Caddo Indian country. Eula Whitehead agrees with me that it is a new species."

I will leave the Latin name to the taxonomists and call it the loveliest of the wild phloxes. The pink flowers are very fragrant. They come into bloom in April (once as early as the seventh) and bloom on until the end of May.

There is an Ozark trillium, too [*T. pusillum* var. *ozarkanum*]. I got it some years ago from Mrs. Mooney of High Mountain Farm in Seligman, Missouri. It has not increased, but it blooms faithfully in early April, a delicate pink flower with a delicious fragrance. Weesie sent me *Trillium decumbens*, an endemic of rocky woods in northeastern Alabama. She sent it in February (the fourth) with its beautifully mottled leaves already up, and the buds of its dark red sessile flowers already sitting on them. It bloomed on Saint Valentine's Day. I have been getting other trilliums from the market bulletin ladies, and between them and the taxonomists, I am getting more and more mixed up.

Because the South Carolina *Market Bulletin* is no longer sent outside the state, I must mention two advertisers that I get interesting wildflowers from: Mrs. Ethel Harmon of Saluda, and Mrs. James Anthony, of Easley. Both are delightful correspondents.

*I know of one source only for
the zenobia, and none for the fetter-bush, which
was collected for me by Belva Bennette who lives
where such things grow, and values them.*
A Southern Garden

Neglected Natives

Dr. Edgar Wherry is still looking for ways to rescue neglected natives. "As you are my only friend in the North Carolina Piedmont country," he wrote last fall, "I am writing to ask you if you can see any way to bring into the rock gardening field the lovely little tradescantia which should bear the name of *Cuthbertia rosea* [*Callisia rosea*], or variety *graminea* [*Callisia graminea*]. My recollections of trips of many years ago are that it is fairly common in grass meadows. I transplanted it into my wild flower garden in Washington, D.C., where it always attracted the attention of visitors—but I gave up that garden 43 years ago!"

Dr. Wells has been urging urging rock gardeners to grow cuthbertia [callisia] since I was his student [at North Carolina State College, now N.C. State University]. He calls it the Sandhills spiderwort, and says it grows in sunny places in the most sterile and dry sands. I got plants from the Clements, at Nik-Nar, but they did not prosper under the white oaks in our Raleigh garden. They were planted in the fall and died before spring. After we came to Charlotte, I found it in bloom at Mr. Crayton's place in Biltmore, and brought it home in bloom. That lasted for two seasons. It bloomed the first year at the end of June, and the next year from May to August. The little triangular flowers were Ridgway's light phlox purple, and the narrow grassy leaves are eight inches long.

I told Mr. Shinn about Dr. Wherry's rescue work, and he wrote, "Our experience with cuthbertia [callisia] has been much the same as yours. It is a sand hill plant, and does not seem to be happy in any other location. I believe one of our troubles was poor drainage. We are trying it now in a somewhat drier spot in a bed of almost pure sand.

"Gathering seed from cuthbertia [callisia] is a rather exacting job.

Since the blooms appear singly, the seed mature in a somewhat similar schedule. You have to be there at the right time to find them ripe. I managed to find a few this year, and I am happy to divide with you. Perhaps Ken Moore has done better than I have."

Under "Tradescantia," our manual lists *T. rosea* [with] a var. *rosea* (*Cuthbertia rosea*) [*Callisia rosea*]; *T. rosea* var. *graminea* (*Callisia graminea*). We saw one of these when we met at Hope Mills [North Carolina] on the eighth of October, 1972, and went to the evergreen shrub bog; but it was out of bloom, of course, so no one knew which it was.

It seems a shame to give cuthbertia to the Tradescants, who have enough honor already; it was named for A. Cuthbert of Augusta, Georgia. The only source I know at present is Mrs. Eugene Polsfuss of Macon.

Dr. Wherry wrote that he thinks our [North Carolina Wild Flower Preservation Society] newsletter is a good place to "call attention to the desirability of bringing this plant into garden use," and, he said, "there is an entirely different plant which I am anxious to obtain. This is *Senecio millefolium*, the lovely laceleaf ragwort. It grows on all the bare peaks along the border of North Carolina and South Carolina." He says he can find no commercial source, and hopes the newsletter can help with this also.

Last fall Dr. Mayer taught me a much needed lesson about jumping to conclusions. He brought me a dried stalk with perfoliate leaves that looked like a eucalyptus, which he said it could not be, as it had the seed pod of a legume. He took it to Julie Moore, who identified it as a *Baptisia perfoliata*. I said it can't be; their leaves are trifoliate and alternate. But this species is an exception: the large round leaves are simple and are joined at the base. It differs in another way: the flowers are solitary instead of in spikes. If I had looked at the key of the bean family, I would have seen that it couldn't be anything else. *B. perfoliata* grows in the sandhills and open woods from the Carolinas to Florida. In Small's *Flora* there is another exception: *B. simplicifolia*.

*I do not suppose there
is any part of the world
in which gardens are not
beautiful in spring.*
A Southern Garden

Morrow Mountain

On the 21st of April [1974], a day of warm sunlight and chilly breezes, I went with the Nowlins to the spring meeting [of the North Carolina Wild Flower Preservation Society] at Morrow Mountain [North Carolina]. On the way, we saw sheets of atamasco lilies in low places along the road, and ditch banks were pink with *Phlox subulata*.

Morrow Mountain was called Naked Mountain after a tornado stripped the timber. Now the trees are grown back to the beginning of a climax forest; the pines are giving way to deciduous trees and the flora that goes with them. There are few flowers in the interval between spring and summer, but the woods were in tender green and the underbrush had been cleared away, leaving the wildflowers alone on the forest floor like designs on a carpet.

We were fortunate in falling in with Ken Moore on the trails, and he named the plants for us. Small clumps of *Oxalis violacea* were dotted along the path and along the clear stream running parallel with it. The leaves were tinged with reddish bronze, and the flowers were rose colored. Years ago, when I checked the color of flowers from a beech wood in Raleigh, they were Chinese violet, so there must be a good deal of variation. The species is scattered across the state from mountains to coast, but I never see it in nurseries or on the lists of wildflower dealers.

Ken showed us *Houstonia purpurea*, which I must have seen before and thought an ordinary weed, but he made me see the tiny pale pink flowers as something precious, and I shall never pass by them again. It is called the mountain bluet, and he says he always thinks of it at Linville Gorge [North Carolina].

I don't think I will forget the name of the veined-leaf hawkweed,

Hieracium venosum, after seeing the beautifully marked reddish purple foliage, but the country people call it rattlesnake weed and believe the leaves laid immediately on a fresh wound will cure snakebite without fail. The juice is supposed to remove warts. The flowers are small yellow daises in wide corymbs on slender stems. Although it is a common weed, it is a distinguished plant when grown as a specimen.

This is also true of the neat little cinquefoil, *Potentilla canadensis*, in perfect scale in miniature gardens of moss- and lichen-covered stones. In April, the compact clumps of five-fingered leaves and solitary golden five-petalled flowers are not at all like the sprawling coarse plants that perhaps they turned into later.

*One of the best points in favor of the
butterfly weed as a garden plant is that it blooms
early in June with the daylilies.*
A Southern Garden
(*in reference to* Asclepias tuberosa)

A Wildflower Garden in August

I wouldn't choose August as a time to see a wild garden, but every season has its lesson in flower, fruit, and leaf. [At Mrs. Herbert Smith's farm called Smithin Farm near Liberty, North Carolina] butterfly weed was in bloom along the roadside, and in the garden there was a single large violet blossom on the butterfly pea, *Clitoria mariana*. There were still a few golden flowers of the wild foxglove, *Aureolaria virginica*, which is called oak leech because it is parasitic of the roots of oak trees. Climbing aconite, button snake root, and pink turtlehead were all in bloom, and the cardinal flower was at its spectacular best. It will thrive in sun or shade in any garden soil. At the Smith's it was blooming well under the trees, but in the bog it was three feet tall with twelve-inch spikes of spectrum red flowers.

The Smith's farm was a wildflower preserve to begin with. When they started their garden many years ago, wild foxglove, pyrola, pipsissewa, the butterfly pea, spotted wintergreen, and the foxtail clubmoss were already growing in the woods. "I can show you fields of the yellow violet (*Viola eriocarpa*) [*Viola pubescens* var. *eriocarpa*]," Mr. Smith said, "and calamus grows down by the bridge." To these have been added, year after year, rare natives from the mountains, the sandhills, and the coast. Mr. Smith likes to grow them from seed, and has even had success with trailing arbutus.

The bog is knee deep in swamp soil, with a plastic sheet at the bottom. Pitcher plants, skunk cabbage, golden club, sea holly, horsetail, and Venus fly traps grow there with Japanese irises. Golden club is *Orontium aquaticum*; the common name calls to mind the curious flowers that come up out of the mud in spring like yellow fingers, not at all like flowers.

Mr. Smith gave me a twayblade (*Liparis liliifolia*). When I planted it under a pine tree, I noticed that his soil matches mine, so I hope it will stay, if the chipmunks don't get it. I remember finding the pretty little brown flowers in the woods near Raleigh the last day of May.

I tried turkey beard (*Xerophyllum asphodeloides*) in my Raleigh garden, but it died without blooming, though it was in just such a shady place as it seems to like in the Smith's garden. He says his bloomed twice. The tall white flowers are called mountain asphodel. The grassy leaves are evergreen, and the plant looks like a clump of fescue.

I had been looking for the climbing milkweed, and there it was in fruit. Lionel Melvin, our consultant [to the North Carolina Wild Flower Preservation Society], says it is probably *Gonolobus suberosus* [*Matelea carolinensis*], though the species seems to be confused. Anyway, it is an angular pod with large decorative fruits and bunches of maroon flowers. Mrs. Smith calls it carrion vine, and Mr. Melvin says that is a good name. He says once when he was collecting where there were many vines in full bloom, the scent was so strong he had to leave.

Mr. Smith says the silk of the common milkweed, *Asclepias syriaca*, is used for insulation in space suits. He has endless bits of odd information and knows the charming country names of native plants. He says *Clematis viorna* is called curly-headed Johnny. Spray is *Leucothoë catesbaei* [*L. axillaris*], which is shipped to Northern florists for funeral sprays and wreaths. Mrs. Smith calls perfoliated bellwort "merrybells," a pretty name that I have heard only in the mountains. Solomon's plume is a prettier name than false Solomon's seal. It is in fruit in August; a little spray of wine-mottled berries drips from the tip of the slender stalk.

*I consider of garden value in
this climate those plants which grow easily
and lustily when their requirements are met
in so far as it is reasonable to do so.*
A Southern Garden

Trilliums

Many years ago, John Lambert of Mena, Arkansas, wrote to ask me about the trilliums in *The Little Bulbs*, and we have been corresponding ever since. In 1976, he had (in his Fork River Arboretum of native plants) thirty-five species and varieties; and now he has forty-six—more than twice as many of those recognized as valid in *Hortus Third*. He has not been able to find a source for *Trillium pusillum* var. *virginianum*, which is uncommon, and *T. persistens*, which is on the endangered list. He would like to hear from anyone who has access to these two trilliums. *T. persistens* is endemic to northeast Georgia and northwest South Carolina. *T. pusillum* ranges from southern Virginia to South Carolina, and from Texas to Missouri. The variety *T. pusillum* var. *Ozarkiana* [*ozarkanum*] came to me from Mrs. Mooney's High Mountain Farm in Seligman, Missouri, and bloomed in deep shade in mid-March or early April for a number of years before being taken over by ivy. The fragrant flowers on ten-inch scapes were white with a faint wine flush on the reverse of the petals.

Mr. Lambert and I both correspond with Weesie Smith, who has a garden full of rare wildflowers in Birmingham, Alabama. "I had a special blessing on January 6th," he wrote in 1977, "a letter from Mrs. Lindsay Smith. She stated that a package of *Trillium stamineum* had been mailed to me the week before. It came on the 12th of January and had been mailed December 24th. The contents were in A-1 condition and of a most generous amount." This rare species was discovered by Michaux and is described by Dr. Small in the first edition of *Flora of the Southeastern United States* (1903) as occurring in Georgia, Alabama, and Mississippi. The dark purple flowers are fetid and sessile.

Weesie sent me *Trillium decumbens*, a dwarf species endemic to northern Alabama and northeastern Georgia. It came on the 4th of February, with a dark red bud sitting peacefully on the three large, round, beautifully mottled leaves. It didn't bloom until the middle of March. Another year it bloomed the first of April, and after that it disappeared. I think it was smothered by a neighbor, *Coreopsis auriculata*, a Southern native that spreads rapidly by stolons and forms an impenetrable mat that is covered with golden daisies from the middle of March into May and is a valuable groundcover for shady places if it is not allowed to take over its betters.

Mr. Lambert is also a friend of Mr. Charlie Moore and the Shinns. "I will never forget Charlie Moore," he wrote in August 1976. "He took me down to the Duke Power Dam site in South Carolina to look for *Trillium vaseyi*. We did not find it, but we collected *T. discolor*, which I still have." *Trillium vaseyi* was one of the five trilliums in bloom when the Wild Flower Society visited Mr. Moore's farm on the 19th of May, 1973. There were four other species, the sweet-scented *T. cernuum* and the ill-scented *T. erectum*, *T. catesbaei*, and *T. discolor*. The *T. grandiflorum* would have been in bloom if the deer hadn't grazed it.

A few weeks after his trip to South Carolina, Mr. Lambert wrote, "Will wonders never cease! Just after I had written to you, a surprise package came from Tom Shinn with two of the needed trilliums. They were *T. vaseyi* (6) and *T. rugelii* (4). *T. rugelii* is a nodding pedicellate type. The petals are white, sometimes with a pale raspberry blush at the base of the petals, otherwise pure white, either way beautiful. This species, he says, was found in the southern Appalachians by Lane Barksdale and published in the *Journal of the Elisha Mitchell Society* [December 1938]. The author has made three collections of this species by the Broad River in the mountains of Henderson County [North Carolina]. It has also been found in Rutherford County [North Carolina]."

Mr. Lambert and I also correspond with Edith Dusek of Graham, Washington, who says trilliums are her old, old love, but now she is making them her specialty. She would like to get in touch with anyone who is interested in sharing information about trilliums and exchanging plants or seeds of unusual forms of these and any other native wildflowers. She is especially interested in the Southern species.

"At present," Mrs. Dusek says, "I have 20 species growing in the garden. Some of these are present in more than one form. Most numerous are examples of our native *Trillium ovatum*. By selecting plants over several states, I have some in flower three months or so. Plants are also selected with an eye to flower size, petal shape, and the colors shown as the flowers age." *T. ovatum* ranges from British Columbia to central California. The fragrant flowers become rosy as they fade.

Edgar Kline of Lake Grove, Oregon, lists *Trillium ovatum* and eleven other American species, among them three forms of *T. sessile*: the Eastern form, the variety *californicum*, and *rubrum*, which is considered a cultivar in *Hortus Third*. "Something called sessile," Mrs. Dusek says, "covers *all* red-flowered sessile trilliums."

Lester Rowntree, in *Hardy Californians*, says the flowers of *T. sessile* are usually white, but sometimes a good mahogany red turns up, and sometimes a "pitiful attempt at being red and green and yellow all at the same time. It can be eight inches tall or two feet."

In *Southern Wild Flowers and Trees*, Mrs. Lounsberry says the leaves of *Trillium sessile* "are nearly orbicular, and about the purplish sessile flower there is a pleasant fragrance. Pennsylvania is the limit of its progress northward." It is strange that botanists never—well, hardly ever— mention fragrance, one of the most desirable characteristics of a plant, and one of the most important in identification. Caroline Dormon used to say she was half hound-dog and recognized things by scent.

Dr. Small describes *Trillium sessile* as having purple flowers and unmarked leaves. In our manual, Dr. Ahles ignores it and describes *T. cuneatum*, which he calls "little sweet Betsy," as the common species in the South with sessile purple flowers and mottled leaves; the variety *cuneatum* includes *T. underwoodii*, *T. hugeri* [*T. cuneatum*], and *T. ludovicianum*. *Trillium luteum*, which is treated as a variety of *T. viride* in *Hortus Third*, becomes a variety of *T. cuneatum*. The plants I grew in Raleigh as *T. luteum* came from the Gardens of the Blue Ridge. The petals were Ridgway's citron yellow, the sepals pale green. The flowers are said to be lemon-scented, but I did not notice any odor. I first saw *Trillium underwoodii* in the Totten's garden in Chapel Hill [North Carolina], and later at Botany Hill in Polk County [North Carolina], where, on a hillside sloping down to the Green River, the flowers filled the warm April air with fragrance.

Mrs. Dusek says, "*Trillium luteum* is *any* species with yellow flowers, be they sessile or stemmed. *Any* green or greenish flower is *T. viride* or *T. viridescens*, which is the same thing." It is not the same thing to Dr. Small, who describes *T. viridescens* as having acuminate bracts and thin petals, mainly purple or red; and *T. viride* as having bracts obtuse, or merely acute, and thick green petals. Mrs. Dusek's notes on *Trillium luteum* in the *Bulletin of the American Rock Garden Society* (Volume 35, Spring 1978) are interesting, and I am looking forward to an article she has just sent to the editor on the Western species.

I find three Japanese trilliums on Mr. Kline's 1978 price list: *T. kamtshaticum*, *T. smallii*, and *T. tschonoskii*. I am always interested in genera, such as *Shortia*, that have species in North American and in Asia, and nowhere else.

6 : Rock Gardens

*Early in September I saw in Mr.
Clement's rock garden a prostrate marigold
that is one of the most charming dwarf
annuals that I have ever come across.*
A Southern Garden

Rock Garden Plants for the Mid-South

Rock gardens are usually made for the cultivation of alpine plants under conditions as nearly as possible like those found where they grow naturally. Because the habitat of alpines is mountain balds, where they are lodged between the crevices of boulders, it is impossible in the mid-South for us to approximate the factors that bring these delicate and brilliant plants to perfection. There they are protected by a heavy blanket of snow in winter and provided with an abundance of moisture from melting snows during the short and favorable growing season. Here, where the open winters, long growing season, and lack of moisture produce the exact opposite of their requirements, it is useless to try to grow alpines other than those not particular as to their environment.

Among those definitely unsuited to our climate are *Armeria laucheana* [*A. maritima* 'Laucheana'], the alpine campanulas, erinus, *Arenaria*, *Achillea argentea* [*A. umbellata*], *Aquilegia alpina*, *Linaria alpina*, the little tufted alpine pinks, and Iceland poppies.

We do not have to forego alpines altogether. Many of them, such as dwarf bearded iris, ajuga, *Nepeta mussinii* [*N. racemosa*], *Veronica incana* [*V. spicata* ssp. *incana*], and *Dianthus graniticus*, adapt themselves perfectly to our climate; and I have no doubt that a number of others will do well in the South. However, we should not strive to make our rock gardens a collection of alpine plants simply because they are the group usually associated with that type of planting, and we should look to other sources for material equally suitable and with which we are more likely to be successful.

Most of the plants found in Northern rock gardens bloom lavishly in the South every spring, but only because they are set out anew each year. *Alyssum saxatile* [*Aurinia saxatilis*], arabis, heuchera, and the Siberian wallflower are so necessary to the spring garden that we are willing if necessary to replace them annually. Arabis, heuchera, and the Siberian wallflower are difficult to keep over the summer because they need moisture but must be well drained.

It is impossible to keep plants moist and well drained in hot, dry weather. Last year, when we had an unusually wet season, the Siberian wallflower (*Cheiranthus allionii*) [*Erysimum × allionii*] continued to bloom throughout the summer instead of drying up by the end of May. The alpine wallflower (*C. linifolius*) [*Erysimum linifolium*], on the other hand, is much more permanent and has the longest season of bloom of almost any rock garden plant. From March until the last of October the small mauve flowers appear among tufts of grayish, linear foliage.

Alyssums are considered particularly resistant to heat and drought. Carl Purdy say that they will all go through a California summer without water. I have found that *A. argenteum* has these qualities, persisting indefinitely in an exposed situation. But *A. saxatile* [*Aurinia saxatilis*] will not live through our summers with water or without it. I am told that another species, *A. sinuatum* [*Aurinia sinuata*], is almost identical with *Alyssum saxatile* [*Aurinia saxatilis*] and will persist. I do not mean to let another year pass without trying it in my garden. *A. serpyllifolium* is not much more persistent than the saxatile alyssum, but it will reseed and bloom the next year.

Although some plants are so valuable as to be worth continued renewal, most of us like a large proportion of our garden flowers to be reasonably permanent. In the South we are in search of plant material able to survive long hard summers rather than long hard winters. There are countless dwarf and trailing plants suitable for planting among rocks and having the qualities that enable them to become established in this section. For the most part they come from temperate regions of Spain, Asia Minor, or the Mediterranean, and from an environment similar to ours.

Pinks, with the exception of some of the alpine species, are a heat-loving tribe. The little calico maiden pinks (*Dianthus deltoides*), the granite pinks (*D. graniticus*), and the cheddar pinks (*D. caesius*) [*D. gratianopolitanus*] are the rock garden species that have proved most successful in the South. The granite pinks are similar to the maiden pinks but bloom over a longer period and are stronger growers. They are useful for filling up space. The cheddar pinks make neat, compact mats of short gray foliage, and their soft lavender flowers are delicately scented and fringed.

The dwarf achilleas, little used with the exception of *A. tomentosa*, are excellent plants for rock gardens and excellent plants for the South. *A. tomentosa*, with its dense mats of woolly finely cut foliage and flat heads of green-gold flowers, blooms from April until late fall. *A. nana* is a dainty yarrow from southern Europe used in making chartreuse. It looks much like the common yarrow except that it is much shorter. It has silvery flower heads and feathery aromatic foliage of a soft green.

To my mind, the most attractive of this group is *A. sibirica*. Its flowers with pure white rays and off-white disks are more like feverfew than yarrow. They grow in short-stemmed clusters above silvery tufts of finely scalloped, linear leaves. It is especially recommended for dry exposed places.

A. argentea, in appearance similar to *A. sibirica*, is an alpine species, and not particularly suited to our climate. I have never seen *A. umbellata*, but it is said to be a good rock garden species and very drought-resistant. I should think it would be a good plant for us to try. All of the above species, except perhaps *A. argentea* [*A. umbellata*], are listed in American catalogues. They are easy to grow, not requiring any special soil and needing only sun and good drainage.

The prostrate veronicas do well here. The best species for us is *V. teucrium* [*V. austriaca* ssp. *teucrium*] and its varieties. By planting *V. teucrium* 'True Blue', which is the last to bloom, with *V. rupestris* [*V. prostrata*], which blooms earlier, we can keep this desirable shade of blue in the garden for several months. *V. repens* requires a continuous supply of moisture. Where a perfectly flat, creeping plant is needed, *Mazus pumilio* is more satisfactory. Two dwarf veronicas, *V. incana* [*V. spicata* ssp. *incana*] with silver foliage and intense blue spikes with drooping tips, and the small, woolly, pink-flowered *V. pectinata* [cv. 'Rosea'] have proved satisfactory with us.

Although most of the dwarf campanulas are worthless in the South, the harebell is one of our best perennials, beginning to bloom in May and continuing throughout the heat of summer. The delicate blue bells on short, wiry stems are not as delicate as they look. They do not seem to mind the cold any more than the heat, and bloom on until the end of October. The name *Campanula rotundifolia* is rather puzzling to one who has seen only the mature linear leaves and not the first small round ones. *C. rotundifolia* has the added value of being tolerant of shade, a quality which is rare in plants also tolerant of heat and drought.

Another wiry little plant that does well for us through the hot, dry weather is *Nierembergia hippomanica*. It is a half-hardy perennial and is said to bloom the first year from seed. It has thread-like foliage and cupped flowers of a blue-tinged white with yellow throats. It blooms well all summer and late into the fall, no matter how dry or how hot it is. This species is creeping and is better suited to the rock garden than *N. frutescens*.

Platycodons are good plants for the South, and the procumbent variety *P. grandiflorus* var. *mariesii* is a good plant for rock gardens. It is permanent and has a long blooming season, beginning in early summer and lasting until late in October. The inflated, five-sided buds are as decorative as the starry flowers. The type is a clear blue, and there is a pure white variety that is very desirable. Platycodons like sun, good drainage, and a light soil.

The prostrate forms of the evening primrose make particularly good rock garden subjects. Most of them come from dry fields and do not demand a great deal of moisture. The only variety seen at all in cultivation in the South (aside from the Texas windflower, which is a pest) is *Oenothera missouriensis* [*O. macrocarpa*]. This lovely primrose with its ephemeral flowers, enormous and pale yellow, is not seen often enough. It is easy to grow if it is given lime and sun. Having for its habitat the barrens of the Southwest, it is immune to drought. It does not like to be encroached upon by other plants. The California catalogues offer a number of varieties of low-growing evening primroses that might reasonably be expected to thrive in our section if they were given a trial.

Stonecrops are important rock garden plants, and many of them, especially those from warm countries, grow well in the mid-South. *Sedum moranense* from southern Mexico is one that flourishes with us. It is an attractive evergreen variety with a pleasing winter color. The flowers are white. *S. anopetalum*, a native of Asia Minor, grows especially well here. It is a desirable variety because its foliage remains in good condition both winter and summer. *S. lydium*, also from Asia Minor, cannot stand our summer sun, but will do well for us if it is given some shade. It is one of the smallest sedums (from two to three inches) making a mat of soft blue-green.

The European stonecrops also do well in the mid-South. The common Old World stonecrop, *Sedum acre*, will grow anywhere. It thrives in poor soil and is used to cover arid places. It is a good plant for rock ledges. *S. acre* is one of the most attractive stonecrops as well as the commonest.

S. sexangulare, another small-leaved species, is much like *S. acre* in habit, but forms heavier clumps. It has yellow flowers and very dark green foliage. *S. reflexum* is one of the best species for the South. It is one of the taller kinds, growing to one foot. Its foliage is good winter and summer.

S. album is an evergreen, creeping species from four to six inches high, forming a mat. It is the round foliage type with thick, waxy leaves and white flowers blooming with us in July. *S. album balticum* is a minute plant for a well-drained rock pocket where it will not get too much sun. Its leaves are green globules. *S. album* 'Purpureum' has purplish foliage. It is a dainty sedum, but it does not stand our summer as well as the type. *S. hispanicum* (in the trade as *S. glaucum* or *S. anglicum*) cannot stand our summer sun, but will do very well if given some shade. It is a charming species, and worth this consideration.

Of the Oriental stonecrops, *S. sarmentosum* has the showiest flowers. It is a rampant sedum, light yellow, and very coarse. *S. ellacombianum* [*S. kamtschaticum ellacombianum*] from Japan is apt to freeze in one of our open winters. This is not because it cannot stand the cold, but because the new growth put out in mild weather gets nipped with low temperature.

We have four native sedums found mostly on rocks in the mountains. *S. nevii*, the cliff stonecrop, ranging from Virginia to Alabama, forms gray rosettes and has white flowers. It is hardy as far north as Massachusetts. *S. ternatum*, one of the best groundcovers for shaded places, also has white flowers. *S. telephioides* [*Hylotelephium telephioides*], taller than the other two, has pink flowers. *S. pulchellum*, widow's cross, is also tall.

Sedum acre, *S. anacampseros* [*Hylotelephium anacampseros*] (which rarely flowers), *S. nicaeense* [*S. sediforme*], and *S. album* are especially recommended for dry situations. *Sedum diffusum* and *S. spurium* are not successful in the South. *S. diffusum* cannot stand our summers.

Houseleeks can be grown in the South if they are provided with afternoon shade. Among those that have proved successful here are *Sempervivum blandum* (*S. rubicundum*) [*S. marmoreum*], a species with pale pink foliage deepening to red in winter; *S. longifolium* [a name of no current botanical standing], better and more compact than *S. blandum*; *S. tectorum*, the common hen-and-chickens; *S. globiferum* [*S. montanum*], a houseleek from Russia, forming rosettes three inches across and having pale yellow flowers; and *S. laggeri* [*S. arachnoideum* ssp. *tomentosum*], a better form of the cobweb houseleek with bright red flowers.

In the South we cannot have more satisfactory plants than the dwarf iris for our rock gardens. We can have spring, beginning the last of February, with the fragrant purple flowers of *Iris reticulata*. The earliest dwarf bearded species come next: *I. pumila* 'Caerulea', a light blue self; the rich purple *I. pumila* 'Atroviolacea' [*I. pumila atroviolacea*]; and the small yellow Hungarian iris, *I. flavissima* [*I. humilis*]. The later-blooming hybrids of *I. pumila* lengthen the season for the dwarf iris until after the first buds of the tall bearded iris are opening in the borders.

Some of the dwarf bearded iris are remontants and should be included in a collection for the rock garden. The remontants are of the greatest value for the South where their fall buds are not in danger of being nipped by the frost. 'Jean Siret', a reliable repeater with yellow flowers, blooms for the first time in March. The soft blues of the intermediate bicolor, 'Autumn King', appear in April with blue flax and *Veronica rupestris* [*V. prostrata*], and again in early October with dwarf pink asters.

There should be wide patches of the dainty native, *Iris cristata*, and a small clump of the rarer Southern species, *I. verna*. *Iris cristata* blooms the second week in April and *I. verna* a little earlier—usually the last of March. *I. verna* is a deeper blue than the crested iris and much more fragrant. Mrs. Wilder says that it is as sweet as a bunch of hothouse violets. It is considered difficult to transplant, but that is probably because it is not given the acid soil that it is accustomed to in its native pine woods. The Japanese roof iris (*I. tectorum*) is another dwarf species that does well in the South. It blooms in April with *I. cristata*, and has the same flat, crested flowers. It is said to be hardy where its foliage is evergreen.

Our climate is a favorable one for botanical tulips, most of which come from warm countries—Greece, Persia, Asia Minor—and require a thorough baking in summer. Of the gay and diverse dwarf species suited to the rock garden, *Tulipa kaufmanniana*, *T. clusiana*, and *T. patens* [*T. celsiana*] are the easiest to grow. *T. kaufmanniana*, the water-lily tulip, blooms first. It is the earliest tulip, coming in March with the dwarf iris. The large, short-stemmed flowers are typically ivory, the petals marked with red on the outside; but there are white, primrose, and red forms.

T. clusiana, the lady tulip, blooms the first of April and lasts for a long time. It is one of the most permanent things in the garden if it is left undisturbed. The slender buds, striped red and white like peppermint candy, never open until late in the day and not at all on cloudy days, but this does not make them less charming. *T. patens* (*T. persica* in the catalogues) [*T. celsiana*], one of the last to bloom, is also one of the smallest. It has yellow flowers.

A good source for plants for the mid-South is the North Carolina sandhills. The apparently fragile wildflowers that grow there in the burning sand can help us to solve the problem of dry summers. In the book *The Natural Gardens of North Carolina*, Dr. B. W. Wells recommends several of them for rock gardens. The sandhill chickweed (*Alsinopsis caroliniana*) [*Minuartia caroliniana*], a distinctive species with starry white flowers and thread-like foliage, and the sandhill spiderworts (*Cuthbertia graminea*) [*Callisia graminea*] and *C. rosea* [*Callisia rosea*]), with their tufts of rose-colored flowers and grassy leaves, are suitable for planting among rocks and like an exposed, sunny situation.

The sandhill moss pink (*Phlox hentzii*) [*Phlox nivalis* ssp. *hentzii*], a distinctly Southern species, is considered superior to *Phlox subulata*. Trailing arbutus (*Epigaea repens*) is found among the turkey oaks on the sandhills, as well as beneath the conifers on mountain slopes. And still it is a difficult plant to cultivate, one worthy of the mettle of the most fastidious rock gardener. The common pyxie moss (*Pyxidanthera barbulata*) grows in moist places; a smaller species (*P. brevifolia*) recently discovered by Dr. Wells, prefers a dry, exposed situation. It forms dense mats, changing from dark green to white in February, when it is in bloom, and to red when the seeds are formed. A rare plant found only in a restricted area in the Sandhills, it may prove difficult in the rock garden; but it is well worth a trial and is already available from at least one nursery.

*For the present, it seems very much
at home on a shady slope in a carefully prepared
pocket of sand and leaf mold, where I hope its roots will
find moisture under the rocks in summer droughts.*
A Southern Garden (*in reference to* Omphalodes verna)

Rules for Rock Gardens

There has been a great deal of controversy about the right and wrong way to make rock gardens; and there will always be discussion of this point, for it is largely a matter of taste and can never be settled for all time. There are, however, certain fundamental rules that apply to all attempts at growing plants among rocks, and it is well to have them in mind before trying to establish these fascinating subjects in a proper setting.

The first rule for a rock garden is that it should be on a slope. The reason for this is practical as well as aesthetic. A slope is better drained than level ground, and it is more natural to rock formation. Where the ground does not slope naturally, it is better to have another type of garden than to try to create an artificial hillside or to pile up stones to resemble an Indian mound.

The second rule is that a rock garden should not follow any regular pattern but should be made to look as if it had come about naturally. This is hard to accomplish on a small city lot bounded by walls and fences, perhaps with the garage on one side and the house on another. Such a situation lends itself to rectangular borders, straight paths, and clipped hedges. In a garden like this, dwarf and creeping plants can be grown among the rock borders of the flower beds or in the crevices of stones of a flagged terrace, or—where there is more than one level—in a retaining wall.

The way to make a rock garden look as if it had come about naturally is to provide a leafy background and to use weathered stone set in the ground in the way it came out of it. For background an informal planting of native cedars, dogwoods, shadblows [any of several species of the *Amelanchier* genus], redbuds, and hollies is the best substitute where a natural growth is lacking. Native stone is good when it has been exposed to wind and sun, but not when it is fresh from the quarry. Rocks should be chosen as carefully as the plants that are to grow among them, preferably by collecting a few at a time from fields and roadsides. And there should not be too many of them. A few of the right kind judiciously set is far more pleasing than a rock pile harboring a few plants.

Use rocks as big as it is possible to acquire and handle, and set them deep in the earth with their heavy sides down in formations that follow the contours of the earth. The rocks should not be all alike, but should vary in shape and size. Skillful gardeners may devise picturesque ledges and miniature ravines, but it is better not to be too ambitious unless one is sure of getting a good effect. Gardens built a little at a time so that the affinities of rocks, plants, and slope may be studied will be more pleasing than those constructed in a day. The trouble with most gardeners is that they are too impatient. We should imitate nature in her deliberation as well as in her skill in achieving effects that are at the same time casual and inevitable.

When the rocks are put in place, the soil should be very carefully prepared, for it cannot be remade as in the perennial border every time a new planting is necessary. First the existing soil must be dug to a depth of two feet or more and mixed with a generous supply of humus. Most rock plants need a humid, porous soil, one that will not dry out completely and will not become soggy in wet weather. A mixture of leaf mold or peat with sand and good loam—the sand to make it porous and the humus to hold moisture—answers the requirements. Manure and commercial fertilizers are not generally recommended; but rock plants need food as well as other plants, and it is best supplied by a top dressing in the fall of one part sand, one part leaf mold, and some bonemeal. A mulch of stone chips helps to keep the crowns of the plants dry, to keep the weeds down, and to keep the moisture from evaporating in hot weather.

The third rule is that the plant material be suitable in character and scale. The original purpose of rock gardens was to provide cool, moist root runs and proper drainage for the cultivation of rare alpines. In our parched Southern climate, it would be foolish to try to make a collection of mountaintop plants, but we can grow some of the less exacting alpines as well as other types of dwarf plants. The important point is to choose trailing and procumbent varieties that lend themselves to filling in crevices and covering broad surfaces, and to choose plants that will be in scale with each other and with the rocks. Scale is all-important because legitimate rock garden material ranges in size from tiny creepers to dwarf shrubs. Too great a contrast in the sizes of the plants and plants too large for the rocks are the easiest mistakes to make.

Instead of wasting time over plants that have to be coaxed, we may as well start with those that will thrive in the South, since all plants suitable for rock gardens are not suitable for our climate. Among those that do well for us, none are lovelier than our native wildflowers. One of the first of these to bloom in the woods is the yellow-flowered chrysogonum, which grows in such neat tufts between flagstones or among rocks and is probably the easiest wildflower to transplant. It grows in any soil, in sun or shade, and is almost everblooming.

The pale hepaticas with their furry buds and prettily mottled leaves are also early. Later, bloodroot pushes pure white buds through the leaf mold. These are among the commonest wildflowers, and are sure to grow in cultivation. To them may be added our dwarf crested iris (*Iris cristata*), wild ginger, foam flower, columbine, cranesbill, anemones, wild coreopsis, meadow rue (*Thalictrum*), atamasco lilies, bluets, bird's-foot violets, partridge berries, and moss pink. More difficult to establish in cultivation are lady's slippers, trilliums, trailing arbutus, and some of the native lilies. It is a pity to take them from the woods unless we are sure of being able to make them live. The delicate dog-tooth violets are not difficult once they are acquired, but the bulbs are unbelievably deep in the ground, and a person who does not know this is apt to destroy the plant without getting them up. They should be dug only with a spade.

Much of the standard rock garden material is likely to be impermanent in this section. *Alyssum saxatile* [*Aurinia saxatilis*], saponaria, *Aquilegia alpina*, *Gypsophila repens*, arabis, and cerastium make wide spreading mats of solid bloom the first season but cannot be counted on for the second. We need not lack, however, for plants that do bloom year after year. For full sun there are nepetas, thymes, dwarf veronicas, pinks, poppy-mallows, and *Tunica saxifraga* [*Petrorhagia saxifraga*]. The last is a rock garden standby. Its mist of pink flowers has the same effect as baby's breath, for which it can be substituted. Of the low-growing veronicas, *V. teucrium* [*Veronica austriaca* ssp. *teucrium*] and its varieties are the most satisfactory ones for the South. They produce sheets of blue in early spring. The maiden pinks and cheddar pinks are our chief dependence for dianthus. For shade we can have certain ones of the trailing campanulas; that old favorite, plumbago, which produces vivid mats of blue all summer and even into fall if it is kept cut back; the indispensable bugle plant (*Ajuga*); prunella; and the pretty alpine aster that scorches if it is planted in full sun.

Many of the small bulbs like rock garden conditions, and most of them do well for us. The spring starflower [*Ipheion uniflorum*], a relative of the onion, is one of the easiest to grow and one of the most rewarding in the quantities of violet-tinted flowers. The brilliant *Iris reticulata* is a rock garden gem and not at all difficult. The charming lady tulips with their peppermint-candy buds open into wide stars when the sun is upon them. The species crocus, more suited to rock gardens than the stodgy horticultural varieties, are especially desirable for the South because they bloom very early, some of them even in winter. The Siberian squill produces very small, very blue flowers early in February. Grape hyacinths make broad splashes of color where there is room for them to become naturalized, but they increase so rapidly that they crowd out other bulbs if they are planted among them.

> *Certainly we should consider
> the appearance of the garden in winter
> as well as in summer, particularly
> in the choice of shrubs.*
> A Southern Garden

Rock Garden Conifers in Southern Nurseries

Ever since I began to collect plants systematically instead of merely taking pleasure in those that chanced to come my way, I have been annoyed when I failed to find in the trade the plant that I wanted. But once, when I was making the rounds of the nurseries, it occurred to me that it would be much wiser to learn what the plantsmen have to offer than to deplore what they lack. Poking about in this amiable frame of mind, I found a number of interesting shrubs that I did not know about and that did not appear in the catalogues. I was particularly delighted with the dwarf conifers.

In a Maryland nursery I found two dwarf plum-yews and a spreading form of the English yew. The Japanese plum-yew, *Cephalotaxus drupacea* [*C. harringtonia* var. *drupacea*], is typically a tree to thirty feet tall, but one form found in the nursery is low and spreading. This is probably what Rehder calls variety *nana*. I saw one eight-year-old plant that had not got above eighteen inches. The other dwarf plum-yew is a form of variety *pedunculata* (or *fastigiata*) listed as *C. pedunculata repandens* [*C. harringtonia*]. Six-year-old plants were less than a foot tall.

The dwarf form of English yew, *Taxus baccata* 'Repandens', is said to grow eventually to three feet, but eighteen-inch specimens have grown no taller in my garden in five years, though they have spread considerably. In the same nursery, I came across specimens of the rare *Cedrus libani* 'Nana' (usually listed as 'Comte de Dijon'), which grows from two-and-a-half to three feet, and two dwarf forms of *Cryptomeria japonica*. The one known as *C. japonica* 'Nana' is a slow-growing pygmy said not to exceed eighteen inches, and less than that in the nursery specimens. The form known as 'Elegans' or 'Compacta' is said to grow at the rate of six inches a year, and so will make a larger shrub. It is not so hardy as the type.

In a Virginia nursery I found *Cryptomeria japonica* 'Vilmoriniana', an enchanting fluffy ball about two feet high. This is very symmetrical and could well be used as an accent in a formal garden. All of the dwarf cryptomerias are light green in color and turn a reddish brown in cold weather. They are easy to grow and like sun.

In a Georgia nursery there were several specimens of *Cedrus atlantica* 'Pygmaea' [*C. libani ssp. atlantica*], stout, bristling little bushes about two feet high. This discovery was my last before gas rationing; when we can take to the road again, I shall set out in search of further treasures.

*There is room even
in a small garden for an
almost infinite variety of
bulbs and border plants.*
A Southern Garden

Some Small Members of the Iris Family

In searching for rock garden material, I have come upon some delightful Southern irids that are new to me. They came from Mrs. James Dormon's garden in Shreveport, Louisiana, where the three natives, *Nemastylis*, *Herbertia*, and *Eustylis* bloom in succession from March through June, and *Cypella herbertii*, from South America, blooms all summer. These bulbs have not been in my garden long enough to tell whether they can be permanently established, but all have come through one winter; and even if they do not prove to be permanent, they are not too expensive to renew from time to time.

The pinewoods lily, *Eustylis purpurea* [*Alophia drummondii*], is like a small, dark-violet tigridia on stems two feet tall. It has the shell-like sheen and texture of the tigridia and like it is fleeting, the flowers coming out in the morning and shriveling before night. With me it blooms for about a month beginning late in May or early in June, but Mrs. Dormon finds that with moisture it will bloom through the summer. She also says that it will stand drying off if left in the ground, but not if taken up. This may mean that it cannot be taken up and stored where it is not hardy, but I should think that any gardener who likes new things would be eager to try it for a season. Bulbs set out in early spring bloomed for me the same summer. The pinewoods lily is native to Louisiana and Texas where it grows in sandy soil or sometimes in clay. It will bloom in sun or half-shade, and the bulbs should not be more than two inches deep.

Nemastylis acuta, so closely related to *Eustylis* that they are sometimes placed in the same genus, has not bloomed for me so far. I mean to keep trying it in various situations, for it is native as far north as Tennessee, and I can see no reason for it not to flourish in North

Carolina though it is not very hardy. In Louisiana it blooms in March, and from Miss Caroline Dormon's illustration in her book *Wild Flowers of Louisiana*, it must be as heavenly blue as its local name, which is "celestials." In cultivation, celestials requires good garden soil in sun or part shade and deep planting—six to twelve inches.

Herbertia drummondiana [*Alophia drummondii*], listed by Miss Dormon as *H. caerulea*, is said to come from "wet prairies," but it did not do so well for me in a wet place, and I did not get the enchanting blue flowers until I planted the bulbs in light soil in a slightly raised border. The flowers are what I call blue, very blue; but, according to Ridgway's classification, they are deep lavender. That is, the showy outer segments are of this hue, while the small, pointed inner segments are a deep, rich violet. With me it is quite a bloomer, coming in April and lasting until June. The bulbs are small and dark and firm like those of zephyranthes, and will stand drying in summer if they are left in the ground, but not if they are taken up. *Hortus Second* gives the herbertia a height of up to one foot, but with me the stems are not over five inches, and the leaves are like those of nut-grass. This is one of the prettiest little bulbs that I have ever had, and worth a great deal more trouble than it has required so far. I think it is going to require some coaxing to get it established.

The fourth of these little irids is *Cypella herbertii*, imported to England from South America in 1823, according to Mrs. Loudon, and named by William Herbert in honor of his brother George. It looks like a yellow tigridia, and has indeed been classed by some as *Tigridia herbertii*. The wide outer segments form a triangle that measures two inches from point to point, and they are indented at the base to form a cup in which the small, curled inner segments form another triangle. The flowers are a deep golden yellow with shell-like markings of maroon. They are produced in quantity, although they last only a day. With me they bloom from early May through the summer, with periods of rest in between. The fugitive flowers are borne on wiry eighteen-inch stems. The slender, plaited, evergreen leaves are like the foliage of the pinewoods lily. The flowers are similar except in color, and both are without fragrance. The bulbs can be lifted in the fall and stored over the winter in regions where they are not hardy outdoors. I have them in full sun in a place where the soil is light.

There is a small white violet in the South that I have not been able to identify. My father brought it to me from some Georgia relatives, and I am trying to pass it on to other gardeners so that it will not be lost.
A Southern Garden

More about Violets

In the violet number of the *Bulletin*,[1] I saw no mention of two Asiatic species, *Viola eizanensis* [*V. dissecta*] and *V. patrinii*.

According to *Hortus Second*, *V. eizanensis* is not known botanically. For all that, it is a distinct and lovely violet; and I wish I could grow it. It does not seem, however, to care for the summer heat and repeatedly disappears from my shady rock garden after blooming very early in March and producing two or three pale green and finely cut leaves. The large, creamy white flowers are on short, slender red stems. The lower petals are delicately marked with fine lines of bright violet, and the upper two are streaked with paler violet. It came to me from Mr. Borsch, who recommends some shade for it and woodland soil. I have read elsewhere that it should have an acid loam with some moisture and full sun. This is one of the prettiest violets that I have ever grown, and I would be willing to take some trouble to get it established if I knew what it really needs in these parts.

I suppose rock gardeners in more favorable climates will turn up their noses at the easily grown Chinese violet, *V. patrinii*. For the South, it is a fine thing with clean attractive foliage and bloom in spring and fall. It is one of the best plants for dry shade where the summers are trying and the winters uncertain, seeding itself freely, but not too freely, for it is nice to have extra plants to give away.

V. jooi from southeastern Europe is another violet that I like, though with me it was transitory and must be tried again before I can tell whether the trouble was the climate or the situation. I planted it in

---

1. The bulletin referred to is the *Bulletin of the American Rock Garden Society* (vol. 4, pp. 94–188).

a dry place on a sunny wall and gave it lime as Mr. Borsch says that it comes from the limestones of Transylvania. It is a real miniature, blooming with me from early spring into summer. The leaves are small and near the ground, and the flowers are lilac.

One of the nicest white violets that I have came from Mr. Osmun as *V. alsophila* [*V. blanda*], said to be native in the Adirondacks. Usually the small pure white flowers appear soon after the middle of March; and when they have finished blooming, the heart-shaped leaves grow broader and taller. This is one of the few white violets that I have been able to grow in dry shade, and it is one of the prettiest that I have seen.

I was glad to see Mrs. Henry's praise of that delightful Southern violet, *V. walteri*, which is so little appreciated here that I first came across it in a Western catalogue. Later Miss Caroline Dormon sent it to me from Louisiana.

Mr. Barr asks if *V. nuttalii* is always a shy bloomer in the East. It is with me, but after reading his account of it, I mean to see if it will not bloom better if I move it from the shade to the sun. It is the only plant of the Great Plains that has so far showed any tendency toward becoming established with me, though Mr. Barr has sent me many over a period of years. I was well pleased with the tiny yellow flowers and shiny pale green leaves; but, of course, I would be even more delighted if I could get it to bloom freely.

Last year, the white hoop-petticoat
daffodil, N. bulbocodium [var.] monophyllus,
said to bloom in January, bloomed in January—not
in someone else's garden but in my own.
A Southern Garden

A Review of Little Daffodils

I have never achieved my ambition to have in a single season a succession of little daffodils from November to May, but, over a period of years, I have had them in bloom each of those months. Once I managed to get a bulb of *Narcissus serotinus* from Drew Sherrard in Portland, Oregon, in order to have bloom in October, but the wretched little thing never bloomed at all, and I have never seen it listed again.

The only little daffodil that has ever bloomed for me in the fall came from Robert Moncure of Alexandria, Virginia, under the formidable name of *N. bulbocodium* 'Clusi Foliosus' [*N. cantabricus* ssp. *cantabricus* var. *folious*]. It bloomed in November or December and persisted for a number of years. I have an idea that I would have it yet if I had not been so careless with the trowel. Such treasures should always be in a tiny rock pocket all to themselves. *N. b.* ssp. *monophyllus* is more difficult, and never persisted for more than two or three years. It blooms in January or February, according to the season. *N. b. citrinus* blooms next. It is more easily established than the white forms, but it increases little. *N. b. conspicuus* blooms last of all, at the end of the daffodil season. The deep yellow flowers and the shiny rat-tail leaves are very plentiful, and the bulbs increase rapidly. This is the easiest of all of the little daffodils.

N. minimus [*N. asturiensis*], the tiniest of the trumpets, bloomed once very early in February, and then disappeared forever. *N. minor*, which blooms in March, is larger and more persistent, but less attractive. The flowers are of a durable substance and stay in bloom for two weeks. *N. lobularis* [*N. minor*] blooms early in March on six-inch stems. The small trumpets are lemon-colored, and the perianths are creamy.

There is so much confusion about the white trumpets that there seems little use in describing them, but all are lovely. I have had three entirely different ones sent to me as *N. moschatus* [*N. pseudonarcissus* ssp. *moschatus*]. "The botanists of the late eighteenth and early nineteenth century," Peter Barr says in the *Bulletin of the Alpine Garden Society*, March 1935, "appear to have applied the name *moschatus* variously to the white trumpet daffodils known as *albicans*, *cernuus*, and *tortuosus*." In old gardens hereabouts, there are a number of white trumpets of varying sizes and shapes that come into bloom any time between early February and the middle of March. I love them all, but I have not found all of them easy to grow. They may grow in wide drifts in one situation and disappear completely when they are transferred to another garden.

The *N. cyclamineus* hybrids are too overpowering for the rock garden, with the exception, perhaps, of 'Beryl' and 'Le Beau'. 'Beryl' blooms rather late, usually early in April. It shows its *cyclamineus* inheritance in its drooping flowers and reflexed petals, and its *poeticus* inheritance in its short, colorful cup. The petals are pale yellow at first, but they become creamy with age. The stem is eight inches. 'Le Beau' is taller, with an exaggeratedly long narrow trumpet and petals turned all of the way back. It blooms in February with the early ones.

The tiny, almost transparent flowers of *N. triandrus* var. *albus* [*N. triandrus triandrus*] are the most appealing of all, but, as Sir William Lawrence says, "Angels' tears are liable to be spilled." The smaller *triandrus* hybrids are the cream of the rock garden daffodils. This year from Mr. Heath I had 'Hawera', a *triandrus* × *jonquilla* hybrid for which I have long been searching. It blooms at the end of March, producing two or three nodding flowers to a scape. The pale flowers are the color of winter sunshine. The cup is small and bowl-shaped, and the winged petals turn back toward the stem. Mr. Heath sent me also 'April Tears', which is similar to 'Hawera', but smaller, of a deeper yellow, and more lavish with its blossoms. The rare and beautiful 'J. T. Bennett Poe' came to me this spring from Carl Krippendorf from his collection in Milford, Ohio. More like the 'Queen of Spain' (but smaller) than 'Angels' Tears', it is pale and as delicate as sea foam, and entirely different from all other daffodils.

The *Jonquilla* hybrids are mostly too big for rock gardens, but 'Tullus Hostilius' and 'White Wedgwood' should, perhaps, be let in, and 'Lintie' is definitely a flower of the rocks. 'Tullus Hostilius' is very sturdy and long lasting, and has a very long period of bloom beginning early in March. The flowers are of the trumpet type, but the color is jonquil yellow. 'White Wedgwood' is similar in shape, but the starry perianth is creamy white and the trumpet is yellow. It blooms late in March or early in April, and very freely. The stems of both of these are about twelve inches. 'Lintie' blooms early in April. The shimmering yellow petals are round like those of the poet's narcissus and slightly reflexed, and the short, fluted cup is rimmed with orange. It is only six inches tall. All three have two flowers to a stem.

A number of jonquils found in old gardens in the South are suitable for rock gardens. The earliest one that I know came to Chapel Hill from Williamsburg and is said to be *N. jonquilla* 'Simplex'. It is not the variety 'Simplex' as I know it, a tall flower that blooms much later. The sweet yellow flowers bloom on short stems at the end of February or in March, when the foliage is short, too, and fine. Later the stems grow to eighteen inches, and the foliage gets coarse. This is the earliest jonquil that I know of. The latest is also a small one. Mr. Heath found it in an old planting in Virginia and lists it as 'Helena'. This year it bloomed for me in the month of April. It is even more perfect for the rock garden than the early one, for it never gets taller than seven inches and the foliage is fine, sparse, and inconspicuous, although it lengthens to twenty inches after the flowers fade.

I have from two different sources a small jonquil which is listed as *N. j.* 'Citrinus', but I can see no difference between this and *N.* × *tenuior* [*N. jonquilla* × *N. poeticus*], which is one of the best of the jonquils—free-blooming, delightful, and growing anywhere.

The other species of the jonquil group have always proved difficult, except for *N.* × *gracilis* [*N.* × *tenuior*], which is too big for the rock garden. "I planted a dozen or so of *N. juncifolius* [*N. assoanus*] about fifteen years ago, but they have gradually dwindled away, and I saw only two or three blooms this spring," Mr. Krippendorf wrote. Fifteen years sounds to me like a mighty long time for little jonquils. I planted this small species twice, but it never held out for more than the season.

The botanical tulips are delightful,
and I have an idea that many of the
species would do well in our gardens.
I wish I knew more of them.
A Southern Garden

Some Notes on Species Tulips

Last year Mr. Moody sent me a collection of forty rock garden tulips, some of which were new to me and some of which I had grown before. This spring, after finding out which had survived the second season, I went through my files to assemble these notes on all of the little tulips that I have grown in Charlotte and previously in Raleigh.

Tulipa acuminata bloomed the first season on April 16th, a total of one flower from the three bulbs, the second season none. Anyway, with its long stringy petals, it is more odd than beautiful.

T. aucheriana opened two seasons in the middle of April and looks happy. It is one of the most delightful kinds, with starry, mallow-pink flowers expanding wide in the sun.

T. australis blossomed once on April 9th. Of the six bulbs planted, not one showed leaf or bud after the first season.

T. batalinii blooms with *T. tarda, aucheriana, hageri,* and *chrysantha* [*T. clusiana* var. *chrysantha*], between the first and middle of April. This distinct and lovely species with urn-shaped buds the color of the horticultural chart's[1] aureolin yellow, seems still satisfied after its second season.

T. biflora flowered once, late in March, and that was the end of twelve bulbs originally planted. On second trial it did not bloom at all. The charming blossom, yellow and white as I remember it and

---

1. The horticultural color chart that Elizabeth Lawrence refers to is not identifiable from the information in this article. She usually referred to the color chart from *Color Standards and Color Nomenclature*, written and published by Robert Ridgway (Washington, D.C., 1912).

something like *T. tarda*, only daintier, was worth the attempt. The species *turkestanica* planted once did not bloom.

T. chrysantha [*T. clusiana* var. *chrysantha*] bears a flower of soft yellow on a very short stem. Though this blossomed well for two seasons, I have no further check on it, nor on others tried at the same time, for I left them behind in Raleigh.

T. clusiana not only persists indefinitely, but increases. It usually offers its pearl-white stars soon after the middle of March, but sometimes not until April. In good soil the stalks may reach eighteen inches, and then it seems a little lanky for the rock garden. Though it is always springing up in odd places, I have never known whether it seeds itself or whether little bulbs scatter when something else is planted.

Neither so reliable nor so persistent, *T. florentina* [*T. sylvestris*] blooms about the same time, a patch sometimes flowering for several seasons. As its name indicates, I think it should be placed in some shade. Also it likes more humus and more moisture than most species. Flowers the colors of buttercups are borne on stems as long as those of *T. clusiana*.

T. fosteriana is very large and showy, much too large for the rock garden, or at least for one that features the smaller species. One year the buds of 'Defiance' were killed by the cold. 'Cantab' opened March 8th; 'Princeps' April 6th.

T. hageri is one of the most satisfactory species and certainly one of the most attractive if it can be planted where its terra-cotta flowers show to advantage. It is very floriferous, usually coming the first week in April.

The water-lily tulip is one of the most precocious. The earliest date I have for it is the first week in March. This is not one of my favorites, as the peppermint-striped flowers seem too big for the short stems. The large and showy multicolored forms and hybrids in the *kaufmanniana* group bloom over a long period, beginning this year with 'Solanus' on the second of March and ending with 'Henriette' on the 22nd, the last coming on into April. Not only long lasting, 'Henriette' is one of the most beautiful, very large and urn-shaped, ivory with rose flames on the outside. To me this is one of the most superb of all tulips. 'Solanus' is lemon yellow with red flecks, the variety 'Coccinea' bright red with a gold center, 'Bellini' white inside and red out, 'Fritz Kreisler' large and pink. 'Cesar Franck', which I have not had, is said to be one of the earliest tulips, blooming even before most of the crocuses. The flowers are deep yellow, with scarlet flames on the outer divisions.

The year I left Raleigh [1948], I had *T. linifolia* for the first time, blooming on April 7th, the cup-shaped flowers scarlet and black.

T. marjoletti bloomed in April, one year the 8th, the following year the 24th, with gay red and yellow flowers on long slender stalks. When I left it behind, it seemed well established.

T. ostrowskiana seems to be a rare one, concerning which I can find nothing except that it comes from Turkestan and is closely related to *T. oculis-solis* [*T. agenesis*]. My single bulb died without flowering.

T. persica [*T. celsiana*], supposed to be one of the late species, bloomed in Raleigh toward the end of March and early in April, which is about midseason. It did very well there, but here in Charlotte died out. Mrs. Wilder says that with her it was the most persistent species. It is certainly one of the prettiest, like a little piece of cloisonné.

Though *T. praecox* sounds like an early one, it did not bloom until the end of March. It has now been with me for two seasons, a very pretty bright red, like a single early, with conical flowers on six-inch stems. This comes from central Europe.

*One of the
delightful qualities of
winter flowers is that
they last so long.*
A Southern Garden

Rock Gardens in Winter

I wish some gardeners would write about bloom in November, December, and January. There must have been some, even in cold gardens, in this very open winter. Mr. Starker wrote on January 8th of heathers, hellebores, and snowdrops in bloom in an Oregon snowstorm, and here it seems to me that we have had more winter flowers than ever before. This may be partly because there is more to bloom as I keep adding new things for this time of year, and partly because the old plants bloom more freely and over a longer period as they get better established; but, most of all, I think it is due to a mild season.

The first week in November, *Zephyranthes candida* was still in bloom along with *Crocus longiflorus, C. ochroleucus,* and *Cyclamen neapolitanum* [*C. hederifolium*]. There were still forget-me-nots that the frost had missed, and several kinds of violets. On the first day of the month [January], *Oxalis bowieana* [*Oxalis bowiei*] began to bloom, but it did not get far before the frost caught it. This is really a fall bulb, and should bloom in September. The Algerian iris came into bloom on the same day, and there have been flowers at intervals ever since. Whenever the thermometer drops below 20 degrees, they stop; but, as soon as it warms up, they come again.

Soon after *Cyclamen neapolitanum* [*C. hederifolium*] bloomed out, *C. cilicium* began, and on a sunny wall there was a rosy flower of *C. vernum* [*C. coum*] on Christmas day.

The white hoop petticoats began to bloom early in December. Now, in the middle of January, 'Nylon' is in bloom, and I see that the first bud of *Narcissus scaberulus* has poked up out of the ground.

Before Christmas two bergenias were in bloom. One is called *Bergenia cordifolia*, but I think it is the wrong plant as the leaves are not at all heart-shaped. The flowers are very pale. The other, with flowers of a deeper pink, is *B. ligulata rosea* [*B. ciliata* 'Rosea']. *Iberis sempervirens* 'Little Gem' has a distinct tendency toward winter bloom. Since early December it has been flecked with white. Mrs. Chrismon says she has in her Greensboro, North Carolina, garden a wild white phlox that blooms all winter, and the rest of the year too. From time to time, I find a round blue periwinkle, and parting the dark leaves of *Viola rosina* [*V. odorata* cultivar] uncover a rosy pink flower.

From Thanksgiving on, the buds of the winter heaths begin to show color, and come what may, you can count on them for an amethyst glow for the rest of the winter. There is also a good white form of *Erica mediterranea*.

Crocus laevigatus cv. 'Fontenayi' began to bloom the fifteenth of November, and *C. minimus* on the third of December. I have had a long search for the latter, and this is the first time it has bloomed in my garden. The violet cups are charming, but no smaller than most winter species. *C. sieberi* is usually the first to bloom after Christmas, but this year *C. chrysanthus* 'E. A. Bowles' was ahead. I found a stray bloom the day after Christmas. Now, in mid-January, there has been a flower of 'Snow Bunting', and the buds of *C. imperati* are waiting for a sunny day. *Galanthus elwesii* also bloomed before the end of the old year. Now the oriental hellebores are in bloom, but where are the snows of yesteryear?

It is by far the loveliest of the heaths
in flower, with long racemes of inverted urns,
very pure white among the pale oval leaves.
A Southern Garden
(*in reference to* Zenobia pulverenta)

Two Wonders

It is a wonder to me that you can spend your life searching out plants, and then come across things you have never heard of and can't find in the books. Two or three years ago, I saw *Cyanthodes colensoi* in Mr. Starker's catalogue, and sent for it to see what it is like, although I didn't expect it to stay with me. This genus comes from New Zealand and Australia, and plants from that part of the world seldom thrive with me, so I didn't expect it to live through the winter; and, when spring found it still there, I didn't expect it to live through the summer. But it still grows, or rather stays—I don't think it has grown much—in the crevice of the garden steps.

Mr. Starker describes it as "an upright shrublet, with small bluegrey leaves, pink at the tips of the branches. Small creamy flowers in clusters are sweet-scented and succeeded by rose-red berries." The plant is something like a tiny Persian candytuft, but so far I have seen no flowers or fruit. The only cultural hint Mr. Starker gives is that it wants sun. From its looks, I should say that it would like a less dry and starved soil than I have given it; and perhaps, like some of the other species, it wants peat.

My other wonder is that such a good shrub as *Indigofera decora* should go unsung. Mr. Bean describes it as a charming dwarf shrub that Fortune found growing in the gardens of Shanghai, the standards of the flowers white marked with crimson, the wings pink. After a long search, I recently found it listed by the Brimfield Gardens. The form I have is the variety *alba*, with pure white flowers, forty to sixty to a slender raceme. The white flowers, the pale green calyces, the slender stems and fine compound foliage, all make a delightfully cool and fresh pattern. In my garden, this species blooms early in May, but I suspect that it is summer-flowering in Connecticut. I think it would have to be used with caution in the choice parts of the rock garden, for it suckers and makes a very thick mat; but it is a charming summer groundcover, although it is cut back to the ground in winter.

My *Indigofera* came to me from Mr. Epstein in exchange for the promise of *Zenobia pulverulenta*. I got the best of the bargain, for the plants I sent for *Zenobia* turned out to be *Rhaphiolepsis!*

7 : Brothers of the Spade

> It is not prepossessing when left to its own devices, but Miss Jekyll contrived a way of pinning the stalks down over the foliage of earlier blooming perennials to encourage the growth of extra flowers all along the stem.
> A Southern Garden
> (*in reference to* Helianthus orgyalis, *now* H. salicifolius)

Miss Jekyll of Munstead Wood

In an age of fine writing and fine gardening, Gertrude Jekyll excelled in both. The advice she gave to gardeners is as sound today as it was when she first offered it to her readers, and I am delighted to see it again in print.

Miss Jekyll was fifty-six when her book was published in 1899, and she was nearing middle age when she gave up painting as a career and turned to horticulture; but before she died, soon after her eighty-ninth birthday, she had written thirteen books and had made plans for, or taken part in the planning of, something like three hundred and fifty gardens.

She had been a gardener all her life, and at twenty-five she made a garden at Wargrave Hill when her family went there to live in 1868. The painter George Leslie described this garden as a wilderness of sweets, where old-fashioned flowers bloomed in profusion and lavender hedges made marvelous growth. "Much interest in garden plants—always collecting," Miss Jekyll wrote in her journal at that time. She had already begun to experiment with new combinations of plants, introducing opium poppies and wildflowers into the flower borders—a radical step in the days of carpet bedding. "Gertrude was a pioneer spirit," her sister-in-law, Lady Jekyll, said. "Long before women had claimed their present independence in the arts and professions, in trade, in travel, in sport, and in many difficult crafts, she had quietly and firmly established her right to self-expression."

Miss Jekyll was born in London in 1843. When she was four, her parents moved to Bramley House, a country place in Surrey where they allowed their children great freedom. She roamed the countryside and learned to know the wildflowers intimately, not only by shape and color, but also by smell. She also knew the garden flowers by their scents and could name the roses with her eyes shut. She always describes scents vividly. Lupines, she says, smell like a very good and delicate pepper; *Lilium pyrenaicum* like a mangy dog; some of the schizanthus are redolent of dirty henhouses; and the scent of bracken is like "the first smell of the sea as you come near it after a long absence."

"When I pick and crush in my hand a twig of Bay," she said, "or brush against a bush of Rosemary, or tread upon a tuft of Thyme, or pass through incense-laden brakes of the Cistus, I feel that here is all that is best and purest and most refined, and nearest to poetry, in the range of faculty of the sense of smell."

Her hearing also was unusually keen. "I can nearly always tell what trees I am near by the sound of the wind in their leaves," she said, "though in the same tree it differs much from spring to autumn, as the leaves become of a harder and drier texture. The Birches have a small, quick, high-pitched sound; so near that of the falling of rain that I am often deceived into thinking it really is rain, when it is only their own leaves hitting each other with a small rain-like patter. The voice of oak leaves is also rather high-pitched, though lower than that of the Birch. Chestnut leaves in a mild breeze sound much more deliberate; a sort of slow slither." The noise of all the Poplars, she adds, is disturbing, but the murmur of Scotch Firs is delightfully soothing.

She thought her unusually keen hearing was by way of compensation for her poor eyesight. Her natural focus was two inches, but she trained herself to close observation and often saw things better that those with perfect vision overlooked. As she drove about in her dog-cart, she never missed the smallest flower along the roadside, and when she found something new, she observed it minutely. In *Children and Gardens*, she says to her young readers: "If you will take any flower you please and look it carefully over and turn it about, and smell it and feel it and try to find out all its little secrets, not of flower only but of bud leaf and stem as well, you will discover many wonderful things."

In this fashion she examines the wood sorrel, "the tenderest and loveliest of wood plants. The white flower in the mass has a slight lilac tinge; when I look close I see that this comes from a fine veining of reddish-purple colour on the white ground. White seems a vaguely indefinite word when applied to the colouring of flowers; in the case of this tender little blossom the white is not very white, but about as white as the lightest part of a pearl. The downy stalk is flesh-coloured and half-transparent, and the delicately formed calyx is painted with faint tints of dull green edged with transparent greenish buff and is based and tipped with a reddish-purple that recalls the veining of the petals. Each of these has a touch of clear yellow on its inner base that sets off the bunch of tiny whitish stamens."

Miss Jekyll's art, like all that is good, grew out of her environment. She was fortunate in that she was able to develop her own style in a part of the country that she had known and loved since childhood. She knew the heath and woodland and the sandy hills, and the yellow-grey sandstone of the quarries; she knew the flowers of the fields and hedgerows, and the plants in cottage gardens. She understood country ways and the craftsmen and their materials. Following the example of William Robinson in his revolt against carpet gardening, she searched gardens and nurseries for old-fashioned hardy plants to replace the bedding-out plants of the glass house.

She was also fortunate in having to work with her an architect equally devoted to the traditions of the district. Edwin Lutyens (later Sir Edwin) was nineteen when they first met, and was at work on his first commission. Miss Jekyll was forty-six, and well established as a gardener and a designer of gardeners. Together they drove about the countryside studying ancient farm houses and cottages.

The knowledge they acquired was put to use in building Miss Jekyll's house at Munstead Wood. When it was finished, it looked as if it had been there for two hundred years, she said, and "seemed to have taken to itself the soul of a more ancient dwelling place." Munstead Wood consisted of fifteen acres across the road from Munstead House, where Miss Jekyll lived with her mother from the time it was built, in 1878, soon after Captain Jekyll's death, until Mrs. Jekyll died in 1895. The garden at Munstead Wood was laid out some time before the house was built, a portion at a time, with no special plan. Later Miss Jekyll fitted the parts together as best she could, and related the whole to the paved court with its tank and stone steps that Sir Edwin designed for the garden side of the house.

(I wrote to Francis Jekyll, Miss Jekyll's nephew and biographer, to ask what has become of Munstead Wood. Mr. Jekyll answered from Munstead Hut, in May 1964. He says the property was sold fifteen years ago and divided into four parts, and the garden as Miss Jekyll created it has ceased to exist. I am glad he is living in the Hut (where

Miss Jekyll lived when the house was being built) and I hope there are some "tabbies" there still. "Dear little Hut!" Miss Jekyll wrote, "How sorry I was to leave it.... How I loved the small and simple ways of living, the happy absence of all complications.... How deliciously simple it all was, how small and few the bills—a pound a week for the house keeping.")

Each section of the garden was devoted to a season, or to some particular kind or type of plant. A place where two woodland paths came together was planted for winter with heaths and hellebores, *Pieris floribunda*, and the large, round, wine-tinted leaves of *Megasea* [*Bergenia*]. There was a spring garden for early bulbs and flowers that bloom from late March to late May; the Hidden Garden for the interval between spring and summer; the June garden around the little cottage called the Hut; the main border for summer; and for October the Michaelmas daisies had a garden to themselves. There was also a nut walk; a rock garden for alpines; a wide, green wood walk; and a network of smaller paths that threaded the woods and led from one delightful planting to another. All were grouped about two wide lawns, and special attention was given to the parts where lawn and woods met.

The chief feature of Munstead Wood was the celebrated south border, eighteen feet wide and a hundred-and-eighty feet long (in another place she describes it as fourteen feet wide and two-hundred feet long), with a high stone wall for background. The color scheme was the same at each end: blue, white, pale yellow, and grey, then purple, white, pink, and grey foliage; the color then changed from both ends through yellow and orange to brilliant red. J. C. N. Forestier describes it in *Bagatelle et Ses Jardins*: "I remember having seen in July a charming border, where the flowers were arranged in tones of chestnut and nasturtium; snapdragons, Indian pinks, zinnias, gaillardias, nasturtiums; *Helenium cupreatum*, coreopsis, dahlias, hollyhocks,—at the end of the border a quantity of *Eryngium amethystinum*, brushing with powder blue the stalks of the hollyhocks. Above all of these pale colors, a slender arch of a climbing rose of luminous color, called Ophire. Miss Jekyll, the skillful artist of Munstead Wood—perhaps to please a Frenchman—called it her 'Pompadour effect.'"

Miss Jekyll liked to use warm colors, reds and yellows, in "graduating harmonies culminating into gorgeousness," and cool colors in contrasts. "Texture plays so important a part in the appearance of colour-surface," she says, "that one can hardly think in colour without also thinking of texture. A piece of black satin and a piece of black velvet may be woven of the same batch of material, but when the satin is finished and the velvet cut, the appearance is often so dissimilar that they may look quite different in color." Her familiarity with braids and brocades, lace and damask, increased her delight in the texture and pattern of leaves: the back of the leaf of *Alchemilla alpina*, she said, is silvery-green satin of the highest quality. "The satin lining, as is plain to see, comes up and over the front edge of the leaf with a brightness that looks like polished silver against the dull green surface." She had also a great feeling for form, both for the individual beauty of such things as acanthus and yucca, and for placing each plant or group so that it would become a part of a harmonious whole. "In gardening," she wrote Mrs. Boyle, "I try to paint living pictures with living flowers, paying attention to throwing them into groups both for form and colour. . . . I wish I could show you some of my garden pictures that seem fairly successful: The Primrose Garden in its season a river of gold and silver flowering through a copse of silver-stemmed young birch trees for a hundred yards or more. Another of this year's pictures that pleased me was a large isolated group of foxgloves with bracken about their base, backed by a dusky wood of Scotch firs."

The primroses were the celebrated 'Munstead Strain', developed by crossing the variety 'Golden Plover' with a very pale, almost white polyanthus found in a cottage garden. The flowers are all white and yellow, but vary greatly in detail. As she herself says, Miss Jekyll never spared herself in the way of actual labor, and one of her chores was dividing the primroses. Every year, when they were taken up, she sat for two days on a low stool cutting them apart, while one boy brought freshly dug plants, and another took the divisions to be carefully replanted in dug-over and freshly manured soil. It was very pleasant to sit there, in a clearing half shaded by oak, chestnut, and hazel, and on one of those days she wrote, "The still air, with only the very gentlest south-westerly breath in it, brings up the mighty boom of the great ship guns from the old seaport, thirty miles away, and the pheasants answer to the sound as they do to thunder. The early summer air is of a perfect temperature, the soft coo of the wood doves comes down from the near wood, the nightingale sings almost overhead . . . but oh, the midges!"

Among other plants she developed and put on the market were Lent hellebores, columbines, double pink poppies, and white foxgloves.

Miss Jekyll felt that plants should be the chief ornaments of a garden, and that such features as were added should be useful as well as beautiful: seats and sundials, pots and tubs for plants, dipping wells, summer houses, and pergolas. She particularly liked the pergola for displaying roses and climbing plants, and often makes use of a photograph of the charming one in her sister's garden in Venice, with rows of white lilies blooming on either side of the path. She made frequent visits to her sister in her younger days, and once, crossing the piazza, she met [John] Ruskin.

Miss Jekyll considered stone the most desirable material for garden features, particularly if it could be had nearby. The garden walls at Munstead Wood were built of Bargate stone from the local quarries, and so was the two-story Thunder House for watching storms as they gathered beyond the fields and chalk hills. She made excellent use of the same stone in the dry walls and steps of the series of terraces at Millmead. Next to her own garden, I think Millmead must be the most perfect example of her style, for in planning it she had only herself to please. She bought a strip of land, seventy-five by four-hundred feet, on a steep hillside, and built the house and laid out the garden before she began to look about for a tenant. Sir Edwin Lutyens designed the house, and together with the garden it was an example of "satisfactory indoor and outdoor planning." Miss Jekyll made the most of the site, allowing the garden to overlook the pretty meadow and the millstream at the foot of the slope, framing the view of the village church and the distant hills, giving a fine old pear tree a little enclosure of its own, and taking advantage of natural springs to make a tank and a stone dipping well. Flowers in careless profusion filled the borders and tumbled over the walls, and even seeded themselves in the stone steps. Miss Jekyll thought these unplanned effects the best of all, and she never liked the garden to be too neat. "I hold the heresy," she said, "of not minding a little moss on the paths, and of rather preferring a few scattered clusters of rose petals on its brown-green velvet." But there was nothing careless in her planning. "In the way it is done," she said, "lies the whole difference between commonplace gardening and gardening that very rightly claims to rank as fine art." She was an artist first, and a gardener second; her training in painting gave her an understanding of design, and a mastery of form and color.

All of the well-known gardeners of the day were welcomed to Munstead Wood. One was the Honorable Mrs. Boyle (E.V.B.) of Huntercombe Manor, with whom Miss Jekyll corresponded, and another was Mrs. C. W. Earle who wrote, in *Pot-Pourri from a Surrey Garden* (1896), "There has been in this year's 'Guardian' a succession of monthly articles on a Surrey Garden, written by Miss Jekyll of Munstead Wood, Godalming. I give her address, as she now sells her surplus plants, all more or less suited to light soils, to the management of which she has for many years past given special attention.... All the plants and flowers about which Miss Jekyll writes she actually grows on the top of her Surrey hill. Her garden is a most instructive one, and encouraging too." I rather suspect that under the guise of giving her free advertisement, Mrs. Earle was putting Miss Jekyll in her place as being "in trade."

Miss Ellen Willmott, whose garden at Warley Place, Essex, was as celebrated as Munstead Woods, was of course a frequent visitor; and in 1909 the Countess von Arnim, the "Elizabeth" of the German garden, was there. I can think of no two gardeners less likely to be charmed with one another than Elizabeth and Miss Jekyll. I should like to know what each one of them wrote in her journal that night.

Mr. Bowles went to Munstead, though I cannot remember any mention of it in his books, and the Reverend C. Wolley Dod, and Canon Ellacombe. In 1880 Dean Hole paid a visit, bringing William Robinson with him. Miss Jekyll had met Mr. Robinson five years before, when she called at his office. She became a regular contributor to his magazine, *The Garden*, and for a short while was on its staff. Mr. Robinson often visited Munstead Wood, and "more than once," Francis Jekyll, her nephew, says in his *Memoir*, "lent his experienced hand in the laying out of the garden."

All of these were welcomed, but as her fame spread, through her books and her honors (The George Robert White Medal of Honor from the Massachusetts Horticultural Society, the Victoria Medal of Honor, and the Veitchian Gold Cup), she was beset by strangers who wanted to visit Munstead Wood, and meet its mistress. By the time she had written her second book, she was begging her readers to stay away. "It is always pleasant to hear from or to see old friends," she wrote in the preface to *Home and Garden*, "and indeed all who work hard in their own gardens, yet, as a would-be quiet worker, who is by no means overstrong, I venture to plead with my kind and numerous, though frequently unknown friends, that I may be allowed a somewhat larger measure of peace and privacy." Later she wrote to a friend, "If I could only know who were the genuine applicants, I would still make exceptions. You can have no idea what I have suffered from Americans, Germans and journalists."

One of these Americans was Edith Wharton, who, with "a hundred questions to ask, a thousand things to learn," went to Great Warley (Surely this is a mistake. She must be thinking of Miss Willmott's place?) in a party of fashionable people, none of whom was interested in horticulture. "I put one timid question to Miss Jekyll," she says in her autobiography, "who answered curtly, and turned her back on me to point out a hybrid iris to an eminent statesman who knew neither what a hybrid nor an iris was; and for the rest of the visit she gave me no chance of exchanging a word with her."

As many of Miss Jekyll's friends were writers, she often appears in their books. George Leslie, in *Our River*, describes her as a lady of singular and remarkable accomplishments: "Clever and witty in conversation, active and energetic in mind and body, and possessed of artistic talents of no common order . . . there is hardly any handicraft the mysteries of which she has not mastered—carving, modeling, housepainting, carpentry, smith's work, repoussé work, gilding, wood-inlaying, embroidery, gardening, and all manner of herb and flower knowledge and culture, everything being carried on with perfect method and completeness."

In Miss Jekyll's house there was a gallery, sixty feet long and ten feet wide, with glassed-in cupboards in which she kept the pretty things "such as are almost unconsciously gathered together by a person of accumulative proclivity." Here, she says in *Home and Garden*, "are memories of many lands of many persons: of countries I shall never see again, for my travelling days are over; of kindly little gifts from friends who are no longer among the living. Some of the small objects are of absolutely no intrinsic value but of a loveliness that is beyond all price, such as beautiful shells and feathers. Then there are tiny ancient tear-bottles, both brilliant and dainty in iridescent colouring of their decaying surface-flakes; a little silver Buddha; delicate pieces of Venetian glass; bronze coins green with age; old Church embroideries of gold and colours upon white silk now faded and discoloured; ostrich eggs of ivory white and emu eggs of dim dusty green; little objects innumerable—eight foot by four of them as a carpenter would say—a life's history in a hieroglyphic writing that is legible to one person only, but that to all comers presents a somewhat pretty show."

In *Reperusals and Recollections*, Logan Pearsall Smith relates how, on a visit to Munstead House, not long before Miss Jekyll died, he was told that she would like to see him. He crossed the road, and taking from its hiding place the key to the door in the garden wall, he let himself in to Munstead Wood; following shady paths until he came to an open lawn, he saw the house before him. No one was about. The silence cast a spell. It was like a scene in a fairy tale: "the locked gate and secret key, the walk through the wood to the beautiful old house which its venerable inhabitant had built for herself so long ago, and over which brooded the silence and solitude of her extreme old age." Standing there alone, he remembered a time when he had walked through the garden with Miss Jekyll herself, and had asked her if she really enjoyed it all. It is difficult, he had said, "to assess one's own possessions"; the artist is apt to see only the imperfections in the thing he has created. Miss Jekyll had agreed. "But," she said, "now and then when I am thinking of something else, I come round the corner suddenly on the house and garden; I catch it unawares. It seems to me all right; and then I enjoy it—I enjoy it very much I can tell you."

Although she traveled widely in her youth, at nineteen going to Rhodes, Constantinople, and Athens with the Charles Newtons, and later spending a winter in Algiers, and often visited her sister in Venice, and spent many summers with the Blumenthals at their chalet above Montreux, Miss Jekyll paid her last visit to London in 1904, and stayed at home more and more as she grew older. She was only fifty-seven when she began to beg her readers to leave her in peace, but she wrote eight years later (in *Children and Gardens*) that she could still, when no one was looking, climb over a five-barred gate or jump a ditch. "I think it is because I have been more or less a gardener all my life," she said, "that I still feel like a child in many ways, although from the number of years I have lived, I ought to know that I am quite an old woman." At seventy-two she was laying out paths on a knoll of Hydon Heath, and directing four Boy Scouts in clearing out the undergrowth. In 1932, she wrote Miss Wilmott that it was very hard not to be able to do "all the little things about the garden that want doing directly you notice them," and to have to be hauled about in a wheel chair instead of having "leisurely solitary prowls of close intimacy with growing things." Even so, she made plans that year for a garden for Mr. Round of Cottage Wood, and had some writing under way when she died, on the eighth of December, 1933, just after her eighty-ninth birthday.

Too much has been made of Miss Jekyll's lack of personal beauty—she has even been called ugly. Logan Pearsall Smith speaks of her "plain but splendid face," and all of her life artists wanted to sketch and paint her. On the voyage to Turkey, Mary Newton made a charming sketch of her in her cabin, a sweet and serious young girl, intent upon her watercolor pad. When she was twenty-one, J. J. Carter sketched her on horseback, a graceful, spirited, slender figure in a becoming riding habit. Susan Mackenzie made a drawing of her as an imposing young woman, rather statuesque in her elaborate black gown. And at seventy-seven, William Nicholson with great difficulty persuaded her to sit for him. "I feel grateful to Providence," he wrote Lady Jekyll, "for the chance she gave me of recording so lovable a character. I am so glad if you think I have put a little of her serene charm into my painting."

No wonder she was serene. All of her happy life was lived in the security of a large, loving, and prosperous family, who had perfect faith in God, themselves, and the British Empire.

*Then it [Zone 8] picks up in
Southern Arizona, goes on to Phoenix, and
wanders in a thin wavy line all the way
up the West Coast and into Canada.*
A Southern Garden *(revised edition, 1967)*

Friends in Oregon

Long ago I joined that friendly society, the Brothers of the Spade, whose founder was Peter Collinson of London. In 1734 he wrote to John Custis of Williamsburg, Virginia, with whom he exchanged letters and plants for more than a decade, begging him for more seeds. "I have already enough for myself," he said, "Yet I think there is no greater pleasure than to be Communicative and oblige others. It is laying an obligation and I seldom fail of Returns for Wee Brothers of the Spade find it very necessary to share amongst us the seeds that come annually from Abroad. It not only preserves a Friendly Society but secures our Collections, for if one does not raise a seed, perhaps another does."

Through correspondence with gardeners in various parts of the world, I have learned that there is a bond between all Brothers of the Spade, and I soon found that those on the West Coast have much in common with those in North Carolina in spite of great differences in conditions and climate. Carl Starker and Drew Sherrard were the first of my letter-writing friends in Oregon. I never met Mrs. Sherrard, but Mr. Starker came to lecture to the Charlotte Garden Club on flower arrangement. When he stood on the terrace and looked down on my garden, he said he felt very much at home among all of those plants from Jennings Lodge.

Drew Sherrard was a pioneer in bringing native plants into Oregon gardens. She learned about them when she traveled with her husband, who was superintendent of Mt. Hood National Forest and who later was Senior Regional Forester for the North Pacific Coast. Her little book *Roadside Flowers of the Pacific Coast* (Binfords and Mort, 1932) had a package of seeds tucked in each copy.

At one time she sent out a list of rare daffodils, and that is how I came to write to her and to get her delightful letters, always telling of something in bloom, whatever the season. When she died, in 1960, Mrs. Sherrard left me a legacy, her neighbor, Louise Gee. Mrs. Gee also looks for flowers in every season, and usually finds them.

"It was Mrs. Sherrard," she says, "who introduced me to the miniature daffodils, and in her garden I learned to know and love the small bulbs of early spring: the scillas and grape hyacinths, the tulip species, and all the little irises. I am always adding to my collection and extending the blooming season. *Oxalis adenophylla* blooms in summer, and I have *Leucojum autumnale* too, such a charming little thing. In my old garden, which was surrounded by Douglas firs and *Cornus nuttallii*, the sternbergias used to bloom every year; but in the eight years I have been here I had no luck with them. Right now (early September) *Cyclamen hederifolium* (*C. neopolitanum*) is beginning to make a show. It will last a long time. *Colchicum autumnale* is in bloom, and also *Colchicum speciosum* and *Crocus speciosus*. *Crocus ochroleucus* comes later. *Crocus asturicus* [*Crocus serotinus* ssp. *salzmannii*] may bloom as late as November, and with it here are often flowers of *Gentiana sino-ornata*. It is a strange combination, the bright gentian blue and the violet, one that I did not like at first, but it grows on me."

Mrs. Gee says many of the rare plants in her garden came from Drew Sherrard: "She was a most generous gardener, and a peaceful person to be with. I used to stop to have tea with her on my way home from work, and I seldom left without some rare bulb or plant. Once she gave me a very old pink rose called 'de Meaux', a miniature form of *Rosa* × *centifolia*. Another time I came away with a rhizome of 'Zua', a bearded iris that I had never seen anywhere else. It has a fragrant ruffled flower of a very pale and subtle shade of blue. Her gifts, like herself, were unusual."

'De Meaux' *is* an old rose. It has been in gardens since 1814. Miss Jekyll calls it a pompon rose and puts it in a class with *Rosa chinensis* 'Minima', the pompon de Paris. Now that the miniatures have come into favor again, I thought I might find it listed; but so far it has not turned up. *Iris* 'Zua' is still in the trade—or was when I wrote this. It was one of the first irises my mother and I had when we started a collection. I think we must have bought it from Robert Wayman, for the description in his 1933 catalogue fits the flower I remember—very large and ruffled and of a uniform soft pearl grey. It is a sport of *Iris* ×

germanica var. *florentina*, and was introduced by Mrs. William Crawford of La Porte, Indiana, in 1914. Mr. Wayman also listed a blue form, which must be the one Mrs. Gee has.

Mrs. Gee is also interested in calochortus [mariposa lily]. "Last spring," she wrote, "I had several species in bloom: *Calochortus tolmiei* (*Calochortus maweanus*), *Calochortus uniflorus*, and one I collected in the Siskiyous of southern Oregon, which I think is *Calochortus elegans* var. *nanus* [*C. coeruleus* var. *nanus*]. It is like a very tiny form of *Calochortus uniflorus*—silky, very pale lavender cups on two-inch stems. I found it in a very wet place with bulbs quite shallow. Usually they are so deep it is a terrible job to dig them. I also had mariposas in bloom, *Calochortus luteus* and *Calochortus venustus*; and the fairy lanterns, *Calochortus albus* and *Calochortus amabilis*. I have the pink form of *Calochortus amabilis*, as well as the typical white, but the yellow has not been with me so long, and I do not know how permanent it will be. The mariposas, of course, are rather fickle, but I have them in a raised bed where I hope they will stay with me."

When Mrs. Sherrard was writing about wildflowers in her Sunday column in the *Portland Oregonian* she went to Stayton to lecture. She went by train and bus, as it was wartime, taking irises from her garden with her. She told the Stayton gardeners that, although there are nine species native to Oregon, she had never found a pure white natural hybrid. She said she was still looking for one, and that the place to find it would be where the pale yellow *Iris chrysophylla* meets the lavender *Iris tenax*. One of the Stayton gardeners, Mrs. Raleigh Harold, took up the search, but it was not until Mrs. Sherrard's death some twenty-five years later that she found what she was looking for. She and her daughter were driving along back roads where irises in tones of blue were blooming along the roadside. "We passed a nice, homey house," she said (in the *Bulletin of the American Rock Garden Society*, January 1964), "with a pool, weeping willows, and a newly made planting of *Azalea mollis* [*Rhododendron molle*]. Then, in a field of about forty acres, among irises of every shade of blue and lavender, we counted eight clumps of pure white ones. We drove back to the house, and my daughter asked the lady if we might dig some of the irises. She said, 'Those blue flowers?,' looking us over to see if were were all there, then said, 'Help yourself.' We took two clumps each and left the others there. If seeds mature, some will be sent to the Seed Exchange."

I have another friend in Oregon, Jonathon Benjamin, who is interested in bringing the Western wildflowers into the garden. He lives in Cheshire, about a hundred miles south of Portland, in Zone 8, I think, where the weather is as changeable as it is in North Carolina. "We have some vicious weather on this ranch," he says, "followed by magnificent mild spells and occasional weak sunshine. The garden in all seasons is kept heavily watered and heavily mulched with a minimum of three inches of sawdust. The only adjustment the plants have to make is to cold, damp, clay soil with a heavy organic content. I find wind damage to be a very real problem, which I have solved by using stones on the surface, or oak limbs upwind. Sometimes little mounds of wet oak leaves form downwind behind these barriers, but contrary to all advice, I have learned that there is no danger in their covering the plants. However, I keep a wary eye on the slugs. I am trying to domesticate the fritillarias and lilies of the Northwest, but so far I have nothing to recommend to you. I don't want to raise your hopes, but if I succeed in domesticating the exquisite *Viola glabella*, I am going to give you a start. It is amazingly tolerant to water and shade, and may serve you well. If you are still interested in a very early white violet, I will send you one that was planted nearly a hundred years ago to border a walkway on a farm in my neighborhood. As we are as far north as southern Maine, the sun is weaker than in North Carolina, so I suggest you give it a good deal of shade. And though it is very drought resistant, please mulch it heavily. If it lives, it will increase rapidly, for it seeds liberally, and has even invaded the crushed rock walks. Don't forget the mulch. We had no success with *Viola rosina* [*V. odorata* cultivar] until we placed stone upwind, and mulched it well."

In the *Bulletin of the American Rock Garden Society* (January 1964), Olga Johnson writes about a garden on a wooded mountainside in Canyonville, Oregon, where Mary Byman grows figs, magnolias, and fuchsias, with rhododendrons, tree peonies, and alpines from the Siskiyous and the Alps.

In the fifty years she has been planting them in her woods, bulbs from the mountains of Europe and the mountains of Oregon have been seeding themselves by the thousands and the tens of thousands. *Cyclamen hederifolium* (*C. neopolitanum*) springs up everywhere in the fall, *Cyclamen coum* takes over in midwinter, and the erythroniums come with the spring. One clump that was already there when Mrs. Byman began her garden in 1914 has hybridized with other species that she has brought in, and now there are multiples of fawn lilies in "yellows, white, lavender, and a whole palette of pinks, some with strong tones of darker color at the base of the perianth segments.

"*Penstemon rupicola* spreads over many square yards in this garden; *Dianthus alpinus* in various color phases blooms in masses; a whole company of the scarlet *Delphinium nudicaule* riots down a lower slope of the garden. The precious small *Trillium rivale*, in both pink and white, has seeded delightful clumps in many a corner. *Gentiana acaulis* occupies a large, specially prepared bed where it blooms freely, grateful for an annual dressing of barnyard manure.

"In a tray atop an old sewing machine stand are several husky plants of *Lewisia rediviva*, the white-flowering ones found in the Columbia Gorge; in this artificial home they burst into prodigal bloom in late May and are easily protected from any unwelcome summer moisture. As for the taller lewisias, it was especially because of her work in hybridizing them that she (Mary Byman) received, in 1959, a citation and cash award for horticultural achievement from the Oregon Federation of Garden Clubs.

"Other garden-worthy natives of the Pacific Northwest grown in this garden include: *Iris innominata* in many brilliant self-hybrids; *Kalmiopsis leachiana* (a collected plant from Marcel Le Piniec), an ericaceous shrub of limited distribution from which the Kalmiopsis Wild Area of southwestern Oregon has its name; *Campanula piperi* from seed collected in the Olympic Mountains (Mrs. Byman says that it is a hard one to grow); *Sedum spathulifolium* 'Purpureum' from the Pacific coast, which is not difficult; *Romanzoffia sitchensis* from shaded stream courses, its attractive scalloped leaves as much an asset as the small white flowers which, surprisingly enough, are often very double. Of our American *Dryas octopetala* she has two forms, one smaller than the other; she also grows *Dryas* × *suendermannii*, and *Dryas minima* [*D. octopetala* 'Minor'] from Switzerland."

But all that is not enough. At eighty-two, Mrs. Byman was still off seed-collecting in the Siskiyous.

> Mrs. Rowntree says that the deep
> blue of C. quamash *[Camassia quamash]*
> is relieved in the camass meadows
> by a yellow owl's clover.
> A Southern Garden

Letters from the West

California gardeners, more than any others, appreciate and preserve their native flora. One of the most ardent protectors of the wildflowers was Miss Charlotte Hoak, whom I met through the Bulb Society. In fact, I think she was "the" Bulb Society, for I have not heard anything of it since she has been unable to get out the quarterly newsletter into which she managed to pack so much horticultural information from all over the world.

Some years ago she wrote to ask my opinion of cocktails, conversation, and organic gardening. Two out of three of the answers must have been satisfactory, for the letters continued. Miss Hoak says the records of her family's garden, on a wooded estate on the Mendocino coast, go back to the mid-nineteenth century. For more than fifty years she had her own garden in South Pasadena.

"You would certainly love my garden," she wrote. "Since 1909 I have tended a space fifty by a hundred feet, and kept careful records. It is so thickly planted I have to consider what to part with before setting out something new. I decide what the new plant is worth, and put it in the place of something worth not quite so much. I have *Sternbergia lutea* which flowers in many feet of golden light. *Allium triquetrum* is a pest, just as you say, but one of the best species for seasoning. *Allium neapolitanum* is naturalized in many Pasadena gardens, and we have dozens and dozens of alliums native to California. My favorite is *Allium dichlamydeum*, a dwarf species from the Mendocino coast. It has deep, rose-colored flowers. The Bermuda buttercup, *Oxalis pes-caprae* (formerly *O. cernua*), has become naturalized in walnut groves and orchards and waste places. Some of the wood sorrels (such as *Oxalis crassipes*) are evergreen, and some of them depart as soon as the spring is over, without leaving a trace. Bright-eyed *Oxalis hirta* is one of the latter."

Miss Hoak sent me reports on the weather, too, and the sandstorms and smog. "We are all sanded up," she wrote in February 1961, "and are keeping our plants alive by continual watering. Foolish people have let the soils get so depleted, and have allowed pesticides to poison our soil as well as our flowers. We are moving up to higher levels where we can get out of the smog, and have plenty of water. The new six-acre garden at Lake Isabella, in Kern County [California], should give us new records for winter bloom and hardiness."

Miss Hoak was a native daughter, and knew every county in the state, and the deserts, high and low. "I am on the job of saving our wildflowers," she wrote, "for they are fast disappearing as their habitats are ruthlessly leveled to build houses for the thousands of Eastern newcomers who don't care a snap about them. I knew Carl Purdy from my childhood days at Comptche, and learned my first lessons from a bit of enchanted woodland which he loved and collected from. It bordered on a field of cloth of gold, where polished buttercups were succeeded by a wealth of little bulbs which took over when the ardent heat of summer reduced the buttercups to windblown chaff. I have gathered together the beautiful wildflowers that he rescued from the destruction of road building, and grew at The Terraces, his place in Ukiah, California. To think that it is now a hunting lodge! I have all his catalogues, from the first one in 1897. How little we valued those precious pages when we got them, and how cheap, indeed, the priceless bulbs he offered!"

Carl Purdy (1861–1945) began commercial bulb collecting when he was seventeen. He became an authority on the native plants of his part of the country, and wrote monographs on *Calochortus, Erythronium, Brodiaea, Fritillaria*, the lilies, and the minor Liliaceae of western North America. In his bulb catalogue for fall 1925 and spring 1926 he describes The Terraces: "It lies in the mountains between Mendocino and Lake Counties, at an elevation of 2,300 feet above the sea, and 1,700 feet above Ukiah Valley. It is a wonderful place from a scenic point of view, and has so many natural beauties that it makes one of the most unique gardens in the world. The Terraces are not of my own making, but are steps in the mountainside built by mineral deposits. Over these a small stream pours, making endless cataracts and cascades, while the gardens follow the stream for well toward half a mile."

The Terraces were acquired by homesteading in 1906, and the site was chosen because a fine stand of *Lilium pardalinum* was already growing there. When other lilies were introduced, they grew equally well. "It is about eight miles from Ukiah to The Terraces," Mr. Purdy said, "the first four are across the valley; the next three miles are up the lower Mill Creek canyon, and then a mile of mountain grade."

In every issue of his catalogue, Mr. Purdy sent a greeting to gardeners everywhere and an invitation to visit The Terraces. The invitation was accepted by botanists, plantsmen, nurserymen, and gardeners, who came from great distances, and often stayed for some time to study the fine collection of plants, and to enjoy the hospitality and the conversation of their host. One of these was Henri Correvon, the Swiss alpine specialist, who came from Geneva to discuss saxatile plants. As M. Correvon's English was no better than Mr. Purdy's French, they often got into difficulties and had to call on the cook to interpret. The cook was Edith Murphey, a worker with the Indian Service, who had an enforced holiday in winter when she was unable to go on field trips. She asked for a job in the nursery in order to learn the native flora, but Mr. Purdy said he had plenty of men to work outside and was badly in need of someone in the kitchen. So she spent her winters at The Terraces, and when spring came she set out to remote Indian reservations in the Rockies, and wherever she went, she collected wildflowers for Mr. Purdy.

In California Mr. Purdy's friends were Dr. Jepson, Luther Burbank, John Muir, John McLaren, and Alice Eastwood. Miss Eastwood, like Mr. Purdy, taught school for a living, while she taught herself botany. Through Alexander Wallace, Mr. Purdy met the great nineteenth-century gardener, William Robinson, and contributed comprehensive articles on *Calochortus* and *Erythronium* to his monthly review, *Flora and Sylva*. He introduced Peter Barr's daffodils into this country, and Mr. Barr paid a visit to The Terraces; so did Lady Byng, and most astonishing of all, the beautiful and capricious Ellen Willmott, the friend of Gertrude Jekyll and Queen Alexandra. A little corner of the garden at The Terraces was devoted to bulbs from Miss Willmott's garden, and Mr. Purdy sent bulbs to her garden at Warley Place in Essex, England. He sent her ten thousand bulbs of *Camassia esculenta* [*C. quamash*] to plant around the lake.

As his customers reported their experiences from all parts of the country, Mr. Purdy found that the Western bulbs do better where the winters are consistently cold—better in Montreal and Vermont than in New Jersey. Even so, Mrs. Wilder tells (in *Adventures with Hardy Bulbs*) of many that grew happily in her garden in Westchester County, New York, and I have had some success in North Carolina. Mrs. Wilder does not mention the lilies, and I have never made any attempt to grow them, but Mr. Purdy thought that with care the following kinds could be grown in Eastern gardens: *Lilium humboldtii*, *Lilium bloomerianum* (*L. humboldtii* var. *bloomerianum*), *Lilium columbianum*, *Lilium pardalinum*, and *Lilium roezlii* [*L. vollmeri*].

The brodiaeas are the most adaptable of the California bulbs. Several settled down in my Raleigh garden, and two of the most faithful species, *Brodiaea laxa* (*Triteleia laxa*) and *Brodiaea coronaria*, the harvest brodiaea, will prosper as far south as the Gulf Coast. Mr. Purdy says (in the *National Horticultural Magazine*, October 1933), "It is probable that all are hardy throughout the East. Several self-seed and go wild in Massachusetts and Delaware, and would doubtless do so elsewhere.... Really all are beautiful and worthwhile. Possibly the following choice of one in each type might comprise the very best: *Brodiaea ixioides* [*Triteleia ixioides*], *Brodiaea laxa* 'Purple King' [*Triteleia laxa*]; *Brodiaea coronaria*; *Brodiaea grandiflora* [no longer a valid name]; *Brodiaea stellaris*; *Brodiaea ida-maia* [*Dichelostemma ida-maia*]; *Brodiaea pulchella* [*Dichelostemma pulchellum*]; and *Brodiaea volubilis* [*Dichelostemma volubile*]."

Brodiaea ida-maia (*Dichelostemma ida-maia*), the firecracker flower, bloomed for me the first year, but I found, as Mrs. Wilder did, that it does not return. In my garden the golden star, *Brodiaea lugens* (*Triteleia ixioides*), is also a transient, but Mrs. Wilder says it stood by her for many years. She says her stock came from a garden in Poughkeepsie, so perhaps the corms were already used to the New York climate. *Brodiaea volubilis* [*Dichelostemma volubile*], the snake lily, is more curious than desirable. The long, slender stem twines around the nearest support, and if it is tall enough will grow to six or eight feet before producing a small umbel of dull pink flowers.

Mr. Purdy's customers, from Michigan and Minnesota to Massachusetts, and from Montreal to the District of Columbia, reported that all of the Western erythroniums colonize successfully. They are not particular as to soil as long as it is well drained and contains some humus, and is shaded but not too heavily so. *Erythronium californicum* seems to be the most dependable, and I have found it so, though it does not carpet the ground in my garden as it does in cooler climates.

"Fires seem to delight erythronium bulbs," Lester Rowntree says, in *Hardy Californians*, "for after a burn they sometimes grow two feet tall and have huge flowers, as many as fifteen on a stalk: Mr. Purdy said fritillarias are always finer the year after a fire, and this seems to be true of Western bulbs in general. After a fire had swept through Santa Barbara, Mrs. de Forest took me to see sheets of mariposa lilies (*Calochortus venustus*) blooming in tall grass on the mountainside, delicate lilac bowls swaying gently on slender stems."

Lester Rowntree was another visitor to The Terraces. Once, when she spent a night with us long years ago, she told me of arriving there unheralded and finding the whole family at lunch under the trees—Mr. Purdy like a patriarch at the head of the long table. Although I have never seen her since, all through the years Lester has written to me from time to time—a note at Christmas or a letter scribbled by the wayside on one of her seed-collecting trips: "I'm on a dusty little country road," she once wrote on her way home from Canada, "and a mechanic from a small town ten miles away is fussing with my car. If he can't fix it, I'll just sleep here—my blessed sleeping bag is always with me. The government experiment stations in British Columbia were most interesting, and the gardeners passed me around so that I saw a lot more than I had planned. Oh, the rock gardens of the Northwest! They can grow all the things there that I grew in England, plus anything that I could grow in northern New Jersey—just the very opposite from California gardening. I'm so glad we live in a country that has so many climates. There are so many places to go, so much to do and learn. I was at home this spring for the first time in twenty years, and I loved watching the plants on my own dear hillside. South African plants do so well there, in spite of the fog."

"How we need rain," she wrote from Carmel on the eleventh of February, "I water and water, and my water bill is higher than my food bill, but it's worth it. Just now my wild and weedy hill is a fragrant dream. There must be thousands of freesias and other small bulbs blooming above the bright green of that devilish *Oxalis cernua* [*O. pes-caprae*], which has somehow sneaked in and now smothers every inch of the hill. Lovely as this oxalis is now, it will soon turn brown, and every year it gets thicker. Now no self-sown annuals, upon which I used to depend for late spring and summer bloom, can struggle up through it. There must be millions and millions of its little dark bulbs underground; they are impossible to eradicate. It will grieve you to hear, as it grieved me to do it, that just as they were at the height of their graceful drippiness, I had to hack out two immense specimens of *Garrya elliptica*. The gas man refused to come up the drive until I took them out."

I do grieve for the garryas, for I remember Lester's writing in her first book, *Hardy Californians*, of her pleasure in finding this shrub growing wild on the gravelly slopes; it reminded her of the walled garden of her childhood in the English Lake Country, where her father grew it as a small formal tree. It was "always a delight to the eye and especially so in spring when the four-inch long silver and gray-green catkins hung down like a multitude of tassels from underneath a neat flat leafy parasol."

Hardy Californians and *Flowering Shrubs of California* are books that I read again and again. When I take one of them from the shelf to look something up, I forget what I am looking for and become lost in Lester's account of her travels. For nine months of every year, she went from desert to mountaintop in search of wildflower seeds. Though she has made her living by lecturing and writing about plants and by selling seed, she has always gardened for love. "Intelligent collecting," she says, "is a conservation measure; indeed the work is legitimate only when done with knowledge and forethought and when the motive is the preservation of the plants themselves. A scrupulous collector always does more good than damage. He never exhausts a stand. When seed is scarce, he sees to it that some is sown in appropriate places not far from the parent growth. . . . Collecting is a pursuit which should be actuated only by love of plants."

Clyde Robin now carries on the work of Carl Purdy, Theodore Payne, and Lester Rowntree. As he lives near Lester, I asked him if he knows her. He says he does indeed. She helped him to get started in collecting and is an invaluable friend and advisor. "As for my work," he wrote, "I roam far and wide over this area where we have in excess of five thousand indigenous plants. I gather the choicest seeds and enlist the help of botanists from universities and botanic gardens here and throughout the world. We are racing with time to preserve these choice plants before our state fills up from boundary to boundary, and the inhabitants stamp the plants out forever. I publish a catalogue every two years, and try to refine the information and plant selection in each one. I always have some unlisted seeds on hand, and collect an order where the size justifies the collection. This is a happy, busy, and constructive work. The only sad note is that I cannot do more to preserve the beauty of our own time for future generations."

Theodore Payne was another pioneer in collecting and distributing the native plants of California. His catalogues do for the shrubs what Mr. Purdy's catalogues do for the bulbs. Mr. Payne was twenty-one when he arrived in California from England and took a job as gardener on Madama Modjeska's ranch in the Santiago Canyon in the Santa Ana Mountains. In front of the long, low ranch house there were two fountains, a rose garden, and a wide lawn bordered with flowers and shrubs. There were Turk's-caps, pink oleanders, and beds of cannas and gazanias, with a wooden fence covered with the blue dawn flower. There were Canary Island date palms, and an Abyssinian banana that was frozen back every winter.

Hummingbirds came to the Turk's-caps. Mr. Payne had never seen hummingbirds before. It was all so different from England—long hours of work in heat he was not accustomed to, irrigating the roses and vegetables and pruning the olive trees. But he was happy with the motley crew of Europeans and Mexicans and the house guests—many of them distinguished actors—who liked to talk with the gardener and dance with the ranch hands. On Sundays he went in search of wildflowers. A stream of clear water ran along the floor of the canyon, falling over boulders, and forming deep pools. At every turn a new vista opened to draw him further on. There were penstemons along the trail, and mariposa lilies; and, in an open place, a great bush of the Matilija poppy [*Romneya*]. He collected poppy seed for the garden, but they never came up. Later he learned that they will germinate only when straw is burned over the ground. In shady places the meadow rue was as high as his head; and at the foot of Elephant's Peak, he stood knee high in maidenhair fern.

He loved it all, but he could not continue to be Madame Modjeska's gardener. As soon as he had saved enough money, he went to look for a job in the seed and nursery business, for which he had never been trained; and in 1903, he started a business of his own and began building up a collection of native plants. His nursery became, as he says in his 1949 catalogue, the first and only one of its kind, and he grew "the largest collection of California native plants and wild flowers ever brought together in a commercial establishment."

In 1961 he turned over his plants and seeds and his files to the Theodore Payne Foundation for Wild Flowers and Native Plants, and wrote his memoir, *Life on the Modjeska Ranch in the Gay Nineties*.

Madame Modjeska loved her rose garden. She never forgot the hours she and her young English gardener spent with the 'Duchesse de Brabant', 'Madame Caroline Testout', 'Paul Neyron', 'General Jacqueminot', and the one she loved best of all, 'Papa Gontier'." When she was playing in Los Angeles she sometimes visited Mr. Payne at his seed store. One Sunday morning in 1908, as she was passing on her way home from mass at St. Vibiana's Cathedral, she saw him inside arranging a flower seed display and stopped to speak to him. "She stayed and chatted a while," he says, "then left for her hotel. That was the last time I was ever to see Madame Helene Modjeska. She died April 8, 1909. . . . She was a great artist, a good woman, and one of the most charming persons I have ever known."

*Mine came from Mr. Tong, who
had it from Mrs. Mitchener, who had
it from some other gardener.*
A Southern Garden
(*in reference to* Helianthus angustifolius)

Brothers of the Spade

I belong to that great fraternity whose members garden for love; they are called Brothers of the Spade. Some own estates, some are directors of botanic gardens, and some have only small back yards. The small back yards sometimes harbor the rarest plants. I like to think of one that I visited in Plainfield, New Jersey, years ago, in which Arthur Osmun grew and propagated a unique collection of violets and an astonishing number of alpines. A few raised beds held the entire stock of The Paramount Gardens, and for years they supplied the wants of plantsmen in various parts of the world.

Though the Brothers of the Spade may be professional gardeners, or nurserymen, or old ladies who sell flowers through the mail, they are all amateurs in the true sense of the word—they garden for love. "Having no greater pleasure than to be communicative and oblige others," they keep in cultivation many a valuable plant that would otherwise be lost. Among them they preserve a reservoir of plants that could never be collected in any one place, even an institution, for the preservation of plants depends upon individual effort, and it is only in private gardens, in lonely farm yards, or around deserted houses that certain plants no longer in the trade are still to be found.

One of the plants preserved in this way is the Persian iris (*Iris persica*), which has been in American gardens since colonial times, but is very seldom seen in catalogues. Alice Morse Earle says (in *Old Time Gardens*) that she found it on a seedswoman's list in a Boston newspaper for March 30, 1760. And Jefferson grew it at Monticello. In 1812, he wrote in his *Garden Book* that, on the 23rd of September, he received "6 Dwarf Persian Iris" from Bernard McMahon, the Philadelphia seedsman. The next record I have is in Ella Porter McKinney's *Iris for the Little Garden*. Her bulbs came to her, she says, from an old garden in Tennessee, where they had been known "since the memory of man," and had made large clumps, and had gone even further afield than Mrs. McKinney's garden in northern New Jersey. From this same stock came the bulbs that Vivian Grapes grows in Big Spring, Nebraska. "I'm sorry you lost *Iris persica*," Miss Grapes wrote. "It bloomed beautifully in my garden this spring. I am sure it is true, for it came from the very place you mentioned, the old garden in Tennessee. It blooms just above the ground with foliage like young corn, and blue-green falls tipped with blue-black velvet." The pretty, sweet-scented flowers were once found in old gardens in North Carolina, but Miss Grapes is the only person I know of who grows them now; and it is some time since I have found them in the trade.

Another little bulb still preserved in gardens is *Moraea polystachya*. It came from California to North Carolina, and was passed about as an iris for a number of years before Elizabeth de Forest identified it for us. "In Santa Barbara," Mrs. de Forest wrote, "it seeds itself everywhere among the rocks, and comes up by the hundreds as soon as the fall rains break the long summer drought. Then spring comes to this part of the world, and *Moraea polystachya* is one of the first flowers. It starts to bloom in November, and keeps right on into February or March. I see, in *A Botanist in Southern Africa*, by John Hutchinson, that it is found in Naude's Pass (4,740 feet), between Kimberly and Capetown, and on the Kaap Plateau of the Kalaharia, a limestone plain. My ground is way over on the alkaline side, and has very sharp drainage, so it thrives with me in spite of some summer waterings."

The bright blue-violet flowers also bloom for me in November and almost make me feel that spring has come to my garden too; they survive a surprising number of frosts, but they do not bloom all winter. In April, when the foliage has dried up, I take up the corms and leave them on the window sill until late summer; then I put them back on the top of the dry wall in a mixture of three parts of sand to one of soil. In northern gardens, I doubt whether corms planted outdoors would produce bloom before frost, but they are recommended for growing indoors.

It is a long leap from my garden in North Carolina to the subzero winters and the hot summers of Big Spring, Nebraska, or to the warm winters and cool summers of Santa Barbara. It is an even longer leap to an almost frost-free garden in New Zealand, where the sun is never hot. Nevertheless, Jean Aldred, editor of the *Auckland Lily Society Bulletin*, says she grows many of the bulbs that I write about, though bulbs from South Africa do better for her than those that need a real winter rest. "For lack of cold," she says, "we are not very successful with the bearded irises, but the Louisiana irises do well in our climate. I have several introduced by someone named Dormon. Is that the Caroline Dormon who wrote *Flowers Native to the Deep South*?"

She is, indeed, the same Caroline. And I sent Mrs. Aldred's letter on to her, for she was always interested in plants from New Zealand, though she says those that she sent to her friend Sam Rix, of Mount Maunganui, fared better than the ones he sent her in exchange. Her most successful import was the hybrid lily, 'Marlyn Ross' (*Lilium dauricum* × *Lilium sulphureum*), bred by D. J. Ross of Hawera. It bloomed well for several years before giving in to the Louisiana summers. "The flowers faced up to the sky, like our *Lilium catesbaei*," Caroline said, "and the form was like it too. But the color was a clear lovely yellow, with a few red spots near the center."

Caroline also sent seeds of American wildflowers to England, Japan, and Australia. And so, she says, our natives are now blooming all around the world.

Mrs. Richard Bradbury, who writes to me about winter bloom in her garden in Vancouver, Washington, is another gardener with international interests. "Sharing plants, bulbs, seeds and pollen," she says, "is a basic part of a gardener's life. My garden consists mainly of large collections: some 200 varieties of daffodils, nearly as many lily species and hybrids, and about 800 kinds of iris. When I look about, I find a great deal of it comes from friends in faraway places. I direct seventeen robins, mostly on lilies, but two on daffodils. They go to forty states and several foreign countries."

Some years ago, Mrs. Bradbury started an international round-robin for the North American Lily Society, with members in some twenty foreign countries. "It made fine progress at first," she says, "going around the world and visiting seven countries on four continents in ninety-two days. Later trips were six to ten months or more, and then about the time of the Mau Mau trouble in Kenya, it was in that area, and never returned. But I hope, soon, to start another international group."

I don't dare join the round-robin myself—it might stop with me, and stay there. But I do try to answer all letters from gardeners, and I think I have answered all but three. One of them was from a farmer in East Carolina, who wanted to know something about draining a swamp. I could not tell him, of course, but I did mean to send him Wiley Long's address on a post card. Only I could not find a post card, and then I misplaced the letter, and when it turned up again I could not find a post card. Then there was a letter from an Australian gardener who wanted seeds of miniature daffodils. I laid it aside until I could collect some seed, but there never seemed to be any when I went out to look for them. The third was from a rock gardener in the Middle West. It was such a good letter, and her problems and interests were so like mine, that I laid it aside for a time when I had leisure to answer at length. I still wake up in the night and think about those unanswered letters.

Gardeners often send me plants they know I want, or think I'd like, and they also ask me to supply their needs and desires. I used to do it gladly before age and rheumatism slowed me up, but I am now trying to learn not to promise what I cannot fulfill. I did, however, get off a package to one gardener who wrote, "You say you give away plants from your garden. Please send me some of Mattie Bell's aster."

Gardeners are generous because nature is generous to them. And because they know what it means to read about something and not be able to get it. To the Brothers of the Spade, a rare plant is above the price of rubies. "If you had sent me 20 times the weight of the seeds in gold, it would not have bin the 20th part so acceptable," John Custis told Peter Collinson. William Cobbett said (in *The American Gardener*) that he preferred a fine carnation to a gold watch studded with diamonds; and E. A. Bowles (in *My Garden in Autumn and Winter*) said he would rather have been the raiser of *Colchicum speciosum* 'Album' than the owner of a derby winner. I am sure Mr. Bowles meant it.

*So often I have left them
in the woods to enjoy another season, and
when the season came, and they were revisited,
woods and plants were gone.*
A Southern Garden

In Memory of Dr. Edgar T. Wherry
No Phlox without a Salutation

Soon after my mother and I came to Charlotte [in 1948], Dr. Wherry and another botanist, his friend, Mr. Benedict, came by on a collecting trip in search of a remarkable new species of cactus that had recently been discovered along the Catawba River [in western North Carolina].[1] Dr. Wherry also wanted to look for the place where a Mr. Crow had told me he had found an albino form of a mossy phlox growing naturally near a bridge over the Catawba River. "If it should be *Phlox subulata*," he wrote, "I want to hunt up the place myself. It could be a most important discovery from the standpoint of plant geographics, since that far south we have authentic records of it only from much higher altitudes." The place was found, but the phlox was no longer there; and the plant that Mr. Crow had transferred to his garden turned out to be *Phlox nivalis*, which is normal for this region.

In the last week of March 1948, Dr. Wherry started on a field trip to collect further data for various species of phlox. From Philadelphia he drove south through North Carolina, then to Louisiana and Texas, and up the West Coast to Washington. The first species he saw was *Phlox nivalis*. It was in bloom at the head of a small springy swamp on the northwest side of the highway just 10 miles northeast of Charlotte. There were no striking color forms in the small colony; however, a few days later, he saw much prettier ones in South Carolina.

---

1. This article was originally published in the *Newsletter of the North Carolina Wild Flower Preservation Society*, as "The Woodlanders and Dr. Wherry." It has been abridged slightly for this printing to keep the focus on its central topics—Dr. Edgar T. Wherry and his phlox explorations.

The colors available in this species from Woodlanders Nursery are pastel pink and lavender; a white form is also listed. It occurs in xeric sites on the coastal plain from Virginia to Florida. The flowers bloom in Aiken in spring and fall, and often in winter; the foliage is evergreen. It needs sun.

In his little folder in 1936, Latta Clement, of Nik-Nar Nursery, listed four named cultivars of *Phlox nivalis*: 'Anne Knight', lavender-flowered; 'Colonel Moore', a sheet of pure white flowers; 'Mary Alice', pale pink with red eye, very neat; 'Sir Guilford', bright pink blossoms with red eye, very showy and handsome. 'Sir Guilford' must have come from Guilford County, which was named for the first Earl of Guilford (1704–1790), an intimate friend of George III and Queen Charlotte. I hope it is still cherished in some garden or nursery. It seems to me meet and right to give flowers historical names, such as naming them in honor of plant explorers, botanists, and horticulturists, but it is useless unless the flower is kept in cultivation.

In his monograph, Dr. Wherry mentioned 'Mary Alice' as one of the named clones that has been in the rock garden trade in recent years, along with 'Azure', which was found by Mrs. J. Norman Henry in Georgia. Most notable, however, is 'Gladwyne', also collected by Mrs. Henry in Georgia, which he considers the best white mossy phlox, and it tends to flower continuously from April to November.

"A vigorous large-flowered plant which appeared spontaneously in the garden of the Henry Foundation in Gladwyne, Pennsylvania, has been named *Phlox henrae* Wherry [*Phlox* × *henryae*]. It combines the characteristics of *P. nivalis* and *P. bifida* . . . and is manifestly a hybrid between them."

In the American Rock Garden Society *Bulletin* (Volume 4, no. 2, 1946), Dr. Wherry says, "There has been so much confusion in the relationships of *Phlox nivalis* that a discussion of its history is in order. It was sent to England in early colonial times and figured by Plukenet in 1691. It was later misnamed by Linnaeus, but was brought permanently into horticulture in 1788. In the early 1820s, a Dr. Wray sent a white-flowering variant from Augusta, Georgia, to the firm of C. Loddiges in England, and they issued a color plate of it under the name of *P. nivalis*—signifying snowy—in 1823." The epithet was validated by Sweet in 1827, but Asa Gray "refused to distinguish *Phlox nivalis* from *P. subulata*, and thereby led Charles Darwin to become confused as to their pollen relations."

And the confusion didn't end there; but Dr. Wherry's epithet, *Phlox nivalis Loddiges*, is upheld by the staff of the Bailey Hortorium in *Hortus Third*. As Dr. Wherry says, "The nomenclatural situation of this taxon is complex."

There seems to be no final word as to the valid name of *Phlox hentzii*. It appears in Dr. Small's *Flora of the Southeastern United States* (1903) as *Phlox hentzii*, in our manual as *Phlox nivalis* var. *hentzii*, and in *Hortus Third* it does not appear at all. Dr. Wherry says it well merits the common name, pine phlox.

In the *Natural Gardens of North Carolina*, Dr. Wells calls *Phlox hentzii* "the Sandhills moss pink" and says, "It differs from the common moss pink (*P. subulata*) in that the plants do not form large, loose mats, but the stems stand stiffly erect in small masses. . . . It is one of the most desirable plants for exposed rock gardens, being much superior to the other species. *P. hentzii* is distinctly southern and is confined to the Sandhills country."

According to Dr. Wherry, Reginald Farrer said the day that saw the introduction of *Phlox subulata* into England ought to be kept as a horticultural festival. That day was the tenth of December, 1745, when John Bartram sent "one sod of the fine creeping spring Lychnis to Peter Collinson in London" (phlox at that time being thought to belong to the genus Lychnis). Dr. Wherry appreciated Farrer's enthusiasm and the importance of his dissertation as to the future of the rock garden, but he deplored his having had only Brand's 1907 monograph at hand. For Brand was a German who had never visited America, and knowing few of the species in living condition, had misinterpreted a good many of them.

Although it doesn't grow naturally any farther south than Atlanta, Caroline Dormon was able to establish *Phlox subulata* at Briarwood. "How can anyone create a rock garden without it?" she asks in *Natives Preferred*. "The tiny leaves are evergreen, so the spreading mats are attractive even in winter. In February (in the deep South) they begin decking themselves in their pretty flowers, white, blue, lavender, and pink. They bloom for weeks, and at the height of their season form carpets of gay color. Dr. Edgar Wherry says *Phlox bifida* has larger flowers, but to most gardeners that species is included in *P. subulata*."

On his way to the West Coast in the spring of 1948, Dr. Wherry stopped at Saline, Louisiana, to visit Briarwood. Caroline took him to a bluff near Shreveport where she had found a large colony of an unusual form of *Phlox divaricata*. When they came to the place, she had difficulty in finding a single clump for him to photograph. "They used to cascade all down that bluff!" she cried. "What became of them?" he asked. She replied, "Diggin' women!" He asked permission to quote her comment. She gave it, but asked him not to mention her name. "Some of my best friends are 'diggin' women" she said, then added, "and now we have 'diggin' men! So many are becoming interested in gardening."

In the deep South, *P. divaricata* is perennial and evergreen. It occurs from Florida to Louisiana and northward. This was another early introduction into European horticulture. It was sent by John Bartram to Peter Collinson about 1739. A plant from Virginia, grown in the Uppsala Botanic Garden and pressed by Linnaeus before 1753, is in the Linnaean herbarium.

Last year, Belden Saur sent me the 1981 price list of the Rocknoll Nursery on U.S. 50, Hillsboro, Ohio. I looked at once for phlox, and he said, "At the moment, we are interested in the genus Phlox, especially in the monograph by Dr. Edgar T. Wherry under *Phlox subulata australis*, the western and more southern form of *P. subulata* as described by Dr. Wherry." Dr. Saur listed 'Maiden Blush', 'Fort Hill', and 'Twin Creek', the latter from Rose County, Ohio.

Phlox subulata australis was found by Dr. Wherry seven miles from Staunton, Virginia, on April 9, 1928. It grows chiefly in neutral to moderately acid soils on open rocky slopes chiefly in the Appalachians and Piedmont. *Phlox subulata* [ssp.] *brittonii*, Britton's phlox, was found on Kates Mountain, West Virginia, in May 1898. Dr. Wherry says, "It grows chiefly in subacid soil over shale in the Appalachians and gneiss in the Piedmont, along the upper New River and the Potomac. It is known south to Ironto and west to White Sulphur Springs."

I never could find Ironto in the atlas, but I learned from the zip code directory that it is in Virginia. (Dr. Wherry expects you to know geography.) *Phlox brittonii* [*P. subulata* ssp. *brittonii*] is listed in the 1982 Rocknoll catalogue and is described as having "light pink flowers over tiny clumps of short needle-like foliage."

"Starting with a small nursery at Foster, Ohio," Mr. Saur said, "rock plants and unusual plants have been my business for many years." I wish I had known him then—over 50 years ago—when he and Carl Krippendorf and Robert Senior were gathering other lovers of saxatile plants together in Cincinnati to form the Ohio Rock Garden Society. That was not very long before I first visited Mr. Krippendorf at Lob's Wood, his woodland acres near Milford, Ohio. At the same time, I was reading Mr. Senior's articles in the early issues of the America Rock Garden Society's *Bulletin*, and getting plants from the Rocknoll Nursery. Many of these plants, Mr. Saur said, came from the large rock garden at the Saur Farm of Hillsboro. They were grown and divided from these plants.

While I was writing all this, the postman brought the Rocknoll catalogue for spring 1982, and with a note from Eleanor Saur. "Dear Miss Elizabeth," she wrote, "I have your letter you wrote to Belden, my husband, but he died on the fourth of November, 1981, out in his garden planting an allium from North Carolina. It is blooming today (June 27) with lovely red flowers.

"Dorothy sent out this catalog in January. An interesting list is published by Allen Bush of Holbrook Gardens, Hendersonville, North Carolina. Belden got the lovely phlox 'Chattahooche' from Allen. We visited the members of the Western North Carolina chapter of the ARGS [American Rock Garden Society] at Hendersonville two years ago. Next week, my daughter and I are going to the national meeting of the ARGS at Boulder, Colorado. I am 76 years old, but hope to put out another list next spring.

"This spring," Mrs. Saur wrote, "we listed 32 varieties of phlox. You will see *Phlox glaberrima* among them. It grows about 15 miles from Hillsboro; there are about five acres of them. You will find this phlox pictured and described in Wherry's phlox book."

Two color forms of *P. glaberrima* 'Interior' ('Status Novus' for uniformity) are offered: one "bright reddish purple to rose, the other, lavender, is selected from plants growing in nearby Pike County, Ohio." The height of them is given as 12 to 15 inches. "We offer quite a few new phlox this spring that have been tested in our garden in Southwest Ohio."

I feel I should mention here the Andre Viette farm and nursery perennial catalogue (1981) as Mr. Viette is a Virginian and as he lists seven named cultivars of *Phlox subulata*, two of them being 'Millstream Daphne' and 'Millstream Jupiter', recently released by the Fosters. As Mr. Viette's farm is near Fishersville, I thought it would be in the Tidewater country, but it is between Staunton and Charlottesville, Dr. Wherry's "happy hunting ground."

The Woodlanders list *Phlox stolonifera*, a lilac-blue selection. Caroline [Dormon] called the flowers light blue. Dr. Wherry described the color as changing with the latitude, the colonies being more violet in the South and "varying from violet to lavender, and from purple to lilac; and northward rather uniformly purple." He says the scent varies in strength and is somewhat like honeysuckle. He says the best color forms are 'Blue Ridge' and 'Pink Ridge'. I found a plant said to be 'Blue Ridge' in a Greensboro garden some years ago; the flowers matched Ridgway's mauve. In my Raleigh garden, I checked the colors of the flowers of *P. stolonifera* from the Gardens of the Blue Ridge for several years. They checked as light phlox purple, Bishop's purple, and Chinese violet; the colors are closely related, as you can see on the Ridgway color standards: the first two have the same plate number—XI, and all have the same color number—65. Dr. Wherry says Ridgway named the color 65b "phlox purple" because the flowers of *Phlox glaberrima* are often of that bright purple hue. Dr. Wherry expects you to know Ridgway.

Phlox stolonifera was discovered in Georgia by John Fraser, an English plant explorer in 1786, but he did not take plants to Europe until his return from his sixth trip to North America in 1801. John Sims described the species in *Curtis's Botanical Magazine* in 1802. The same species was found in our mountains by Michaux, who named it *Phlox reptans*, a name no longer valid but still in use when Mrs. Lounsberry traveled in North Carolina mountains at the turn of the century and wrote about Southern wildflowers and trees.

"*P. reptans*," she wrote, "crawling phlox, a beautiful dwarf form, shows its large flowers in one of the pink or purple shades, and through our range is to be found mostly in the mountains where, on moist slopes or valleys it sometimes covers the ground."

I have seen this species in bloom in April at Botany Hill, a nature preserve in Polk County [North Carolina], a few miles west of Charlotte, and heard of it growing naturally as far east as the hills of Randolph County. It occurs in the Appalachians, from central Pennsylvania to Atlanta, and a little way into Tennessee.

When Dr. Wherry left Philadelphia (in late March 1948) on a field trip to collect additional data on some species of the genus Phlox, he drove south and first came upon *Phlox nivalis* in bloom in North Carolina; as he went on to the Gulf Coast, he found *P. amoena* and *P. pilosa* along the way to the Southwest.

Phlox amoena (Sims) was discovered in South Carolina along the Santee Canal in 1786 by John Fraser and illustrated and published by John Sims, editor of the *Botanical Magazine*, in 1810. John Fraser was a celebrated botanist and plant collector and a friend of Thomas Walter, a South Carolina botanist and author of *Flora Caroliniana*, 1781, "which was written entirely in Latin, and composed *Ad Ripas Fluvii Santee*."

Phlox amoena is usually called the hairy phlox, but I prefer Dr. Wherry's name—chalice phlox. He says it requires more acid soils than are maintained in most gardens, and is rarely cultivated. What dealers offer under this name is a natural hybrid of *P. stolonifera* and *P. subulata*, the correct name for which is *P.* × *procumbens*. Mrs. Saur lists *P.* × *procumbens* and also a form with bright pink flowers, four inches, and also 'Timmy Foster', a pink selection. This is evidently not the plant that Mrs. Wilder had because she described it as "easy and useful, gay and very willing."

Mr. Clement claimed that he grew the true species, *P. amoena*, [with] rosy red flowers, and twelve inches high. The Woodlanders offer a pale lavender selection, and whatever I had in my Raleigh garden as *P. amoena* produced flowers of a hue close to Ridgway's mallow-purple with a dark purple eye. I think this was the one I had from Carl Purdy in 1945. It bloomed on the eighth of March in 1946, and again from late October to December. Mrs. Henry selected a bluish-flowered form of *P. amoena* (not *P.* × *procumbens*), propagated it, and put it on the market, along with clones of other species that she considered to be of horticultural value, such as *P. amoena* 'Tallapoosa'.

Phlox pilosa was one of the three figures published by Plukenet in 1691; it was later described by Linnaeus, and is recognized in *Hortus Third* as *P. pilosa*. Its range is from Connecticut to Florida, and west to Texas and Wisconsin. "The color most often seen," Caroline Dormon says, "is a rather hard magenta pink," but she says her sister-in-law, Ruth Dormon, found a lovely, almost magenta-pink form growing on her place near Shreveport.

In Dr. Wherry's article, "Rock Garden Phloxes," there is a photograph of *P. pilosa ozarkana* that he made in Shreveport, "native in Mrs. James Dormon's wild garden." Caroline was indignant when he named this variety (or subspecies) *ozarkana* because he found it in the Ozark Mountains. "I call it the Caddo phlox," she wrote when she sent it to me. "It grows in sheets in Caddo Parish in Louisiana."

Ruth sent me the typical *P. pilosa*, and later on Caroline sent me "Minnie Colquitt's 'Peach Blossom'—different from Ozarkana." I see no difference in any of these, and I no longer know which is which; but whatever colony I have is increasing (though not encroaching) in a raised border facing northwest where it blooms usually from late April through May, or some seasons not until the first of May. Caroline said it is too tall for a rock garden, but the slender stems lean gently together to form a low mass that glows in the late afternoon sunshine; and in my garden, it is the loveliest and most beloved of all low-growing perennials.

In the same issue of our rock garden society bulletin, Dr. Wherry discusses *Phlox ovata* and relatives. "The first reference to this species," he says, "was made by Plukenet in 1700; the species epithet was assigned to it by Linnaeus in 1753. . . . The name mountain phlox has been allotted to the present species because of its abundant occurrence in the Appalachian Mountains from northern Georgia to east central Pennsylvania."

In May 1929, Dr. Wherry drove "through the hills of Walker County, Alabama, on the lookout for interesting native plants," and he discovered near the village of Oakman "a spectacular relative of *P. ovata*. This bears abundant large soft-pink flowers, and was duly named *P. ovata* var. *pulchra* [*Phlox pulchra*]."

Oakman is about 40 miles northwest of Birmingham, so I was not surprised when Weesie Smith sent me from her wildflower garden a small plant labeled "*Phlox pulchra*—not *P. ovata pulchra*."

Weesie's phlox arrived on the 4th day of February, 1974, and bloomed early in May. It bloomed early in May again the next year, and I haven't seen it since. The flowers were Ridgway's mauvette, a very pale tint of Chinese violet; they were a little more than an inch across and faintly fragrant. Dr. Wherry says *P. pulchra* thrives in a few gardens. Mine must not be one of them, but he photographed it in a garden in Pennsylvania. I first had *P. pulchra* from the Nik-Nar Nursery in 1940, as "a new variety of *P. ovata*, and by far the most beautiful of our native phlox—large heads of soft pink."

I never saw it in the trade again until it appeared on the Woodlanders list: *P. pulchra*, Alabama phlox.

I believe Dr. Wherry considered the finding of "the so-called *Phlox texensis*" in its native haunts and being able to prove it to be typical *P. nivalis*, separated from the Alabama-Florida colonies by a gap of over

500 miles, the most important accomplishment of his entire 1948 trip exploring for phlox. The habitat of *Phlox nivalis* is open pine-oak woods on sandy slopes, and it is endemic in the coastal plain and known only from Woodville, Texas, and adjacent areas.

In April 1950, Dr. Wherry wrote, "Yesterday I was in Washington and went out on a trip with Mr. Benedict, who was my companion when we visited you last summer. We talked over further trips together, but we feel inclined to go northward this year. But you can rest assured that whenever circumstances lead me to within reach of Charlotte, I will call to see you."

He never did get within reach of Charlotte again, but letters were exchanged; and I know he would no more overlook a friend in his travels than he would pass by a phlox without a salutation. Once he wrote from Georgia, "This afternoon we saw some rocks on a hill northwest of Marietta where 10 years ago I had seen *Selaginella rupestris*, so I climbed up, and there it was!"

All the while I was writing this, I was thinking about Dr. Wherry and feeling uneasy. Just now I found the American Rock Garden Society *Bulletin* for summer 1982. In it was an announcement of his death on May 19, 1982. I was not surprised; I had known it all along.

This delightful amaryllid from Chile is perfectly hardy in North Carolina where it has been generously and enthusiastically distributed by Billy Hunt.
A Southern Garden
(*in reference to* Rhodophiala bifida)

On William Lanier Hunt

When my sister was a student at the University of North Carolina, she said to my mother, "There is a boy here that you would like; he brought his garden with him when he came to Chapel Hill." And that is how we came to know William Lanier Hunt, F.R.H.S. [Fellow of the Royal Horticultural Society], gardener and garden consultant, horticulturist and botanist; lecturer, writer, bibliophile; promoter and instigator of foundations, botanic gardens, and arboretums, and all good works in horticultural circles, here and abroad.

When Bill went to Chapel Hill in 1926, he was already a seasoned gardener. He was born (he says) and grew up in the celebrated Lindley Nursery in Greensboro, North Carolina. The nursery fields were his garden, and the greenhouses his playroom. He began to assemble his plants when he was a small boy and continued to add to his collections when he went to the Woodberry Forest School in Virginia. When he was ready to go to the university, two trucks were needed to transport his plants and rare bulbs to Chapel Hill. He rented a lot for his large iris collection, and he farmed out his bulbs and other plants in private gardens in the village. It was in these gardens that I first saw the oxblood lily, the roof iris (*Iris tectorum*), and *I. japonica*, formerly *I. fimbriata*, a fitting name, as its petals are finely fringed; it was under this name when Bill gave it to me. He called the oxblood lily *Amaryllis advena*, but Dr. Hamilton Traub calls it *Hippeastrum bifidum* [*Rhodophiala bifida*]. It was once called *Rhodophiala*, and Dr. Traub has named a hybrid of the oxblood lily and another species of the same genus *Rhodophiala* × *huntiana* and described it in the *Amaryllis Year Book* (1964) as "*floribus intense rubris usque ad rhodamino-rubellis.* Holotypus: Traub no. 817 a + b (TRA)."

In those days, when spring came to Chapel Hill, everyone—students, professors, botanists, horticulturists, gardeners and nature lovers, and most of the village—used to walk to Laurel Hill to see the rhododendron in bloom on the slope above Morgan Creek. They called the flowers laurel, but they were really the rosebay, *Rhododendron catawbiense*, though *Kalmia latifolia*, commonly called mountain laurel, also grows nearby. Here in the Piedmont, the flora of the mountains meets the flora of the coastal plain, and in addition to the plants growing here already, Dr. Ritchie Bell, the director of the North Carolina Botanical Garden, is establishing the major plant communities of the Carolinas so the flora from the coast to the boreal forest can be studied and enjoyed in one place; otherwise, as he says, it could be seen only by traveling two hundred miles.

One spring morning Bill joined the walkers to Laurel Hill; when he saw Morgan Creek in its wooded slate valley with the remarkable native plants growing under the trees, he realized that the property must be preserved for the university and the state and that no time must be lost in doing it. He made up his mind to devote himself to this seemingly hopeless undertaking, although it would mean endless difficulties, disappointments, and sore distress. It took twenty years and a world war (he said) to accomplish what he had set out to do, but the property was bought and paid for at last. In the meantime, he had grown dozens of specimens of *Magnolia grandiflora* from seeds of superior clones found on the university campus, and he introduced exotics from countries where the climate and growing conditions are similar to ours.

Then, in 1960, he began to transfer the land to the university, as the Hunt Arboretum, to be administered under the new North Carolina Botanical Garden. When the gift was announced in 1961, Burke Davis wrote in his "Tar Heel Notebook" (*Greensboro Daily News*, November 26), that it was "one of the greatest gifts to the public weal, to be remembered as long as we are spared the thermonuclear torch. A handsome gesture indeed."

Laurel Hill as an arboretum seemed merely a dream when I first saw it. Robert Moncure, one of our rock garden correspondents who lived in Alexandria, Virginia, wrote that he would like to come to Raleigh on the Seaboard Pullman on Saturday night, to spend Sunday with us, and return Sunday night. My mother and I drove him to Chapel Hill Sunday afternoon. Bill took us to Morgan Creek, where we stood on the highest hilltop, looking down on the clear, brown waters that sang as they swirled around Thomas Wolfe's rock, a ledge of purple slate two hundred feet below. The air was so still, the only sound to be heard was the sound of water, until the four o'clock chimes rang out from the Bell Tower. "Think of it," Bill said. "One hundred acres of woods and fields on the edge of the campus, and in hearing of the Bell Tower, and it's older than Kew."

In those days, there was much going back and forth between gardens in Raleigh and gardens in Chapel Hill. When our garden correspondents came to visit, Bill and I passed them on. Violet Walker was our first and favorite. Bill had spent much of his school days in her garden at Woodberry, Virginia. "We called her Violent," he said—meaning that she was as passionate as he was about plants and gardens. I call to mind these early days because Bill's writings go back to that time, when first Violet Walker and then Elizabeth Rawlinson was the editor of *Garden Gossip* (the organ of the Garden Club of Virginia); and we all wrote for it and for each other.

Sometimes visitors came from the West: one day Lester Rowntree turned up at our door, having driven across the county in her collecting car which had only one seat—the driver's. In it she drove thousands of miles every year. She drove over hills and deserts, through forests, and along the seashore, from one end of the Pacific Coast to the other. Bill and I had never seen Lester before, but we had been in correspondence with her since we read in the *Atlantic Monthly* about her camping trips in the desert, and when she arrived in North Carolina, we were already friends for life. I said, "You must go to Chapel Hill to see Bill Hunt." Lester said, "Please let me sit down a minute first." My mother said, "We are expecting you to spend the night." The next morning we went to Chapel Hill.

When we got there, Bill said to Lester, "You must go to Biltmore to see Latta Clement at the Nik-Nar nursery." Lester gave me a despairing glance. We went to the Botanical Garden and Laurel Hill and had lunch at the [Carolina] Inn. Then Bill gave Lester directions and a well-marked road map, and sent her on to Biltmore [at Asheville, North Carolina].

Soon after that, Bill brought Camilla Bradley to have dinner with us in Raleigh. Camilla was the editor (and moving spirit) of that remarkable and short-lived magazine, *Home Gardening for the South*, for which we both wrote, along with Caroline Dormon and her sister-in-law, Mrs. James Dormon and Inez Conger and their friends in Shreveport and Jo Evans from her garden at Haphazard Plantation. And we all wrote to each other, all of the Confederacy united as in The War. Contributors and subscribers were practically the same.

When my mother and I came to Charlotte to live, I thought we would see less of Bill, but as it turned out we saw him more often. He came, bringing with him young botanists, students or faculty of the university; he came, bringing bulbs and plants for my new garden, and once he brought a rectangular block of slate from Morgan Creek valley. We set it in, like a jewel, in a low stone wall. The valley slate is dark gray when dry, but when it rains it reveals tones of mulberry, mauve, and perilla purple.

Between visits there were letters: "We certainly do have lots of things to work on, don't we?" Bill wrote in July 1976. "In the meantime, what source do you now know for *Iris unguicularis*? You will not believe how beautiful the new walks are, here in the arboretum below my apartment. We have made them right out into space, and dug luscious beds up and down the slopes where no one but a few botanists have been—ever, because they are so very steep. From the paths you can look out into treetops, and look down on the huge trunks of forest trees." I can vouch for the steepness of those slopes, for I have been dragged up and down them many times. I have seen all those cyclamens too, and the glowing yellow host of *Sternbergia lutea*.

While Bill was acquiring the land for his arboretum, and laying out trails, and bringing in new plants, he was also spending summers in England attending the meetings of the Royal Horticultural Society, visiting Graham Thomas's roses, and the gardens of other distinguished Fellows of the society, and haunting the London bookshops in search of rare herbals and other old English garden books, weighty volumes, mostly of folio or elephant size, some illustrated with woodcuts, and some with plates engraved, and colored by hand. "Thank Heaven," Bill wrote recently, "I had the sense to sacrifice and buy Dean Herbert's *Amaryllidaceae* years ago."

Bill is not one to rest on his laurels: "At long last," he wrote in 1981, "we are going to start the Southern Garden History Society. Some months back, I re-worked the bylaws of the English society to suit fifteen Southern states. Flora Ann Bynum, John Flowers, and I held several meetings winter before last, as we got the organization planned. Now, I think the first meeting could be at the Garden Symposium at

Old Salem next May. Last fall I went to Natchez with Jo and Cleo to start planting the things that go with those period houses. Guess you know about the new Society at 'Calline's place.' They got it going this spring, and we are going to establish a garden of old roses there. I think I will be in Natchez this fall, and I look forward to visiting Briarwood, New Orleans, Jo Evans at Haphazard, and maybe Cleo Barnwell in Shreveport." They will be in the book.

Conclusion

A Garden of One's Own
Letters from Elizabeth Lawrence to a Friend
BOBBY J. WARD

On an autumn day in the mid-1950s, Linda Mitchell Lamm of Wilson, North Carolina, and her sister Laura Mitchell Braswell accepted an invitation to tea at Elizabeth Lawrence's home on Ridgewood Avenue in Charlotte. It was the first of many visits for Mrs. Lamm and Miss Lawrence and the beginning of an enduring friendship that would span some 30 years until Miss Lawrence's death in June 1985. It was a friendship born of their mutual love of gardening and horticulture. It extended to an intimate sharing of common interests in literature, art, and languages. It was a fellowship consisting of regular visits, many telephone calls, and frequent correspondence—the majority of which Mrs. Lamm has saved.

Reading through the several scores of letters written by Elizabeth Lawrence to Mrs. Lamm (between October 1960 and December 1984) is an education in itself; to understand and to appreciate the correspondence fully sometimes requires scurrying to a reference book. It is not unusual to find a quote from the *Oxford English Dictionary*, a remark about an article in the *New Yorker* magazine, a brief poem, a phrase in idiomatic French, a thought about Francis Kilvert's diaries, a reference to a specific page in *Bartlett's Familiar Quotations*, or a quote from Eudora Welty's writings. Mrs. Lamm recalls that Elizabeth (as she preferred to be called) was consumed with the world around her—with a classical mind and with great recall. "She could fit a reference from a book or magazine article into anything around her," she says.

Her letters contain the usual personal communication between close friends about family matters; at times they would record marriages and sickness as well as the passage of time and life itself. But the heart of Miss Lawrence's letters is a passion, a quest for horticultural and botanical knowledge: queries of her own or answers to questions from Mrs. Lamm, who, at the time, was newsletter editor of the North Carolina Wild Flower Preservation Society (for which Miss Lawrence occasionally wrote articles).

Through those decades she rarely used a typewriter—the majority of the letters being written in a penmanship that requires close inspection and, at first blush, is difficult to decipher. The envelopes were often stuffed by Miss Lawrence with ads, leaves, or seed; the letters were frequently started and finished over a period of days, sometimes shifting from pen to pencil or back again. The vast majority of her letters were signed "Aff—her abbreviation for 'Affectionately'—Elizabeth." Regrettably *none* of her letters are dated; however, the postmarks on the majority of the envelopes are legible. An additional half dozen or so with illegible or incomplete post marks can be dated rather approximately based on the postage affixed to the envelopes.

The following excerpts from these letters give continued evidence that Elizabeth Lawrence was consumed with a passion for gardening, even in her most casual and personal moments.

DESIGNING LINDA LAMM'S GARDEN

Miss Lawrence designed a terrace and woodland garden for Mrs. Lamm's home in Wilson in the 1960s and was inspired by Gertrude Jekyll when she wrote, "I have been rereading Gertrude Jekyll on woodland gardens since I got interested in yours, and the parallel is uncanny: the sitting-room windows she says, '*look straight up a wide grassy way, the vista being ended by a fine old Scotch Fir*'—just like your pine. I was afraid to say too much to you, for that is so confusing, but I felt that all of the woods needs thinning, especially the part toward the house, and that this is something you should think about as you sit in it or walk through it. Miss Jekyll has much to say on this point, especially that it has to be done with the most careful watching and that it must 'cause interest, not confusion.' So easily said, so hardly done. You can't decide it in a minute. You must brood."

Later Elizabeth would write, "I was so relieved to have your letter, and to find that the sketch for the terrace was not too late. I had open urns in mind, but perhaps the lead ones would be better so you won't have to worry about plants. Proportion is all. If you could set something up in each corner—even a bucket—and see how it looks as to size. I used to think myself feeble-minded because I had to try before deciding, and then I found that all the big gardens are done that way—just as the French design clothes on the person, the garden designers first make what they call mock-ups of garden features to see what they will look like on the spot."

As her thoughts on Linda's garden continued to develop, she again wrote, "When I sat down to my typewriter I looked out the window and saw that the Korean daisies are beginning to bloom. They spill over the path with the weedy ageratum. I put it on the list of things to give to you. I have put a card in the box on my desk: '*Boltonia*, Japanese aster and *Arum italicum*.' Let me know when I see you at the meeting if I left anything off.

"I am still thinking about the questions I didn't answer. How would it do to put the large hosta in that point left vacant in front of the late azaleas? How about putting a yucca (instead of a shrub) on either side of the gate, and then putting plume poppy (*Bocconia*) [*Macleaya*] in place of the large hosta? The *Bocconia* would make a stunning plant all summer, and there would be the yucca in winter. I can give you the *Bocconia* [*Macleaya*], and I put down on your list the lovely white *Iris tectorum*; I have enough to give you a start. If you can find room for it under the bird bath it would be the thing. You should not have given me all of that beautiful moss. I put it in the stone steps at the back of the garden, and it looks as if it had been there always.

"How would it do to plant hyacinths and tulips in pots, since they won't grow in the beds. There isn't really anything else that I can think of for spring. Have you tried the St. Brigid anemones? How about rubrum lilies? The daylily 'Hypericum'? Or *Sedum spectabile*? I feel I let you down on that little square under the guest room window. Don't let me persuade you not to do a little formal bed there if you really want it. You could send me the dimensions and I could draw it. But I see it as filled with flowers. I didn't see any *Rhodea japonica* in your garden— one of the nicest winter greens, but it must not get any sun at all.

"This year I had a lot of feverfew in the borders, and it made them shine for weeks and weeks. When I cut them back, John [Miss Lawrence's gardener] worked up a little place in the back of the bed and stuck down a lot of cuttings for next year. Another standby [for your garden] is sweet rocket. And I think I said columbines? I like those white ones—not too long-spurred.

"If you have a Tillotson catalog, look in it for *Rosa gallica officinalis*. I have written to ask whether [they have] budded plants. I think we should have four in your garden—one in each of the triangles around the wheel. The peonies should also be *officinalis*. I have written to the Mission Gardens to ask whether they still list *Paeonia officinalis rubra*. If not, I am sure we can get it somewhere.

"I think *Iris florentina* would be the best, and I will get it from Sunnybrook Farms [Chesterland, Ohio], but let's plant the old white iris, too. They send a tiny rhizome of *I. florentina*, and it takes it so long to grow—if it does grow.

"*Lavandula officinalis* [*L. angustifolia*] is the same as *L. spica* and *L. vera*. Sunnybrook lists *L. vera officinalis* at 50¢. They would be very small plants. If you can find a locally grown lavender, it would really be best. Let's put lavender in each of the points.

"The enclosed sprig is *Salvia leucantha* in case you do not know it. I always get a couple of plants . . . in spring, as they do not last through the winter—or at least I can't count on it."

A TRIP TO ENGLAND

On a "castle and garden" tour to Europe in 1968 with her close friend from Charlotte, Hannah Withers, Elizabeth wrote of her visit to Gertrude Jekyll's house. She revealed her disappointment in seeing it for the first time when she wrote, "We told Mr. Rivers [the driver] we wanted to see Miss Jekyll's house [and] he said it had just been sold again, and it would be all right to go by, as no one was living there. There was a gardener working in some borders, and I am sure he would have let us walk around, but I could see that there is not much left of what was. Just wide lawns and grown up shrubs (rhododendrons). Miss Jekyll would die at the turn-about at the entrance, and the garages built at the side, so you look right into the service area. Remember how she said (in *Home and Garden*): 'My house is approached by a footpath from a quiet, shady lane, entering by a close paled hand-gate. There is no driving road to the front door. I like the approach to a house to be as quiet and modest as possible, and in this case I wanted it to tell its own story as the way into a small dwelling standing in wooded ground.'

"The quiet shady lane is still there, and must be just as it was fifty years ago, but there is no gate, and the front of the house is open to public gaze—not that many people ever pass. As we went back along the lane, I said, 'The thunder house.' And there it was looking exactly as it does in *Garden for Small Country Houses*, with its fortress-like walls and pointed roof. I should like to have climbed to the second story, though I doubt whether you could see the storms gathering over the chalk hills, for the land was closed in like a tunnel. We drove down the lane, and around by another to the third side where we could see the Hut through an overgrown tangle of vines and shrubs. That is where Francis Jekyll [her nephew] was living when he wrote to me, and where he died about a year ago. We got out of the car, and peered through the wire fence and the bushes, but we couldn't see much. Mr. Rivers took us by Miss Jekyll's church (where his daughter was married), and I wanted to see her grave, but he said we would never find it."

On the same trip Elizabeth visited Vita Sackville-West's Sissinghurst, and she noted, "Sissinghurst was exactly as I knew by heart, and everything in bloom, even the Florentine iris and the tall white foxtail lilies against the yew. But I didn't know how beautiful the weald would be, and that you could see it from all parts of the garden, with cloud shadows moving across."

ELIZABETH'S FLOWER AND WEATHER REPORTS

Miss Lawrence regularly reported in her letters on flowers and the weather and how the latter was affecting her garden and plants. The detailed information she collected (and published) on blooming dates for plants in her garden (in Raleigh and later in Charlotte) has become valuable information for Southern gardeners. Here are typical examples she wrote to Mrs. Lamm: "The first flower of *Amarcrinum howardii* [× *A. memoria-corsii*] is open. The rains have brought it out. The earliest date I have is the 27th of July and the latest the 18 of November. *Crinum moorei* is one of its parents and is about to open, too."

Or in this exchange, "The quince was frozen, but is coming out again. It is warm and sunny again and something new every time I go in the garden: yesterday February Silver [a bicolor *Narcissus cyclamineus* hybrid] and *Anemone patens* [*Pulsatilla patens*] (like a large and more deeply-colored hepatica)."

Linda recalls that on her first visit to Elizabeth's home in Charlotte, she saw *Cobaea scandens* for the first time ever. She immediately fell in love with it, and through the years they exchanged seed and plants with each other. On one occasion Miss Lawrence wrote, "The cobaea you sent me is growing fast. It spread over the holly at the end of the terrace instead of climbing into the tree." And later, "We escaped our usual last of October frost, but we had a black one last night, and that is the end of the cobaea. It has been magnificent and was in full bloom yesterday. Dr. Meyer, the botanist in charge of the U.S. Arboretum's Herbarium, came down in October to make an inventory of the garden . . . and was much impressed to see it [the cobaea] climbing high in the locust. He came years ago to talk to the garden club. [He] also corrected the names of several things in the garden. I hope he is right."

In further correspondence on her fascination for cobaea, she wrote, "I have been writing and going into the garden and coming back and writing some more. Last night I looked up and saw the first flowers of *Cobaea scandens*. They are off-white the first day, faintly violet flushed the second, deeper violet the next, and finally deep purple."

And in another letter to Linda, "The bloom has been erratic and made little show in the garden but the red spider lilies—the early ones were better than ever, and some amaryllids that hadn't flowered for years produced a scape or two: one was a pale pink *Crinum* that hadn't bloomed since we left Raleigh."

While continuing to record the passage of the seasons from her Charlotte garden, in a spring note she wrote, "This is the loveliest and rarest time of year and the loveliest the early spring has turned for many years. The yulan [*Magnolia denudata*] is almost fully out. It usually gets killed or whipped by wind as soon as the first buds come."

Similarly, the following summer she reported, "I haven't had a single hummingbird this year. They usually come to the bright blue Mexican sage [*Salvia patens*] outside the kitchen window. Remind me to send you some (sage, not hummingbirds!). They will come when the pineapple sage [*Salvia elegans*] blooms by the terrace. They love that, too, and will come to it while we sit there."

In a typical seasonal winter note, she told Mrs. Lamm, "I found the first winter iris last week [and] did you see the magnificent sunset; I think it was Wednesday night?"

THE GARDEN LADIES

Her correspondence with her "garden ladies" (as Elizabeth affectionately referred to the various Southern farm women with whom she exchanged seed and plants) was often mentioned in her letters to Mrs.

Lamm. The correspondence with these rural women became the basis for Miss Lawrence's posthumous book *Gardening for Love: The Market Bulletins* (Duke University Press, 1987). In a typical example, she wrote to Linda, "I didn't know you, too, had had plants from Mrs. Hides [*Mississippi Garden Bulletin* correspondent]. I would like to hear about them. I have just sent her a bunch of questions, and I have identified most of the plants, but you can't take anything for granted, no matter how obvious the plants appear. For instance, is her *Houstonia* [a] bluet? It is not likely to be the pink one or the rare boreal species, *H. serphyllifolium* [*H. serpyllifolia*], that grows on the highest mountains. She said, 'I have the little lily, too.' That is not likely to be *L. grayi* which is also boreal and grows only on top of Roan Mountain and perhaps a few other places, so I feel sure that it is *L. michauxii*. I asked her to look in *Wildflowers in North Carolina*. The wood anemone is *A. quinquefolia*. She sent that to me with a few leaves left. Ladies' wash board is bouncing Bet—did I tell you that?—*Saponaria officinalis* it is, of course!"

Miss Lawrence frequently received plants, often parts of twigs and leaves, for identification from her correspondents. In one letter to Mrs. Lamm, she reported on having received a plant that was identified as *Justicia americana*. Elizabeth described the plant as "an undistinguished plant but with delicate little orchid-like flowers." As an afterthought she noted that the woman who had sent the plant is "just like us. She *has* to know [all the plant names] too."

On another occasion she wrote, "I think the twig Laura [Linda Lamm's sister] brought me from Chapel Hill must be the English cherry laurel *Prunus laurocerasus*—a narrow leafed form of it. But I will take it with me to Chapel Hill when we go and ask Bill Hunt to find out for certain. Laura also brought me some snowdrops. My fall one, *Galanthus corcyrensis* [*G. reginae-olgae*], hasn't bloomed yet."

In sending Linda an envelope stuffed with two market bulletins for plant sources, Elizabeth penned a postscript: "What do you think the flora on the [6¢ South Carolina commemorative] postage stamp is—yellow jessamine and cotton? I do hope I included enough postage."

WRITING *THE HERB GATHERERS*

Elizabeth Lawrence mentioned frequently the progress on her own writings, particularly her work on *The Herb Gatherers*, which was published as one of the chapters in *Gardening for Love: the Market Bulletins*.

Mrs. Lamm had read drafts of the material that Elizabeth sent to her, and in one of the letters she wrote to Linda as follows: "The main things I want to know [from you] are whether I have put in too much about the herbalists—I got so carried away it is hard to stop quoting. At times, I thought it sounded like the Department of Fuller Explanation because I was trying to explain it to myself. I felt I had to explain Gerard, Parkinson, Theophrastus—not to mention others I had never heard of myself—to the general reader (which is me). I'd like to know where your attention flags, or it gets too monotonous.... [I'm] glad I got a captive audience for [reading] the *Herb Gatherers*. Please don't be in any hurry to send it back. I am now starting all over with the last of the manuscript—*The Herb Gatherers* being less that half.

"*The Herb Gatherers* is (at present, at least it has turned out to be) *not* a book. It is a section of my original Market Bulletin Book, *Gardening for Love*. Probably *not* a good title so far as publishing is concerned, but that is what it is about, because, as you know, that is what my old ladies do."

Receiving a response from Linda, Elizabeth wrote, "*The Herb Gatherers* came back in the morning's mail. I am grateful for your attention, and it is all most helpful. You are the one who called my attention to Eudora's [Eudora Welty] writing about the market bulletins in *The Golden Apples*. I read it so carelessly that I missed all that. I don't seem ever to have made it clear that *The Herb Gatherers* is just one section of the book about the market bulletins, *Gardening for Love*. It is the last section, and so Caroline Dorman, Eudora [Welty], and Mrs. [Ethel] Harmon are already introduced in their respective states. It was Caroline who introduced me to the Louisiana Bulletin and wrote me about it. And she is quoted throughout that part. The first two sections have to be rewritten as I have so much more material than I had when I sent it around to the publishers the first time, so there is no question of publishing it now. I am appalled at what I have to do to get it in shape. The herbs were merely touched on in the first writing (I have done all that in the last three or four years) along with taking notes and writing bits about the various states and the flowers.

"As soon as I can redo the introduction, telling about the market bulletins and my old ladies, I am going to send . . . the part already done about the Mississippi bulletin and Eudora Welty to [a publisher]. There is more market bulletin material in [Eudora's] *Losing Battles*—'Grannie's Birthday Presents.'"

OTHER PLANNED BOOKS
A Garden of One's Own and *Flowers of the Church*

Miss Lawrence wrote several articles for the North Carolina Wild Flower Preservation Society's newsletter when Linda was its editor. As they exchanged letters relating to these articles and on other writing projects, Elizabeth noted, "The book I am working on is ... about gardeners. The one about 'A Garden of One's Own' is not the one I've been working on now. I mean to do that next."

And she wrote of other possible future books after Linda had sent her a print of a flower painting, "I love it. It will add to my material for a book on 'Flowers of the Church.' There is a flower for each virtue, and most of them medicinal. I wonder if I'll ever live to get to that. You have given me so much help, and in such a delightful subject."

THE POETRY OF GARDENING

Elizabeth Lawrence's letters often freely mixed literature and poetry with her passion for gardening in her correspondence with Linda Lamm. Prompted by a newspaper clipping that Linda had sent her about Hope Plantation in northeastern North Carolina, Elizabeth recalled her first visit there and agreeing to do the garden; she recommended including sweet bay and sassafras because she had seen it growing along the roadside and knew that it would grow in the Hope Plantation garden. The owner was delighted.

Elizabeth wrote Linda that a few days after she got home from Hope Plantation she found in chapter eleven in *Jane Eyre* just how the grounds should look at Hope: "I figured that Thornfield could be about the same period as it was an old house when *Jane Eyre* was written, and from the roof Governor Stone would have seen the same sort of thing that Jane saw when she went with Mrs. Fairfax up the ladder and through the trap door: '*The bright and velvet lawn closely girdled the gray base of the mansion; the field, wide as a park, dotted with its ancient timber; the wood, dun and sere, divided by a path visibly overgrown, greener with moss than the trees were with foliage....*' As there is nothing to go on, I thought the planning should be simple and informal, and largely of plants already growing there, which *could* have been used, even if they *weren't*." Elizabeth went on to say that she hoped that the garden committee at Hope would accept her complete planting plans for the garden design.

On another occasion, Elizabeth sent Linda a few lines of poetry that she had been sent by a friend from an eighteenth-century garden book, called *Digging and Squatting*:

> If my garden grows
> The whats,
> It grows on
> Squats. Spades and rakes
> Do truly not
> Beat a squat.

A shared pleasure between Elizabeth and Linda was a book of the nineteenth-century diaries of Francis Kilvert, a vicar at Saint Harmon near the Welsh border in England. His diaries over a ten-year period recorded the landscape and the people of his parish.

"Kilvert's is just what I am looking for, and I have sent to England to ask about it. It is all about country parishes, old ladies, and flowers for the altar," she wrote Mrs. Lamm on one occasion after Elizabeth had attended a reading of excerpts from the diaries that had been arranged by Linda's sister Laura in Charlotte.

Elizabeth frequently mentioned articles she had read in various magazines, including the *New Yorker*, for which Linda's brother, Joseph Mitchell, wrote. If there were an article on plants, gardens, or horticulture, it was sure to come up in the correspondence.

"I am reading [Katharine White's] *Onward and Upward in the Garden*—just published and edited by Mr. [E. B.] White with a delightful introduction. It is a remarkable book.

"I read somewhere that Mr. Bowles is being reprinted and it would probably be better than the old editions—mine are falling apart. I don't know Mr. Bowles's yellow hellebore—or any yellow. I looked in the books, but I didn't find it."

In planning for Mrs. Lamm's daughter's wedding, Miss Lawrence found an appropriate note to pen her: "I feel sure that I will have some Lenten roses [*Helleborus × orientalis*] for the wedding The problem is to make them keep, but I shall try Miss Jekyll's method of slitting the stems—and as she says, '*They are inclined to droop; it is the habit of the plant.*'"

THE LAST LETTER

In the last letter, written the winter before her death, Elizabeth told Linda, "I had no idea you were leading the Herb Society 'onward and upward' or how far they had been led. Thank you for sending me that beautifully drawn plant; it helps me remember how it (*Ageratum*, isn't it?) looked when I saw it in that blazing hot afternoon in Padua—don't you think shade looks cooler in Italy than anywhere else? The little patches of brick path are as beautiful as a Leonardo's bat wings. She (the artist) should have more than her initials to identify her. The drawings in Edith Wharton's *Italian Gardens and their Villas* are good for the villas, but I am glad Maxfield Parrish didn't draw the Botanical Garden. Can't you just see how he would do it?

ELIZABETH LAWRENCE'S LEGACY

Twelve years after her death, Elizabeth Lawrence continues to have devotees and admirers. Now we are enjoying a regional renaissance as "new" gardeners are discovering her writings. Her first book, *A Southern Garden*, is in its fourth edition some 50 years after its first publication, and three other books of her writings have been published since her death in 1985. Of special interest to Southern rock gardeners is *A Rock Garden in the South* (Duke University Press, 1990). With the exception of 144 of her original articles from *The Charlotte Observer*, which were published in *Through the Garden Gate* (UNC Press, 1990), none of the remaining 576 Sunday columns have been readily available. Thus, there is still material to be unearthed for a contemporary generation of gardeners.

In one of her letters to Linda Lamm, Elizabeth unwittingly summed up her own life in a quote about the King Arthur legend that she had stumbled upon in Aldo Leopold's *A Sand County Almanac*:

> Whether you will or not
> You are a King, Tristram, for you are one
> Of the time-tested few that leave the world,
> When they are gone, not the same place it was.
> Mark what you leave.

Elizabeth Lawrence was, indeed, one of the time-tested few that left a mark on the world of garden writing.

APPENDIX I

Bibliography of Elizabeth Lawrence's Published Works

This chronological bibliography of the published writings of Elizabeth Lawrence gives some idea of just how much she wrote about gardens and gardeners. What it does not show is that, along with all of the works listed here, she produced 720 weekly newspaper columns for *The Charlotte Observer* between 1957 and 1972 and carried on an extensive correspondence with other gardeners.

1932 "A Good Flower Show Exhibit," *Garden Gossip* (July)
1933 "Summer-Flowering Bulbs," *Garden Gossip* (December)
1934 "Outdoor Hardy Crinums," *Garden Gossip* (December)
1936 "Twenty-One Plant Facts for Gardeners in the Middle South," *House & Garden* (January), the first of a series of articles
"Perennials Suitable for the Mid-South," *House & Garden* (July)
"Diverse Bulbs for the South," *House & Garden* (September)
"Annuals Down South," *House & Garden* (December)
1937 "Rock Garden Plants for the Mid-South," *House & Garden* (May)
"Broad-Leaved Evergreens for the Mid-South," *House & Garden* (October)
"Narcissi for Next Spring's Garden," *The American Home* (October)
1938 "Milk and Wine Lily," *Garden Gossip* (January)
"Garden Phlox," *Southern Home and Garden* (April)
"*Torenia bailloni*," *Garden Gossip* (October)
"Rules for Rock Gardens," *Southern Home and Garden* (November)
1939 "Some Crotalarias for the Mid-South," *Garden Gossip* (March)
1942 *A Southern Garden: A Handbook for the Middle South* (Chapel Hill: University of North Carolina Press)
1943 "The Onset of Spring," *The Home Garden* (February)
"Permanent Perennials," *Flower Grower* (September)
"Elizabeth Lawrence—An Autobiography," *Herbertia* (September)
"Amaryllids in a Southern Garden," *Herbertia* (September)
"Handsome Wild Indigos," *Horticulture* (November)
1944 "Ornamental Alliums in North Carolina," *Herbertia* (September)
1945 "Gardens of the South," a study guide for the University of North Carolina Library Extension Service
"Rock Garden Conifers in Southern Nurseries," *Bulletin of the American Rock Garden Society* (January/February)

"In Quest of Autumn-Blooming Bulbs," *Bulletin of the American Rock Garden Society* (September/October)
"Daylily Trials in North Carolina," *Herbertia* (September)

1946 "Some Small Members of the Iris Family," *Bulletin of the American Rock Garden Society* (January/February)
"Here Are Blossoms for Southern Evergreens," *The Home Garden* (February)
"Hybrid Crinums," *Home Gardening for the South* (September)

1947 "Further Notes on Hybrid Crinums," *Home Gardening for the South* (February)
"A Review of the Iris Family," *Home Gardening for the South* (April)
"More about Violets," *Bulletin of the American Rock Garden Society* (September/October)
"Daylily Trials in North Carolina," *Herbertia* (September)

1948 "Tender Bulbs for Summer Bloom," *Plants and Garden* (Summer)
"My Best Twenty-Five Daylilies," *Herbertia* (September)

1950 "A Review of Little Daffodils," *Bulletin of the American Rock Garden Society* (July/August)

1951 "Some Notes on Species Tulips," *Bulletin of the American Rock Garden Society* (July/August)

1955 "Rock Gardens in Winter," *Bulletin of the American Rock Garden Society* (Spring)

1957 *The Little Bulbs: A Tale of Two Gardens* (New York: Criterion Books)
"The Curtain in Your Garden," *Popular Gardening* (May)
The first installment of a regular Sunday column for *The Charlotte Observer* first appeared in August

1958 "Groundcovers," *Popular Gardening* (April)

1959 "Two Wonders," *Bulletin of the American Rock Garden Society* (Winter)

1960 "Ivy: Cool Green in Summer, Warm Green in Winter," *Popular Gardening* (August)

1961 *Gardens in Winter* (New York: Harper and Brothers, 1961)
"*Pinckneya pubens*," *The American Horticultural Magazine* (April)
"Habranthus," *The American Horticultural Magazine* (October)

1963 "*Zephyranthes smallii* in North Carolina," *The American Horticultural Magazine* (April)
"Butcher's-Broom—*Ruscus aculeatus*," *The American Horticultural Magazine* (October)

1964 "Miss Jekyll of Munstead Wood," in Gertrude Jekyll, *The Gardener's Essential* (New York: Macmillan, 1964)
"Some Trees and Shrubs of the Southeast," *The American Horticultural Magazine* (October)

1971 *Lob's Wood* (Cincinnati: Cincinnati Nature Center)

"Native Plants for the Country Doctor's Garden," *The Newsletter of the North Carolina Wild Flower Preservation Society* (Fall)

1972 "Pennyroyal," *The Newsletter of the North Carolina Wild Flower Preservation Society* (Spring)

1973 "Southern Endemics," *The Newsletter of the North Carolina Wild Flower Preservation Society* (Spring)

1974 "Neglected Natives," *The Newsletter of the North Carolina Wild Flower Preservation Society* (Spring)

"Morrow Mountain," *The Newsletter of the North Carolina Wild Flower Preservation Society* (Fall)

1976 "A Wildflower Garden in August," *The Newsletter of the North Carolina Wild Flower Preservation Society* (Spring)

1977 "Friends in Oregon," *Pacific Horticulture* (Summer)

1978 "Letters from the West," *Pacific Horticulture* (Spring)

1979 "Trilliums," *The Newsletter of the North Carolina Wild Flower Preservation Society* (Spring)

1981 "Brothers of the Spade," *Pacific Horticulture* (Winter)

1982 "On William Lanier Hunt," in William Lanier Hunt, *Southern Gardens, Southern Gardening* (Durham, N.C.: Duke University Press)

"The Woodlanders and Dr. Wherry" [reprinted in the present volume as "In Memory of Dr. Edgar T. Wherry: No Phlox without a Salutation"], *The Newsletter of the North Carolina Wildflower Preservation Society* (Fall)

1986 *Gardening for Love: The Market Bulletins*, ed. Allen Lacy (Durham, N.C.: Duke University Press)

1990 *Through the Garden Gate*, ed. Bill Neal (Chapel Hill: University of North Carolina Press)

A Rock Garden in the South, ed. Nancy Goodwin with Allen Lacy (Durham, N.C.: Duke University Press)

APPENDIX 2

A Circle of Gardeners

The following list provides brief identifications of the correspondents and authors—and one pet—whom Elizabeth Lawrence mentions, with a characteristic tone of polite familiarity, in her magazine and bulletin articles.

Dr. Harry E. Ahles: native plant enthusiast, Chapel Hill; coauthor of *Manual of the Vascular Plants of the Carolinas* (1964).
Gordon Ainsley: correspondent, bulb dealer, source of amaryllids.
Jean Aldred: correspondent, New Zealand; editor of the *Auckland Lily Society Bulletin*.
Mrs. James Anthony: correspondent, Easley, South Carolina; source of native plants.
Lane Barksdale: contributor to the *Journal of the Elisha Mitchell Scientific Society*.
Claude A. Barr: native plant enthusiast, author of *Jewels of the Plains: Wildflowers of the Great Plains, Grasslands, and Hills* (1983).
Peter Barr: contributor to the *Bulletin of the Alpine Garden Society*.
Mr. Bartholomew: correspondent of Canon Ellacombe (Henry Nicholson), ca. 1900.
William Jackson Bean: author of *Trees and Shrubs Hardy in the British Isles* (1914).
Dr. C. Ritchie Bell: coauthor of *Manual of the Vascular Plants of the Carolinas* (1964).
Mattie Bell: correspondent, source of plants.
Jonathon Benjamin: correspondent, Cheshire, Oregon.
Robert Beverley: author, *History and Present State of Virginia* (1705).
Mr. Borsch: correspondent, source of *Viola eizanensis*.
E. A. Bowles: author of *My Garden in Autumn and Winter* (1944) and many other books about his garden in England.
Mrs. Boyle: correspondent of Gertrude Jekyll who gardened at Huntercombe Manor in England.
Mrs. Richard Bradbury: correspondent, Vancouver, Washington; contributor to the North American Lily Society international round-robin.
Camilla Bradley: correspondent, New Orleans; editor of *Home Gardening for the South*.
Miss Isabel Busbee: correspondent, Raleigh; sister of Jacques Busbee, Jugtown Pottery, Seagrove, North Carolina.

Gordon Butler: wildflower and shrub specialist, proprietor of Butler's Nursery near Fayetteville, North Carolina.

Mrs. Mary Byman: gardener in Canyonville, Oregon; subject of an article in the *Bulletin of the American Rock Garden Society* by Olga Johnson.

Mr. Cayce: a springer spaniel owned by Elizabeth Lawrence while she lived in Raleigh.

Mrs. Florence Chrismon: correspondent, Greensboro, North Carolina; garden columnist for the *Greensboro Daily News*.

Latta Clement: correspondent, Nik-Nar Nursery near Asheville, North Carolina.

William Cobbett: author, *The American Gardener* (1821).

Peter Collinson: author of "Brothers of the Spade" correspondence, with John Custis, 1734–46.

Mr. Cory: correspondent, source of information on habranthus.

William Craig: Contributor to the *Bulletin of the American Rock Garden Scoiety*.

Mrs. William Crawford: correspondent, La Porte, Indiana; iris grower.

Mr. Crayton: correspondent, western North Carolina, near Asheville; "an old mountaineer who knew every leaf and blade from Virginia to Florida."

Mr. Crow: correspondent, western North Carolina.

John Custis: correspondent of Peter Collinson in "Brothers of the Spade," correspondence, 1734–46.

Elizabeth de Forest: correspondent, Santa Barbara, California; writer and artist.

Miss Caroline Dormon: correspondent, Saline, Louisiana; author of *Flowers Native to the Deep South* (1958) and other books on her garden called Briarwood.

Mrs. James Dormon (Ruth): correspondent, Shreveport, Louisiana; sister-in-law of Caroline Dormon.

Dr. J. Y. Dortch: author, reported medicinal use for *Datura* (ca. 1846).

Edith Dusek: correspondent and nursery owner, Graham, Washington; contributor to the *Bulletin of the American Rock Garden Society* on western trilliums.

Alice Morse Earle (Mrs. C. W.): author of many books about gardens, including *Old Time Gardens* (1901).

Canon Ellacombe (Henry Nicholson): author of many books on gardening, including *The Plant-Lore and Garden-Craft of Shakespeare* (1896).

Clarence Elliott: correspondent, England; author of *Rock Garden Plants* (1935), nursery proprietor.

Harold Epstein: Correspondent, source of dwarf shrubs, contributor to the *Bulletin of the American Rock Garden Society*.

Mr. W. O. Freeland: correspondent, Columbia, South Carolina.

Louise Gee: correspondent, Oregon.

Mr. Giridlian: correspondent, source of information about irises.

Vivian Grapes: correspondent, Big Spring, Nebraska.

Paul Green: playwright, Chapel Hill; author of *The Lost Colony*.

Colonel Grey: author; possibly Charles Hervey Grey, author of *Hardy Bulbs* (1938).

Mrs. Maud Grieve: author, *A Modern Herbal* (1931).

Ethel Harmon: correspondent, Saluda, South Carolina; source of native plants.

Mrs. Raleigh Harold: correspondent, Stayton, Oregon; contributor to the *Bulletin of the American Rock Garden Society*.

Wyndham Hayward: correspondent, source of crinums and lycoris.

Mr. Heath: correspondent, Virginia; source of bulbs, relative of Brent Heath, owner of the Daffodil Mart in Gloucester, Virginia.

Mrs. J. Norman Henry (Mary): correspondent, Gladwyn, Pennsylvania; contributor to the *Bulletin of the American Rock Garden Society*, founder of the Henry Foundation, a native plant collector who selected many superior forms of native plants, including *Itea virginica* 'Henry's Garnet'.

William Herbert, Dean of Manchester: British gardener who specialized in observing and writing about bulbous plants, author of a book entitled *Amaryllidaceae* (1837). The International Bulb Society's journal, *Herbertia*, and its Herbert Medal (which Elizabeth Lawrence received in 1943) are named for him.

Charlotte Hoak: correspondent, Pasadena, California; editor of a quarterly newsletter for the Bulb Society.

Mr. Hohman: correspondent, proprietor of Kingsville Nursery, Kingsville, Maryland.

Cecil Houdyshel: correspondent, LaVerne, California; breeder of amaryllids, including crinums.

William Lanier Hunt (Billy): correspondent, Chapel Hill; author of *Southern Gardens, Southern Gardening* (1982), columnist for the *Durham Herald*, developer of the Hunt Arboretum in Chapel Hill.

W. M. James: contributor to *Herbertia*, the journal of the International Bulb Society.

Francis Jekyll: correspondent, England; nephew of Gertrude Jekyll, author of *Gertrude Jekyll: A Memoir* (1935).

Miss Gertrude Jekyll: author of many books about her gardens at Munstead Wood in England, including *Home and Garden* (1926).

Olga Johnson: writer, Canyonville, Oregon; contributor to the *Bulletin of the American Rock Garden Society*.

Fred Jones: contributor to *Herbertia*, the journal of the International Bulb Society (1953).

Miss Willie May Kell: correspondent, Texas; contributor to *Herbertia*, the journal of the International Bulb Society.

Edgar Kline: correspondent, Lake Grove, Oregon; grower of native American bulbs, cofounder of Siskiyou Nursery.

Carl Krippendorf: correspondent, Milford, Ohio; subject of *Lob's Wood* (1971).

John Lambert: correspondent, owner of Fork River Arboretum, Mena, Arkansas.

Linda Mitchell Lamm: correspondent, Wilson, North Carolina; editor of *The Newsletter of the North Carolina Wild Flower Preservation Society* during the 1970s.

Sir William Lawrence: author and founding president of the Alpine Garden Society in Great Britain, who gardened in Surrey, south of London.

Wiley and Caroline Long: correspondents, Roanoke Rapids, North Carolina; owners of Long Plantation.

Mrs. Jane Loudon: Author of many books on gardening in Great Britain, including *Practical Instructions in Gardening for Ladies* (1841) and *Botany for Ladies* (1842), and wife of John C. Loudon, botanist and author of *An Encyclopedia of Gardening* (1822), which Mrs. Loudon edited for republication in 1850.

Mrs. Alice Lounsberry: author of *Southern Wild Flowers and Trees* (1901).

Robert McCartney: correspondent, Woodlanders Nursery, Aiken, South Carolina.

Ella Porter McKinney: author, *Iris for the Little Garden* (1927).

Julia MacKintosh: correspondent, Woodlanders Nursery, Aiken, South Carolina.

The Honorable Henry McLaren: writer featured in the first volume of *Herbertia*, the journal of the International Bulb Society.

Bernard McMahon: Philadelphia seedsman, correspondent of Thomas Jefferson.

Mrs. McMillan: correspondent, North Carolina; source of hymenocallis bulbs, former president of the Garden Club of North Carolina.

Dr. Walter B. and Helen Mayer: friends in Charlotte.

Lionel and Lucy Melvin: correspondents and nursery owners, Pleasant Garden, North Carolina; Lionel served as a consultant to the North Carolina Wild Flower Preservation Society.

Jack Mitchell: correspondent, Fairmont, North Carolina; brother of Linda Mitchell Lamm and a keeper of bees.

Madame Helene Modjeska: actress who owned gardens in the Santa Ana Mountains in California; subject of *Life on the Modjeska Ranch in the Gay Nineties* by Theodore Payne (1961).

Robert Moncure: correspondent, Alexandria, Virginia.

Mr. Moody: correspondent, source of species tulips.

Mrs. Mooney: correspondent, High Mountain Farm, Seligman, Missouri.

Charlie Moore: correspondent, South Carolina; native plant enthusiast.

Julie Moore: member of the North Carolina Wild Flower Preservation Society.

Ken Moore: member of the North Carolina Wild Flower Preservation Society, assistant director of the North Carolina Botanical Garden at Chapel Hill.

Benjamin Yoe Morrison: correspondent, Pass Christian, Mississippi; author of a book on azaleas, first head of the National Arboretum and a member of the National Arboretum advisory council, Washington, D.C.

Dr. Henry Nehrling: author of *The Plant World in Florida* (1933).

Mr. and Mrs. Nowlin: members of the North Carolina Wild Flower Preservation Society.

Arthur Osmun: correspondent, Plainfield, New Jersey; owner of The Paramount Gardens, contributor to the *Bulletin of the North American Rock Garden Society*.

Major Pam: contributor to *Herbertia*, the journal of the International Bulb Society.

Theodore Payne: gardener for Madame Modjeska and owner of his own nursery growing California plants; author of *Life on the Modjeska Ranch in the Gay Nineties* (1961).

Mrs. Peters: correspondent, Alexandria, Louisiana.

Mrs. Eugene Polsfuss: correspondent, Macon, Georgia.

Anne Pratt: author of *The Flowering Plants, Grasses, Sedges, and Ferns of Great Britain* (1870).

Carl Purdy: native plant expert, Ukiah, California; authority on Liliaceae, source of bulbs, contributor to the *Bulletin of the American Rock Garden Society*.

Elizabeth Rawlinson: correspondent, Virginia; editor of *Garden Gossip*, Richmond, Virginia.

Sam Rix: correspondent, Mount Maunganui, New Zealand; friend of Caroline Dormon.

Clyde Robin: correspondent near Carmel, California.

F. F. Rockwell: author of a gardening guide for *House & Garden* magazine (November 1930) and of numerous other garden publications, including *10,000 Garden Questions*.

D. J. Ross: correspondent, source of bulbs, breeder of hybrid lilies.

Lester Rowntree: correspondent, California; author of *Hardy Californians* (1936) and other books on plants of the western United States.

Belden and Eleanor Saur: correspondents, owners of Rocknoll Nursery, Foster, Ohio.

Robert Senior: contributor of many articles to the *Bulletin of the American Rock Garden Society*.

Mrs. Olin Sheets: correspondent, Reidsville, North Carolina.

Drew Sherrard: correspondent, Portland, Oregon; author of *Roadside Flowers of the Pacific Coast* (1932), columnist for the *Portland Oregonian*.

Tom and Bruce Shinn: correspondents, Leicester, North Carolina; Tom wrote about insectivorous plants for the *Bulletin of the American Rock Garden Society* and discovered *Phlox stolonifera* 'Shinn's White' (also known as 'Bruce's White').

Mrs. Slaughter: correspondent, Houston, Texas.

Dr. John K. Small: author of *Flora of the Southeastern United States* (1903) and numerous other books about native plants.

Mr. and Mrs. Herbert Smith: members of the North Carolina Wild Flower Preservation Society, owners of Smithin Farm, Liberty, North Carolina.

Mrs. Louise G. Smith (Mrs. Lindsay Smith, or "Weesie"): correspondent, Birmingham, Alabama.

Carl Starker: correspondent, Oregon; author of books on flower arrangement, including *Western Flower Arrangements*; contributor to the *Bulletin of the North American Rock Garden Society*.

George M. Tong: nursery owner, Raleigh (ca. 1932). Mr. Tong's nursery was purchased in 1933 by Amos Fowler and became Fowler's Nursery.

Dr. Henry Totten: professor at the University of North Carolina in Chapel Hill, coauthor of *Trees of the Southeastern States* (1934), cofounder of the North Carolina Wild Flower Preservation Society in 1951.

Dr. Hamilton Traub: correspondent; daylily breeder; author of *The Amaryllis Manual* (1958).

Andre Viette: Owner of Andre Viette Farm and Nursery, located between Staunton and Charlottesville, Virginia.

Violet Walker (Mrs. Joseph G.): correspondent, Woodberry, Virginia; first editor of *Garden Gossip*, Richmond, Virginia; member of the James River Garden Club.

Robert Wayman: correspondent, nurseryman, and iris grower.

Dr. Bertram W. Wells: author of *The Natural Gardens of North Carolina* (1932), former head of the Botany Department at North Carolina State University.

Cynthia Westcott: author of *The Plant Doctor* (1940) and other books on plant diseases.

Edgar T. Wherry: correspondent, botanist, author of many books on native plants, including *Wild Flower Guide, Northeastern and Midland United States* (1948). He was associated with the University of Pennsylvania and Morris Arboretum and was the most prolific contributor to the *Bulletin of the American Rock Garden Society*, of which he was the editor from 1943 until 1948.

Mrs. Louise Beebe Wilder: Author of several books about her garden called Balderbrae near Suffern, New York, including *My Garden* (1916) and *Colour in My Garden* (1918).

Mrs. Wilson: correspondent, Anne Arundel County, Maryland.
John C. Wister: writer, Philadelphia; author of many garden books, including *Bulbs for American Gardens* (1930).
Hannah Withers: friend and source of plants, Charlotte.
Dr. George B. Wood: coeditor of *The Dispensatory of the United States* (1943).
Dr. Donald Wyman: author of many books for American gardeners, including *Trees for American Gardens* (1951) and *Wyman's Gardening Encyclopedia* (1977).

BIBLIOGRAPHY

Works Referred to by Elizabeth Lawrence

American Joint Committee on Horticultural Nomenclature. *Standardized Plant Names*. 2d ed. Harrisburg, Pa.: J. Horace McFarland Co., 1942.
Bailey, Liberty Hyde. *Hortus Second: A Concise Dictionary of Gardening, General Horticulture, and Cultivated Plants in North America*. Compiled by L. H. Bailey and Ethel Zoe Bailey. New York: Macmillan, 1941.
———. *The Standard Cyclopedia of Horticulture*. New York: Macmillan, 1928.
Bean, William Jackson. *Trees and Shrubs Hardy in the British Isles*. 3 vols. London: J. Murray, 1914.
Beverley, Robert. *The History and Present State of Virginia . . . by a Native of the Place*. London, 1705. Reprint, edited with an introduction by Louis B. Wright. Chapel Hill: University of North Carolina Press, 1947.
Bowles, E. A. *My Garden in Autumn and Winter*. London: Lindsay Drummond, 1944.
Britton, Nathaniel Lord, and Hon. Addison Brown. *An Illustrated Flora of the Northern United States, Canada and the British Possessions*. 3 vols. New York: New York Botanical Garden, 1943.
Burnett, Frances Hodgson. *The Secret Garden*. Philadelphia: J. B. Lippincott Co., 1949.
Chapman, Alvan W. *Flora of the Southern United States*. New York: Ivison, Blakemon, Taylor & Co., 1884.
Cobbett, William. *The American Gardener*. London: C. Clement, 1821.
Collinson, Peter. "Brothers of the Spade: Correspondence of Peter Collinson of London & John Custis of Williamsburg Virginia." *Proceedings of the American Antiquarian Society*. Vol. 58. Worcester, Mass., 1949.
Dormon, Caroline. *Flowers Native to the Deep South*. Baton Rouge, La.: Claitor's Bookstore, 1958.
———. *Natives Preferred*. Baton Rouge, La.: Claitor's Bookstore, 1965.
———. *Wild Flowers of Louisiana*. Garden City, N.Y.: Doubleday, 1934.
Earle, Alice Morse. *Old Time Gardens*. New York: Macmillan, 1901. Reprint, Detroit: Singing Tree Press, 1968.
Ellacombe, Canon. *In My Vicarage Garden and Elsewhere*. London: Edward Arnold, 1896.

Farrer, Reginald J. *The English Rock-Garden*. London and Edinburgh: T. C. & E. C. Jack, 1926.

Forestier, J. C. N. *Bagatelle et ses jardins*. 2d ed. Paris: Librairie agricole de la Maison rustique, ca. 1923.

Gerard, John. *The Herbal: Or General History of Plantes*. London, 1596. Reprint of 2d ed. (London, 1633), New York: Dover, 1975.

Grieve, Maud. *A Modern Herbal: The Medicinal, Culinary, Cosmetic, and Economic Properties, Cultivation and Folklore of Herbs and Grasses*. Edited by Hilda Leyel. New York: Harcourt Brace, 1931. Reprint, New York: Dover, 1971.

Jefferson, Thomas. *Garden Book, 1766–1824, With Relevant Extracts from His Other Writings*. Annotated by Edwin Morris Betts. Philadelphia: American Philosophical Society, 1944.

Jekyll, Francis. *Gertrude Jekyll: A Memoir*. Northampton, Mass.: Bookshop Round Table, 1935.

Jekyll, Gertrude. *Children and Gardens*. New York: C. Scribner's Sons, 1934.

———. *The Gardener's Essential*. New York: Macmillan, 1964. Reprint, Boston: David R. Godine, 1986.

———. *Home and Garden*. London: Longmans, Green, and Co., 1926.

Justice, William S., and C. Ritchie Bell. *Wild Flowers of North Carolina*. Chapel Hill: University of North Carolina Press, 1968.

Leslie, George. *Our River: Personal Reminiscences of an Artist's Life on the River Thames*. London: Bradbury, Agnew, & Co., 1888.

Lounsberry, Alice. *Southern Wild Flowers and Trees*. New York: F. A. Stokes, 1901.

McKinney, Ella Porter. *Iris in the Little Garden*. Boston: Little, Brown, 1927.

Massachusetts Horticultural Society. *Plant Buyer's Guide of Seed and Plant Materials in the Trade*. 6th ed. Boston: Massachusetts Horticultural Society, 1958.

Maxwell, Sir Herbert. *Memories of the Months*. London: Edward Arnold, 1897.

Nehrling, Henry. *The Plant World in Florida: From the Published Manuscripts of Dr. Henry Nehrling*. Collected and edited by Alfred and Elizabeth Kay. New York: Macmillan, 1933.

Parkinson, John. *Paradisi in Sole: Paradisus Terrestris. A Garden of All Sorts of Pleasant Flowers*. London: Lownes and Young, 1629. Reprint, New York: Dover, 1976.

Payne, Theodore. *Life on the Modjeska Ranch in the Gay Nineties*. Los Angeles: T. Payne Publishing, 1961.

Pratt, Anne. *The Flowering Plants, Grasses, Sedges, and Ferns of Great Britain* 5 vols. London and New York: Warne, 1870.

Radford, Albert E., Harry E. Ahles, and C. Ritchie Bell. *Manual of the Vascular Plants of the Carolinas*. Chapel Hill: University of North Carolina Press, 1964.

Rehder, Alfred. *Manual of Cultivated Trees and Shrubs*. New York: Macmillan, 1940. 2d ed. Portland, Ore.: Dioscorides Press, 1986.

Ridgway, Robert. *Color Standards and Nomenclature*. Washington, D.C.: published by the author, 1912.

Rowntree, Lester. *Flowering Shrubs of California and Their Value to the Gardener*. Stanford, Calif.: Stanford University Press, 1939.

——. *Hardy Californians*. New York: Macmillan, 1936. Reprint, Salt Lake City: Peregrine Smith, 1980.

Sherrard, Drew. *Roadside Flowers of the Pacific Coast*. Portland, Ore.: Metropolitan Press, 1932.

Small, John K. *Flora of the Southeastern United States*. 2d ed. New York: John K. Small, 1913.

Smith, Logan Pearsall. *Reperusals and Recollections*. London: Constable & Company, 1936.

Traub, Hamilton. *The Amaryllis Manual*. New York: Macmillan, 1958.

Walter, Thomas. *Flora Caroliniana*. Cambridge, Mass.: Murray Print Co., 1946. Reprint of the 1788 ed. published by J. Fraser, London.

Westcott, Cynthia. *The Plant Doctor: The How, Why, and When of Disease and Insect Control in Your Garden*. Rev. ed. New York: F. A. Stokes, 1940. 3d ed. Philadelphia: J. B. Lippincott, 1950.

Wells, Bertram Whittier. *The Natural Gardens of North Carolina*. Chapel Hill: University of North Carolina Press, 1932.

Wherry, Edgar T. *The Genus Phlox*. Philadelphia: Morris Arboretum, University of Pennsylvania, 1955.

——. *Wild Flower Guide, Northeastern and Midland United States*. Garden City, N.Y.: Doubleday, 1948.

Wilder, Louise Beebe. *Adventures with Hardy Bulbs*. New York: Macmillan, 1936.

——. *Pleasures and Problems of a Rock Garden*. Garden City, N.Y.: Garden City Publishing Company, 1937.

Wister, John Casper. *Bulbs for American Gardens*. Boston: Stratford Co., 1930.

Wood, George Bacon, and Franklin Bache, eds. *The Dispensatory of the United States of America*. 1st ed. Philadelphia: Grig & Elliot, 1833. 23d ed. Philadelphia: J. B. Lippincott, 1943.

Wyman, Donald. *Trees for American Gardens*. New York: Macmillan, 1951.

——. *Wyman's Gardening Encyclopedia*. New York: Macmillan, 1977.

Works Used by the Editors

Halfacre, R. Gordon. *Carolina Landscape Plants*. Raleigh, N.C.: Sparks Press, 1971.

Hortus Third: A Concise Dictionary of Plants Cultivated in the United States and Canada. Revised and expanded by the staff of the Liberty Hyde Bailey Hortorium. New York: Macmillan, 1976.

Hunt, William Lanier. *Southern Gardens, Southern Gardening*. Durham, N.C.: Duke University Press, 1982.

Index of Garden Plants [of the Royal Horticultural Society]. Edited by Mark Griffiths. Portland, Ore.: Timber Press, 1994.

Kartesz, John T. *A Synonymized Checklist of the Vascular Flora of the United States, Canada, and Greenland*. 2d ed. Portland, Ore.: Timber Press, 1994.

Lawrence, Elizabeth. *Gardening for Love: The Market Bulletins*. Edited by Allen Lacy. Durham, N.C.: Duke University Press, 1987.

———. *Gardens in Winter*. New York: Harper and Brothers, 1961. Reprint, Baton Rouge, La.: Claitor's Bookstore, 1977.

———. *The Little Bulbs: A Tale of Two Gardens*. New York: Criterion Books, 1957. Reprint, Durham, N.C.: Duke University Press, 1986.

———. *Lob's Wood*. Cincinnati: Cincinnati Nature Center, 1971.

———. *A Rock Garden in the South*. Edited by Nancy Goodwin with Allen Lacy. Durham, N.C.: Duke University Press, 1990.

———. *A Southern Garden: A Handbook for the Middle South*. Chapel Hill: University of North Carolina Press, 1942. Rev. ed. Chapel Hill: University of North Carolina Press, 1967.

———. *Through the Garden Gate*. Edited by Bill Neal. Chapel Hill: University of North Carolina Press, 1990.

Leopold, Aldo. *A Sand County Almanac and Sketches Here and There*. New York: Oxford University Press, 1949, and reprint, 1987.

Ogden, Scott. *Garden Bulbs for the South*. Dallas: Taylor Publishing Company, 1994.

Seaton, Beverly. "Elizabeth Lawrence," in *American Women Writers: A Critical Reference Guide from Colonial Times to the Present*. Vol. 2. Edited by Lina Mainiero. New York: Frederick Ungar Publishing Co., 1980.

U.S. Department of Agriculture. *Bibliography of Agriculture*. Vols. 3–39. Washington, D.C.: Government Printing Office, 1943–75.

INDEX

Note: In cases where the botanical nomenclature used by Miss Lawrence has become outdated, plants are indexed by their current genus and species names.

Abelia grandiflora, 21
Abyssinian banana, 212
Acca sellowiana, 17
Achillea, 101, 102, 161, 163; *A. filipendulina*, 102; *A. millefolium* 'Rosea', 101, 102; *A. nana*, 163; *A. sibirica*, 163; *A. tomentosa*, 163; *A. umbellata*, 161, 163
Aconite, 104; climbing, 153; winter, 12
Acorus calamus, 141–42
Aesculus parviflora, 34; *A. pavia* var. 'Humulis', 34, 35
Agapanthus, 72; *A. africanus* 'Mooreanus', 72; *A. praecox* ssp. *orientalis*, 72
Agathaea (*Felicia amelloides*), 107
Agavaceae, 48n
Ageratum, 46, 76, 105, 106, 107, 109, 110, 245
Ainsley, Gordon, 60, 61, 68
Ajuga, 130, 161, 171; 'Pink Spire', 130; *A. brockbanki*, 130; *A. reptans*, 130
Akebia quinata, 129
Alabama croton (*Croton alabamensis*), 146
Albizia julibrissin, 6–7; 'Charlotte', 7n; 'Tryon', 7n
Alchemilla alpina, 195
Alliaceae, 49n, 70–71
Allium, 10, 70–71, 77–78; *A. caeruleum*, 71; *A. christophii*, 77; *A. dichlamydeum*, 206; *A. karataviense*, 71; *A. moly*, 71, 77; *A. neapolitanum*, 71, 206; *A. ramosum*, 78; *A. rosenbachianum*, 71; *A. senescens*, 77; *A. sphaerocephalum*, 81; *A. subroseum*, 77; *A. tanguticum*, 77–78; *A. triquetrum*, 206; *A. tuberosum*, 78; *A. validum*, 71, 77
Almond, flowering, 13

Alophia drummondii, 90, 174
Alstroemeria 71, 73; *A. aurea*, 71, 73; *A. brasiliensis*, 73; *A. chilensis*, 71, 73; *A. ligtu*, 73
Alyssum: saxatile (*Aurinia saxatilis*), 162; sweet, 109, 111
Alyssum, 99, 100, 101; *A. argenteum*, 162; *A. rostratum*, 101; *A. serpyllifolium*, 162; *A. wulfenianum*, 13
× *Amarcrinum*, 80; × *A. memoria-corsii*, 239
× *Amarygia parkeri*, 65
Amaryllidaceae, 45, 60, 70n, 72n
Amaryllis (*A. belladonna*), 45–46, 60–73; common (*Hippeastrum* × *johnsonii*), 45; garden (*Hippeastrum* × *johnsonii*), 45; Hall's (*Lycoris squamigera*), 45; hardy (*Lycoris squamigera*), 45
Amaryllis belladonna, 41, 45–46, 61, 63, 65, 73; 'Major', 65; 'Minor', 65; 'Rosea', 65
Amaryllis Society, xv, 60, 68
Amelanchier, 168
American Home, xiv
American Horticultural Magazine, xv, 32n, 238
American Rock Garden Society, xvi
Anchusa capensis, 106, 110
Andromeda, mountain (*Pieris floribunda*), 25–26
Anemone (*Anemone*), 170; Japanese, 104–5; St. Brigid, 237
Anemone, 105, 239, 241; *A.* × *hybrida* 'Kønigin Charlotte', 105; *A. quinquefolia*, 241
Angel's tears (*Narcissus triandrus triandrus*), 56n
Annuals, 106–12
Aquilegia alpina, 161, 170
Arabis, 13, 99, 110, 162, 170; *A. alpina*, 13
Arborvitae (*Thuja*), 18
Arbutus, trailing (*Epigaea repens*), 153, 167, 170

263

Arctotis, 107, 108
Arenaria, 161
Aristea capitata, 89; *A. ecklonii*, 89
Aristolochia macrophylla, 129
Armeria maritima 'Laucheana', 161
Artemisia lactiflora, 102, 104
Arum italicum, 237
Asclepias syriaca, 154; *A. tuberosa*, 153
Asphodel, mountain (*Xerophyllum asphodeloides*), 154
Aster, 80, 104, 105; alpine, 171; dwarf, 166; rough-leaved (*Aster macrophyllus*), 105; Japanese, 237
Aster macrophyllus, 105; *A. novae-angliae*, 104; 'Roseus', 104; *A. tartaricus*, 80
Aucuba japonica, 23
Aureolaria virginica, 153
Aurinia saxatilis, 99, 100, 162, 170; *A. sinuata*, 162
Autumn glory (*Helianthus angustifolius*), 105

Babiana, 89
Baby's breath, 5, 170
Bailey's *Cyclopedia*. See *Cyclopedia of American Horticulture*
Balloon vine (*Cardiospermum halicacabum*), 128
Banana-shrub (*Michelia figo*), 26
Baptisia, 100–101, 120–21, 139–40; *B. alba*, 139; *B. australias*, 100–101, 120–21, 139–40; *B. bracteata*, 139; *B. cinerea*, 140; *B. lactea*, 139, 140; *B. perfoliata*, 139, 150; *B. simplicifolia*, 150; *B. tinctoria*, 140
Barr, Peter, 179, 208
Barrenwort, Persian (*Epimedium* × *versicolor* 'Sulphureum'), 131
Bartram, John, 220, 221
Bay: loblolly (*Gordonia lasianthus*), 22, 26–27, 36; poison (*Illicium floridanum*), 36; sweet (*Magnolia virginiana*), 22, 243
Bayberry (*Myrica pensylvanica*), 17
Bean, William J., 32, 186
Belamcanda chinensis, 86; *B. flabellata*, 86
Bell, C. Ritchie, 228
Bellevalia ciliata, 12
Bellflower, Chinese (*Platycodon*), 102
Bergenia, 184, 185; *B. ciliata* 'Rosea', 185; *B. cordifolia*, 184
Bessera elegans, 70, 92
Beverley, Robert, 142, 143

Bitter-bark (*Pinckneya pubens*), 30
Black-eyed Susan, 113, 114
Black snakeroot (*Cimicifuga racemosa*), 142
Bleeding-heart (*Dicentra spectabilis*), 99, 100, 122
Bloodroot, 170
Bluebonnet, Texas (*Lupinus subcarnosus*), 106, 111
Blue dawn flower (*Ipomoea indica*), 212
Bluet (*Houstonia*), 170, 241; mountain (*H. purpurea*), 151
Blue-eyed Mary (*Omphalodes verna*), 13
Boltonia, 80, 119, 237; *B. asteroides*, 104; var. *latisquama*, 46, 104
Bouncing Bet (*Saponaria officinalis*), 119, 241
Bowles, E. A., xii, 32, 54, 197, 217, 244
Brachycome, 107
Bradley, Camilla, 229
Briarwood, 29, 220. See also Dormon, Caroline
British soldiers (*Nerine sarniensis*), 10
Brodiaea, harvest (*Brodiaea coronaria*), 71, 209
Brodiaea, 45, 49–50, 71, 207, 209; 'Purple King', 209; *B. grandiflora*, 209; *B. stellaris*, 209
Browallia, 106, 109, 111; *B. americana*, 109; *B. speciosa* 'Major', 109
Brunsvigia, 61, 63, 65; *B. major*, 65; *B. minor*, 65; *B. rosea*, 61, 63, 65; × *Amarygia parkeri*, 65
Buckeye: bottlebrush (*Aesculus parviflora*), 34; red (*A. pavia*), 34
Buddleia, 22
Bugle plant/weed (*Ajuga*), 130, 171
Bulletin of the American Rock Garden Society, xv, 158, 203, 204, 219, 222
Butcher's-broom (*Ruscus aculeatus*), xvii, 19–20, 31–32
Buttercup, Bermuda (*Oxalis pes-caprae*), 206, 210
Butterfly pea (*Clitoria mariana*), 153
Butterfly weed (*Asclepias tuberosa*), 153
Button snake root, 153
Bynum, Flora Ann, 230

Calamus, 153
Calamus root (*Acorus calamus*), 141
Calendula, 106, 111
Calico bush (*Pinckneya pubens*), 30

Callicore rosea, 61, 63, 65, 73
Callisia graminea, 149, 150, 167; *C. rosea*, 149, 150, 167
Calochortus, 203, 207, 210; *C. albus*, 203; *C. amabilis*, 203; *C. coeruleus* var. *nanus*, 203; *C. luteus*, 203; *C. tolmiei*, 203; *C. uniflorus*, 203; *venustus*, 203, 210
Camassia, 99, 123, 208; *C. leichtlinii*, 100, 123; 'Alba', 123; *C. quamash*, 208
Camellia japonica, 21; *C. sasanqua*, 21; *C. sinensis*, 22, 27–28
Campanula, 104, 161, 171; *C. elegans*, 104; *C. piperi*, 205; *C. rotundifolia*, 163
Campernelle (*Narcissus* × *odorus*), 99
Campion, rose, (*Silene armeria*), 108
Campsis radicans, 129; 'Mme. Galen', 129
Candytuft, 9, 13, 99; Persian, 186
Canterbury bells, 49
Cardinal flower, 153
Cardiospermum halicacabum, 128
Carrion vine (*Matelea carolinensis*), 154
Caucasian scabiosa (*Scabiosa caucasica*), 108
Cedar, 168
Cedrus libani, 172, 173; 'Comte de Dijon', 172; 'Nana', 172; ssp. *atlantica*, 173
Celestials (*Nemastylis acuta*), 175
Cephalotaxus harringtonia, 172; var. *drupacea*, 172
Cerastium, 170
Ceratostigma plumbaginoides, 103–4, 132
Cercis, 168
Chaenomeles japonica, 12
Charlotte Observer, xvi, 245
Chasmanthe aethiopica, 88; *C. antholyza*, 88
Chickweed, Sandhill (*Minuartia caroliniana*), 167
Chimaphila maculata, 142
Chionodoxa, 12
Chlidanthus fragrans, 41, 61, 72
Chrysanthemum, 105; 'Christmas Gold', 105
Cimicifuga racemosa, 142
Cinquefoil (*Potentilla canadensis*), 152
Cladrastis lutea, 33–34
Clammy locust (*Robinia viscosa*), 34
Clarkia, 106
Clematis, 91; *C. viorna*, 154; *C. virginiana*, 129
Clement, Latta, 149, 219, 224, 229
Cleome, 106, 107, 111
Clethra acuminata, 36

Clitoria mariana, 153
Clock vine (*Thunbergia alata*), 128
Cobaea scandens, 239
Codiaeum variegatum, 146
Colchicum, xii, 74–75, 76, 78, 202, 217; 'Premier', 75; *C. autumnale*, 75, 202; *C. bornmuelleri*, 75; *C. giganteum*, 75; *C. speciosum*, 75, 202; 'Album', 75, 217; *C. variegatum*, 75
Collinson, Peter, 201, 217, 220, 221
Columbine, 42, 101, 170, 238
Cooperia smallii, 96
Coral drops (*Bessera elegans*), 92
Coreopsis, 106, 107, 109, 170; *C. auriculata*, 156
Cornus nuttallii, 202
Cosmos, 103, 106, 111; Klondyke, 110; 'Orange Flare', 109, 126
Cotoneaster, 18, 22, 23; *C. horizontalis*, 23; *C. salicifolius* var. *floccosus*, 23
Cowslip, 49, 110; English (*Primula veris*), 99, 100
Crab-apple, flowering, 13
Cranesbill, 170
Crape myrtle (*Lagerstroemia indica*), 9–10, 22
Crayton, Mr., 29, 35, 149
Creeping spring lychnis (*Phlox subulata*), 220
× *Crinodonna howardii*, 63
Crinum, milk-and-wine, 63, 64, 79. See also Lily, milk-and-wine
Crinum, 10, 45, 47–48, 61–63, 79–82, 83–84, 240; 'Cecil Houdyshel', 63, 64, 80, 81; 'Christopher Lily', 61; 'Ellen Bosanquet', 63, 81; 'Empress of India', 62, 79; 'H. J. Elwes', 82, 83–84; 'J. C. Harvey', 82; 'Peachblow', 82; 'Sophie Nehrling', 84; 'Virginia Lee', 63, 80, 82, 84; *C. americanum*, 41, 43, 61, 64; *C. asiaticum*, 42, 44, 85; *C. augustum*, 61, 62, 85; *C. bulbispermum*, 41, 43, 47, 61, 62n, 63, 73, 81; 'St. Christopher', 62n; *C. erubescens*, 41, 44, 61; *C. fimbriatulum*, 41, 42, 43; *C. jagus*, 61, 62, 84–85; *C. kirkii*, 42, 44, 61, 63; *C. kunthianum*, 61, 63; *C. moorei*, 42, 44, 61, 63, 73, 81, 82, 85, 239; *C.* × *powellii*, 61, 62–63, 73, 80, 81; 'Album', 41, 44; 'Krelagii', 81; 'Louis Bosanquet', 81; 'Roseum', 44, 81; 'White Queen', 63,

80; *C. sanderanum*, 47; *C. zeylanicum*, 41, 43, 61, 62
Crocosmia, 49, 88, 89; 'Hereward', 89; 'His Majesty', 89; *C.* × *crocosmiiflora*, 49, 88
Crocus (*Crocus*): autumn, 75–76; fall (*Sternbergia lutea*), 93, 41; saffron (*Crocus sativus*), 76; summer (*Zephyranthes candida*), 48
Crocus, 3, 10, 12, 74, 75–76, 87, 171, 202, 184, 185, 202; 'Snow Bunting', 185; *C. angustifolius*, 12, 87; *C. chrysanthus* 'E. A. Bowles', 185; *C. imperati*, 185; *C. kotschyanus*, 76, 87; ssp. *kotschyanus*, 76; *C. laevigatus* 'Fontenayi', 185; *C. longiflorus*, 76, 87, 184; *C. minimus*, 185; *C. niveus*, 75, 87; *C. ochroleucus*, 184, 202; *C. sativus*, 76; *C. serotinus* ssp. *salzmannii*, 87, 202; *C. sieberi* 76, 12, 87, 185; *C. speciosus*, 75, 87, 202; 'Globosus', 76; *C. tommasinianus*, 87
Crotalaria, 107, 110, 111, 117–18; *C. argyrea*, 117; *C. brevidens* var. *intermedia*, 118; *C. incana*, 118; *C. juncea*, 117; *C. lanceolata*, 118; *C. retusa*, 107, 117; *C. rotundifolia*, 118; *C. spectabilis*, 8, 107, 117; *C. verrucosa*, 118; *C. zanzibarica*, 118
Croton alabamensis, 146
Cryptomeria japonica, 172; 'Compacta', 172; 'Elegans', 172; 'Nana', 172; 'Vilmoriniana', 172
Curly-headed Johnny (*Clematis viorna*), 154
Custis, John, 201, 217
Cyanthodes colensoi, 186
Cyclamen cilicium, 184; *C. coum*, 184, 204; *C. hederifolium*, 184, 202, 204
Cyclopedia of American Horticulture (Bailey), 85, 118, 146
Cypella, 88, 90; *C. herbertii*, 89, 174, 175
Cyrilla racemiflora, 36
Cyrtanthus, 70; *C. angustifolius*, 70; *C. brachyscyphus*, 70; *C. elatus* 70; *C. mackenii*, 70; var. *cooperi*, 70

Daffodil (*Narcissus*), 3, 13, 51–59, 73, 99, 178; autumnal (*Narcissus viridiflorus*), 59; fall (*Sternbergia lutea*), 93; hoop-petticoat (*Narcissus bulbocodium*), 59; Peruvian (*Hymenocallis narcissiflora*), 47; rush-leaved (*Narcissus assoanus*), 59;
sea (*Pancratium maritimum*), 68; swan's neck, 53; winter (*Sternbergia lutea*), 93
Dahlia, 105
Daisy: African (*Arctotis, Gerbera*), 106, 107, 111; 'Jewel of the Veldt', 106; 'Monarch of the Veldt', 107; 'Ursinia', 106; 'Venidium', 107; Alaska (*Leucanthemum maximum*), 102; elder, 101; English, 100; Korean, 237; Michaelmas, 104, 194; painted, 49; Swan River (*Brachycome*), 107
Date palm, Canary Island, 212
Datura stramonium, 142
Daylily (*Hemerocallis*), 73, 79, 125–27; Lemon, 139
Decumaria barbara, 35–36
De Forest, Elizabeth, 210, 215
Delphinium, Chinese, 5, 105; hybrid, 5
Delphinium 'Tom Thumb', 105; *D. nudicaule*, 205
Devil-wood (*Osmanthus americanus*), 20
Dianthus, 111, 122, 162, 205; *D. alpinus*, 205; *D. deltoides*, 162; *D. graniticus*, 162; *D. gratianopolitanus*, 162
Dicentra spectabilis, 99, 100, 122
Dichelostemma ida-maia, 50, 71, 209; *D. pulchellum*, 209; *D. volubile*, 209
Dictamnus, 122–23
Dierama, 90
Dietes, 89
Dimorphotheca, 107, 108; *D. sinuata*, 107
Dogwood (*Cornus*), 13, 168; summer (*Stewartia ovata*), 27
Dormon, Caroline, 29, 30, 90, 147, 157, 175, 177, 216, 220, 223, 224, 229, 230, 242
Dormon, Ruth (Mrs. James), 67, 89, 90, 91, 174, 224, 230
Doronicum, 11, 99, 100
Dryas octopetala 'Minor', 205; *D.* × *suendermannii*, 205
Dutchman's pipe (*Aristolochia macrophylla*), 129

Earle, Alice M., 197, 214
Echinocystis lobata, 128
Elaeagnus, 18, 146; *E. macrophylla*, 20; *E. pungens*, 20; 'Fruitlandii', 20; *E.* × *reflexa*, 20
Ellacombe, Canon. *See* Nicholson, Henry
Elm, Chinese (*Ulmus parvifolia*), 9

Epigaea repens, 167
Epimedium × *versicolor* 'Sulphureum', 131
Erica mediterranea, 185
Erinus, 161
Erysimum × *allionii*, 162; *E. linifolium*, 162
Erythronium, 204, 207, 209, 210; *E. californicum*, 209
Euonymus, 23, 24, 129, 132; *E. fortunei*, 24, 129, 132; 'Coloratus', 24; var. *vegetus*, 24; *E. japonicus*, 23; *E. kiautschovicus*, 23
Euphorbia corollata, 5
Eustylis, 90, 174
Evening primrose (*Oenothera*), 164
Evergreens, broad-leaved, 17–24

Fairy lantern (*Calochortus*), 203
Farrer, Reginald, 147, 220
February silver (*Narcissus cyclamineus*), 239
Felicia amelloides, 107
Fetter bush (*Pieris floribunda*), 25–26, 149
Feverfew, 237
Fever tree (*Pinckneya pubens*), 30
Firecracker flower (*Dichelostemma ida-maia*), 209
Firethorn (*Pyracantha*), 22–23
Flax, blue (*Linum perenne*), 111, 166
Fleabane (*Hedeoma pulegioides, Mentha pulegium*), 144, 145
Flora of the Southeastern States (Small), 146, 150, 155, 220
Flower Grower, xiv
Flowers, John, 230
Foam-climber (*Decumaria barbara*), 35
Foam flower, 170
Forget-me-not, xv, 184
Forsythia, 12, 13
Fortune, Robert, 122, 187
Foxglove, 114; wild (*Aureolaria virginica*), 153
Foxtail clubmoss, 153
Franklinia alatamaha, 27
Freesia, 89, 90, 92, 210
Fritillaria, 207
Funkia (*Hosta*), 121

Gaillardia, 104, 105; 'Burgundy', 105 'The Bride', 105; *G.* × *grandiflora*, 104
Galanthus elwesii, 70, 185; *G. ikariae*, 70; *G. nivalis*, 70, 241; 'Scharlokii', 70; *G. plicatus* ssp. *byzantinus*, 70; *G. reginae-olgae*, 241
Galtonia candicans, 42
Garden Club of Virginia, xv, 43n, 229
Garden Gossip, xv, 43n, 229
Gardenia augusta, 22
Gardening for Love (Lawrence), xi, xvi, 241
Gardens in Winter (Lawrence), xii
Garrya elliptica, 211
Gas-plant (*Dictamnus*), 122
Gazania, 212
Gelsemium sempervirens, 10
Gentiana acaulis, 205; *G. sino-ornata*, 202
Georgia bark (*Pinckneya pubens*), 30
Gerbera, 107
Geum, 100
Ginkgo, 9
Gladiolus, 49, 88, 92, 101; *G. callinthus*, 88; *G. communis* ssp. *byzantinus*, 42
Golden club (*Orontium aquaticum*), 153
Golden star (*Triteleia ixioides*), 209
Gordonia lasianthus, 22, 27, 36
Green, Charlotte Hilton, xiv
Grey, Colonel, 64, 65, 72, 77–78, 81
Grieve, Maud, 141, 145, 253
Groundcovers, 130–32
Gypsophila repens, 170

Habranthus, 94–95; *H. brachyandrus*, 69, 94; *H. robustus*, 69, 93, 94–95; *H. tubispathus*, 69
Harebell (*Campanula*), 163
Hayward, Wyndham, 62, 64, 65, 72, 73, 84, 96
Heath, winter, 185
Heavenly bamboo (*Nandina domestica*), 6
Hedeoma pulegioides, 144
Hedera, 134; 'Albany', 134; 'Glacier', 134; 'Hahn's Self-Branching', 134; 'Maple Queen', 134; 'Marmorata', 134; 'Pittsburgh', 134; 'Star', 134; *H. canariensis*, 134, 135; 'Fleur-de-lis', 135; 'Gloire de Marengo', 135; *H. helix*, 131, 133, 134; 'Conglomerata', 134; 'Erecta', 134; 'Gracilis', 131; 'Meagheri', 133, 134; 'Pedata', 133, 134
Hedychium coronarium, 9
Helenium, 104; 'Riverton Gem', 104; 'Riverton Jewel', 104
Helianthus angustifolius, 105
Heliopsis helianthoides 'Pitcherana', 103

Heliotrope, 106
Hellebore (*Helleborus*), 185
Helleborus × *orientalis*, 244
Hemerocallidaceae, 73n
Hemerocallis, 73, 103, 120, 125–27;
   'Apricot', 100; 'Bagdad', 120; 'Berwyn',
   127; 'Boutonniere', 126; 'Carnival',
   126; 'Chandra', 127; 'Daylily Wolof',
   120; 'Dorothy McDade', 127; 'Dr.
   Regel', 100, 126; 'Dr. Stout', 125–26;
   'Dumortieri', 127; 'Fire Red', 127;
   'Florham', 102; 'Gaiety', 120; 'George
   Yeld', 120; 'Golden Dream', 120, 127;
   'Golden Sceptre', 120; 'Golden West',
   120; 'Goldeni', 120, 127; 'Hypericum',
   237; 'Hyperion', 120, 125; 'Iowa',
   127; 'J. A. Crawford', 127; 'Lidice',
   127; 'Margaret Perry', 119; 'Mayor
   Starzynski', 127; 'Mikado', 120, 127;
   'Mrs. B. F. Bonner', 127; 'Ophir',
   119–20, 127; 'Potentate', 127; 'Queen
   of May', 127; 'Queen Wilhelmina',
   127; 'Starlight', 127; 'Tejas', 127;
   'Theron', 120; 'Victory Montevideo',
   127; 'Victory Taierhchwang', 126–27;
   H. dumortieri, 126; *H. lilio-asphodelus*,
   xv, 100; *H. thunbergii*, 103; 'By State',
   103 'J. A. Crawford', 103
Hen-and-chickens (*Sempervivum tectorum*),
   166
Henry, Mary, 61, 67, 177, 219
Hepatica, 170
Herbert, William, 81, 175, 230
Herbertia (International Bulb Society
   journal), xv, 60, 64, 70, 73, 82, 96,
   125n, 237
Herbertia, 90, 174, 175
Herb Gatherers (Lawrence), 241, 242
Hermodactylus tuberosus, 88
Heuchera, 101, 162
Hibiscus, 80; *H. moscheutos*, 121–22;
   'Mallow Marvels', 80, 121
Hieracium venosum, 152
Hippeastrum × *acramannii*, 65, 73;
   H. × *johnsonii*, 45, 65; *H. puniceum*,
   65; *H. striatum*, 65
Hoak, Charlotte, 206, 207
Holly (*Ilex*), 24, 168; knee (*Ruscus
   aculeatus*), 31; sea, 153; sweet (*Osmanthus
   heterophyllus*), 28; yaupon (*Ilex
   vomitoria*), 24

Home Garden, xiv
Home Gardening for the South, 84, 229
Honeysuckle, 10
Horse-chestnut (*Aesculus*), 34
Horse-tail, 153
Horticulture, xiv
Hortus Second (Bailey), xiv, 34, 77, 78, 90,
   116, 119, 140, 175, 176
Hortus Third (Bailey Hortorium), xiv,
   51n, 155, 157, 220, 224
Hosta, 121, 237; *H. japonica*, 121;
   H. lancifolia, 121; *H. plantaginea*, 121;
   H. subcordata grandiflora, 121;
   H. ventricosa, 121
Houdyshel, Cecil, 64, 66, 67, 80, 82, 90
House & Garden, xiii, xiv, xv, 11
Houseleek (*Sempervivum*), 165
Houstonia purpurea, 151; *H. serpyllifolia*, 241
Humulus japonicus, 128
Hunnemania, 106, 109, 110, 111
Hunt, William Lanier, xiii, xiv, 60, 87,
   227–31, 241
Hyacinth (*Hyacinthus*), xi, 3, 12, 99,
   237; Dutch, 13, 50; grape, 13, 49, 171;
   summer (*Galtonia candicans*), 42
Hyacinthus, 45; 'Electra', 13
Hydrangea: climbing (*Hydrangea
   petiolaris*), 129; silver-leaf (*Hydrangea
   arborescens* ssp. *radiata*), 35
Hydrangea arborescens ssp. *radiata*, 35;
   H. petiolaris, 36, 129; *H. quercifolia*, 35
Hylotelephium anacampseros, 165;
   H. telephioides, 165
Hymenocallis, 47, 65–68; *H. caribaea*, 68;
   H. caroliniana, 41, 66; *H. galvestonensis*,
   66; *H. narcissiflora*, 47, 68; *H. rotata*,
   66; *H.* × *festalis*, 73
Hypericum crux-andreae, 142;
   H. perforatum, 142

Iberis sempervirens 'Little Gem', 185
Ilex glabra, 24; *I. opaca*, 24; *I. vomitoria*, 24
Illicium floridanum, 36
Indian pipes, 53
Indigo: false (*Baptisia australis*), 120; wild
   (*Baptisia*), 139–40
Indigofera alba, 186; *I. decora*, 186
International Bulb Society. *See* Amaryllis
   Society
Ipheion uniflorum, 10, 45, 49–50, 171
Ipomoea indica, 212

268 Index

Iridaceae, 45
Iris (*Iris*): Algerian, 184; bearded, 119; delta, 139; dwarf bearded, 161; dwarf crested (*I. cristata*), 170; Evansia, 87; Florentine, 239; German, 7–8; Hungarian (*I. humilis*), 166; Japanese, 80, 102, 114, 120, 153; Japanese roof (*I. tectorum*), 166; Louisiana, 80, 102; Persian (*I. persica*), 214; Roof (*I. tectorum*), 227; Siberian, 102, 120; Spuria, 102; vesper (*Pardanthopsis dichotoma*), 87; winter, 240
Iris, 13, 79, 86–91, 110; 'Ambassadeur', 100; 'Autumn King', 105, 166; 'Bluette', 100; 'Caesar's Brother', 120; 'Emperor', 102; 'Florrie Ridler', 120; 'Frieda Mohr', 100; 'Gold Bound', 120; 'Jean Siret', 166; 'Mme. Dorothea K. Williamson', 101–2; 'Mme. Gaudichua', 100; 'Morning Magic', 120; 'Mrs. Rowe', 120; 'Periwinkle', 120; 'Perry's Blue', 120; 'Prosper Laugier', 100; 'Purissima', 8; 'Snow Queen', 120; 'Souvenir de L. Michaud', 100; 'Zua', 202; *I.* × *albicans*, 100; *I. chrysophylla*, 203; *I. cristata*, 166, 170; *I. germanica*, 100; *I.* × *germanica* var. *florentina*, 202; *I. humilis*, 166; *I. innominata*, 205; *I. japonica*, 87, 227; *I.* × *kochii*, 100; *I. orientalis*, 102; *I. pallida pallida*, 101; var. *dalmatica*, 100; *I. persica*, 214, 215; *I. pumila*, 100, 166; 'Caerulea', 166; *atroviolacea*, 166; *I. reticulata*, 13, 166, 171; *I. stylosa*, 87; *I. tectorum*, 166, 227, 237; *I. tenax*, 203; *I. unguicularis*, 87, 230; *I. verna*, 166
Ivy (*Hedera*), 9, 133–35; Algerian (*H. canariensis*), 135; Baltic, 133, 134; Bird's-foot (*H. helix* 'Pedata'), 133–34; Boston, 129; clustered (*H. helix* 'Conglomerata'), 134; English, 133; Irish, 134
Ixia, 90
Ixiolirion tataricum, 72

Jamestown weed (*Datura stramonium*), 142
Japanese hop (*Humulus japonicus*), 128
Jasmine: Cape, 22; winter (*Jasminum nudiflorum*), 7

Jasminum floridum, 7; *J. mesnyi*, 7; *J. nudiflorum*, 7
Jekyll, Francis, 193, 197, 239
Jekyll, Gertrude, xii, xiii, 26, 191–200, 208, 235, 238
Jessamine, yellow (*Gelsemium sempervirens*), 10, 241
Jew's-myrtle (*Ruscus aculeatus*), 31
Jimson (*Datura stramonium*), 142
Jonquil (*Narcissus jonquilla*), 57, 179; Queen Anne's (*N.* × *odorus*), 59
Juniperus sargentii, 132
Justicia americana, 241

Kalmia latifolia, 228
Kalmiopsis leachiana, 205
Kell, Willie May, 82, 84, 95
Kilvert, Francis, 235, 244
Kniphofia, 50; cv. 'Pfitzeri', 50; *K. angustifolia*, 42
Krippendorf, Carl, 179, 221, 222

Laceleaf ragwort (*Senecio millefolium*), 150
Lacy, Allen xi, xvi
Ladies' wash board (*Saponaria officinalis*), 241
Lady's slipper, 170
Lagerstroemia indica, 9–10
Lamm, Linda Mitchell, 235–45
Lapeirousia, 86
Larkspur, 5, 80, 101, 102, 106, 107, 111, 139
Laurel: Carolina cherry (*Prunus caroliniana*), 19; English (*Prunus laurocerasus*), 19; English cherry (*Prunus laurocerasus*), 241; mountain (*Kalmia latifolia*), 227
Laurustinus (*Viburnum tinus*), 21
Lavandula angustifolia, 238
Lavender (*Lavandula*), 9
Leatherwood (*Cyrilla racemiflora*), 36
Lenten rose (*Helleborus* × *orientalis*), 244
Leucanthemum maximum, 102
Leucocoryne ixiodes, 70
Leucojum aestivum, 70; *L. autumnale*, 70, 202; *L. vernum*, 70
Leucothoë axillaris, 154; *L. fontanesiana*, 37; *L. populifolia*, 36–37
Lewisia rediviva, 205
Ligustrum, 18, 19; *L. indicum* 19; *L. japonicum*, 18, 19; 'Rotundifolium', 19; *L. lucidum*, 18, 19

Lilac (*Syringa*), 13; cut-leaf Persian (*Syringa* × *laciniata*), 6; French hybrid, 5; Persian (*Syringa* × *persica*), 5–6
Liliaceae, 45, 70n, 72n, 73n
Lilium catesbaei, 216; *L. columbianum*, 209; *L. dauricum* × *L. sulphureum*, 216; *L. grayi*, 241; *L.* × *hollandicum*, 108; *L. humboldtii* var. *bloomerianum*, 209; *L. michauxii*, 241; *L. pardalinum*, 208, 209; *L. pyrenaicum*, 192; *L. vollmeri*, 209
Lily: asphodel (*Crinum jagus*), 85; atamasco (*Zephyranthes atamasca*), 48, 68, 151, 170; Barbados (*Hippeastrum puniceum*), 65; butterfly (*Hedychium coronarium*), 9, 80; canna, 212; Christopher (*Crinum giganteum*), 61, 74; delicate (*Chlidanthus fragrans*), 72; fairy (*Zephyranthes*), 48; foxtail, 239; ginger (*Hedychium coronarium*), 9; Guernsey (*Nerine sarniensis*), 10, 46; hurricane (*Lycoris aurea*), 64; Jacobean (*Sprekelia formosissima*), 72; madonna, 114, 122; Mariposa (*Calochortus*), 212, 203; milk-and-wine (*Crinum*), 41–42, 43–44, 47–48, 63, 64; Nassau (*Crinum*), 41; oxblood (*Rhodophiala advena*, *Rhodophiala bifida*), 65, 95, 227; pinewoods (*Alophia drummondii*), 174; plaintain (*Hosta*), 121; plaintain, August (*H. plantaginea*), 121; plaintain, blue (*H. ventricosa*), 121; plaintain, narrow-leaved (*H. japonica*), 121; rain (*Zephyranthes candida*), 48, 81, 93, 96; rubrum, 237; snake (*Dichelostemma volubile*), 209; spider (*Hymenocallis*, *Nerine*, *Lycoris aurea*, *Pancratium*), 46, 66, 80, 240; spider, dwarf (*Pancratium*), 67; spider, Gulf Coast (*Hymenocallis galvestonensis*), 66; spider, tropical, 67–68; tiger, 102; torch (*Kniphofia*), 50; turk's-cap, 212; zephyr (*Zephyranthes*), 69, 70, 92, 93, 96. See also *Lilium*
Lily turf (*Liriope spicata*), 131
Limonium sinuatum, 109
Linaria alpina, 161
Linum perenne, xii, 101
Liriope muscari, 103; *L. spicata*, 131–32
Little Bulbs (Lawrence), 155
Little sweet Betsy (*Trillium cuneatum*), 157
Lobelia, 104, 107

Lob's Wood, 222. *See also* Krippendorf, Carl
Loosestrife, 80
Lounsberry, Alice, 35, 141, 142, 157, 223
Lupine (*Lupinus*), 110
Lupinus subcarnosus, 106, 111
Lychnis, 220; *L. coronaria*, 101
Lycoris, 45, 64, 73; *L. aurea*, 47, 64; *L. incarnata*, 64; *L. radiata*, 64, 95; *L. sanguinea*, 64; *L. sprengeri*, 64; *L. squamigera*, 41, 45, 61, 64; 'Purpurea', 64

Macleaya, 237
Magnolia: saucer, 13; red (*Illicium floridanum*), 36
Magnolia denudata, 240; *M. grandiflora*, 17, 228; *M. virginiana*, 22
Mahonia aquifolium, 24; *M. bealei*, 17, 24
Maiden's blushes (*Pinckneya pubens*), 30
Mallow (*Hibiscus*), 103; poppy-, 170; rose (*H. moscheutos*), 121, 124
Marigold, 10, 106, 109, 110; Cape (*Dimorphotheca sinuata*), 107; African, 111
Matelea carolinensis, 154
Matthiola, 106, 111
Mazus pumilio, 163
Meadow rue (*Thalictrum*), 170, 122, 123
Mentha pulegium, 144
Merrybell, 154
Mexican star (*Milla biflora*), 92
Michelia figo, 26
Milkweed: climbing (*Matelea carolinensis*), 154; common (*Asclepias syriaca*), 154
Milla biflora, 70–71, 92
Mimosa (*Albizia julibrissin*), 6–7
Minuartia caroliniana, 167
Mr. Cayce, 83–84, 125
Mock orange, 13
Modjeska, Helene, 212, 213
Monarda didyma, 80; 'Salmonea', 81; *M. fistulosa*, 80
Moncure, Robert, 178, 228
Montbretia (*Crocosmia*), 42, 48, 88
Moore, Ken, 150, 151
Moraea, 89, 90; *M. aristata*, 90; *M. polystachya*, 215; *M. ramosissima*, 90
Moss pink (*Phlox subulata*), 13; Sandhill (*P. nivalis* ssp. *hentzii*), 167; Sandhills (*P. hentzii*), 220

Mother of thousands (*Saxifraga stolonifera*), 132
Mullein, giant (*Verbascum olympicum*), 101
Munstead Wood, 193, 194, 197
Myosotis alpestris, 110
Myrica pensylvanica, 17

Nandina domestica, 6
Narcissus (*Narcissus*): angel's tears (*N. triandrus triandrus*), 179; February silver (*N. cyclamineus*), 239; gardenia-flowered (*Narcissus poeticus* 'Plenus'), 59; paperwhite, 57; pheasant's eye (*Narcissus poeticus* var. *recurvus*), 58; poet's (*Narcissus poeticus*), 58; small-cupped (*Narcissus* × *incomparabilis* × *N. poeticus*), 53
Narcissus, 51–59, 73; 'April Tears', 179; 'J. T. Bennett Poe', 179; 'Mrs. R. O. Backhouse', 52; 'Nylon', 184; 'Queen of Spain', 179; 'Sarchedon', 52; 'Serphine', 52; 'Silver Bells', xi; 'Yellow Poppy', 54; bicolor, 54, 55; classification of, 51–52; divisions of, 51; double, 58–59; miscellaneous, 51; species, 58; various, 59; white, 53, 59; wild, 58; *N. albicans*, 179; *N. assoanus*, 180; *N. asturiensis*, 178; *N.* × *barrii*, 52, 55, 58; 'Acida', 55; 'Bath's Flame', 55; 'Bonfire', 55; 'Brilliancy', 55; 'Conspicuus', 55; 'Dragoon', 55, 'Firetail', 52, 55; 'Glitter', 55; 'Pride of Virginia', 55; 'Red Huzzar', 58; 'Southern Star', 55; *N. bulbocodium*, 59, 178; *citrinus*, 59, 178; *conspicuus*, 178; *monophyllus*, 59; ssp. *monophyllus*, 178; *N. cantabricus* ssp. *cantabricus* var. *folious*, 178; *N. cernuus*, 179; *N. cyclamineus*, 57, 59, 179, 239; 'Beryl', 52, 57, 179; 'February Gold', 57; 'February Silver', 239; 'Le Beau', 179; 'Orange Glory', 57; *N.* × *incomparabilis*, 54–55, 58; 'Fortune', 52, 54; 'Frank Miles', 54; 'Gloria Mundi', 54; 'Havelock', 52, 54; 'Holbein', 54; 'John Evelyn', 55; 'Kennack', 55; 'Loudspeaker', 54; 'Lucifer', 54–55; 'Orange Phoenix', 58; 'President Viger', 54; 'R. M. Tobin', 55; 'Sir Watkin', 54; 'Sulphur Phoenix', 58; 'Will Scarlet', 54; *N. incomparabilis* × *N. poeticus*, 55; *N. jonquilla*, 57, 179; 'Buttercup', 57; 'Citrinus', 180; 'Golden Scepter', 57; 'Helena', 180; 'Lintie', 179, 180; 'Orange Queen', 57; 'Primrose', 57; 'Simplex', 180; 'Trevithian', 52, 57; 'Tullus Hostilius', 179, 'White Wedgwood', 179, 180; × *N. poeticus*, 180; *N.* × *leedsii* (*N.* × *incomparabilis*), 52, 55–56, 58; 'Albania', 56; 'Beatrice', 56; 'Cicely', 56; 'Evangeline', 56; 'Mermaid', 56; 'Mitylene', 52, 56; 'Queen of the North', 56; 'Salmonetta', 56; 'Silver Salver', 56; 'Snow Sprite', 58; 'Southern Gem', 56; 'Tenedos', 56; 'Tunis', 52, 56; 'White City', 56; 'White Lady', 56; 'White Pearl', 56; *N.* × *medioluteus*, 58; *N. minor*, 178; *N.* × *odorus*, 13, 59; *N. poeticus*, 57–58, 59, 179; 'Dante', 58; 'Herrick', 58; 'Homer', 58; 'Horace', 58, 'Juliet', 58; 'Plenus', 59; 'Rupert Brooke', 58; var. *recurvus*, 58; *N. pseudonarcissus*, 179; ssp. *moschatus*, 179; *N. scaberulus*, 184; *N. serotinus*, 178; *N. tazetta*, 57–58; 'Aspasia', 58; 'Cheerfulness', 59; 'Elvira', 58; 'Glorious' 52, 58; 'Hameon', 58; 'Laurens Koster', 58; 'Orange Cup', 58; var. *polyanthos*, 57; 'Grand Monarque', 57; 'Soleil d'Or', 57; *N. triandrus*, 56–57, 59, 179; 'Agnes Harvey', 57; 'Angels' Tears', 179; 'Harvest Moon', 57; 'Queen of Spain', 57; 'Silver Chimes', 57; 'Thalia', 57; *triandrus*, 59, 179; × *jonquilla* 'Hawera', 179; trumpet *Narcissus*, 52, 53–54, 58; 'Beersheba', 52, 53; 'Dawson City', 52, 53; 'Duke of York', 53; 'Emperor', 53; 'Empress', 54; 'Glory of Sassenheim', 54; 'Golden Spur', 53; 'Herod', 54; 'Holland's Glory', 58; 'Imperator', 53; 'John Cairns', 53; 'King Alfred', 52, 53; 'Mrs. E. H. Krelage', 54; 'Robert Sydenham', 53; 'Mrs. Robert Sydenham', 53; 'Olympia', 53; 'Sanctity', 53; 'Serphine', 53; 'Silver Bells', 53; 'Vanilla', 54; 'William Goldring', 53; *N. viridiflorus*, 59
Nasturtium, 106, 111
Neal, Bill, xvi
Nemastylis, 174; *N. geminiflora*, 90–91

Nemesia, 106, 109, 111
Nemophila, 8, 12, 106, 109, 110, 111
Neomarica, 91; *N. gracilis*, 91
Nepeta, 170; *N. racemosa*, 161
Nerine, 45, 46–47; *N. bowdenii*, 65; major, 73; *N. filifolia*, 65; *N. fothergillii*, 65; *N. sarniensis*, 10, 46, 65; *N. undulata*, 64, 95
Newsletter of the North Carolina Wild Flower Preservation Society, xv, 150
Nicholson, Henry (Canon Ellacombe), 94, 197
Nicotiana, 106, 111
Nierembergia frutescens, 164; *N. hippomanica*, 164
Nigella, 106–7, 111
Night-blooming cereus, 62
Nik-Nar Nursery, 149, 219, 225
Ninebark (*Hydrangia arborescens* ssp. *radiata*), 35
North American Lily Society, 216
North American Rock Garden Society, xvi
North Carolina Botanical Garden, 227, 229
North Carolina State University, xv, 3, 149; Arboretum, xvii
North Carolina Wild Flower Preservation Society, 151, 154, 156, 236, 243
Nothoscordum, 95

Oak leech (*Aureolaria virginica*), 153
Oenothera macrocarpa, 164
Oleander, 212
Oleaster, Japanese (*Elaeagnus*), 20
Olsynium douglassii, 88
Omphalodes verna, 13
Ornithogalum arabicum, 50; *O. thyrsoides*, 50
Orontium aquaticum, 153
Osmanthus americanus, 20; *O. fragrans*, 20, 28; *O. heterophyllus*, 20, 28; *O.* × *fortunei*, 20, 28
Oxalis adenophylla, 202; *O. bowiei*, 184; *O. crassipes*, 206; *O. hirta*, 206; *O. pescaprae*, 206, 210; *O. violacea*, 151

Pachysandra, 131, 132; 'Silver Edge', 132
Pacific Horticulture, xvi
Paeonia lactiflora, 8; 'Baroness Shroeder', 8; 'Edulis Superba', 8; 'Felix Crousse', 8; 'Festiva Maxima', 8; 'Louis Van Houtte', 8; 'M. Jules Elie', 8; 'Mikado' 8; *P. officinalis rubra*, 238
Pancratium, 47; *P. illyricum*, 73; *P. maritimum*, 67, 68
Pansy, 13
Pardanthopsis dichotoma, 87
Parkinson, John, 31, 75, 144, 242
Partridge berry, 170
Payne, Theodore, 211, 212
Pearl bush, 13
Pennyroyal (*Hedeoma pulegioides*, *Mentha pulegium*), 144–45
Penstemon, 212
Penstemon barbatus, 108; *P. rupicola*, 205
Peony (*Paeonia*), 8, 13, 101, 122
Pepperbush, sweet (*Clethra acuminata*), 36
Perfoliated bellwort, 154
Periwinkle (*Vinca minor*), xi, 131
Petrorhagia saxifraga, 170
Petunia, 105, 106, 108, 109; 'Martha Washington', 109
Phacelia, 106, 110, 111; *P. campanularia*, 108
Phlox (*Phlox*), 101, 102, 103, 113–15, 119, 218–26; Britton's (*Phlox subulata* ssp. *brittonii*), 221; Caddo (*Phlox pilosa ozarkana*), 224; chalice (*Phlox amoena*), 224; Drummond, 106, 111, 112; hairy (*Phlox amoena*), 224; mountain (*Phlox ovata*), 225; Ozark (*Phlox pilosa* ssp. *ozarkana*), 147; pine (*Phlox hentzii*), 220
Phlox: 'Chattahooche', 222; 'Flora Reedy', 103; 'G. F. Wilson', 147; 'Jules Sandeau', 81; 'Millie Hoboken', 108; 'Mrs. Jenkins', 103; 'Mrs. Millie Van Hoboken', 80; 'Peach Blossom', 147; 'Rhinelander', 81; 'Vivid', 147; *P. amoena*, 223, 224; 'Tallapoosa', 224; *P.* × *ardensii*, 114; 'Hilda', 114, 'Kathy', 114; 'Louise', 114; 'Marianne', 114; *P. bifida*, 219, 220; *P. carolina*, 114; *P. divaricata*, 99, 100, 221; *P. glaberrima*, 222, 223; 'Interior' ('Status Novus'), 222; *P.* × *henryae*, 219; *P. nivalis*, 218–19, 223, 225, 226; 'Anne Knight', 219; 'Azure', 219; 'Colonel Moore', 219; 'Gladwyne', 219; 'Mary Alice', 219; 'Sir Guilford', 219; ssp. *hentzii*, 167, 220; *P. ovata*, 146, 147, 225; *P. paniculata*, 114–15; 'Beacon', 114; 'Firebrand', 114; 'Flora Reedy', 114; 'Jules Sandeau', 115;

'Mrs. Jenkins', 114; 'R. P. Struthers', 115; 'Rheinländer', 115; 'Thor', 115; *P. pilosa*, 223, 224, 225; 'Peach Blossom', 225; ssp. *ozarkana*, 147, 224; *P.* × *procumbens*, 224; 'Timmy Foster', 224; *P. pulchra*, 146, 225; *P. reptans*, 223; *P. stolonifera*, 223, 224; 'Blue Ridge', 223; 'Pink Ridge', 223; *P. subulata*, 13, 147, 151, 167, 218, 220, 222, 224; 'Millstream Daphne', 222; 'Millstream Jupiter', 222; *australis*, 221; 'Fort Hill', 221; 'Maiden Blush', 221; 'Twin Creek', 221; ssp. *brittonii*, 221; *P. suffruticosa*, 114; 'Magnificence', 114; 'Miss Lingard', 114; 'Perfection', 114; 'The Queen', 114

Photinia, 18; *P. serratifolia*, 20–21
Physostegia virginiana 'Vivid', 80, 104, 105, 108
Phytolacca americana, 142
Pieris floribunda, 25–26, 194; *P. japonica*, 26
Pinckneya pubens, 29–30, 35
Pineapple guava (*Acca sellowiana*), 17
Pink (*Dianthus*), 170; alpine, 161; calico maiden (*Dianthus deltoides*), 162; cheddar (*Dianthus gratianopolitanus*), 162, 171; Chinese, 109; granite (*Dianthus graniticus*), 162; maiden, 171; moss, 170; mullein (*Lychnis coronaria*), 101
Pipewood (*Leucothoë populifolia*), 37
Pipsissewa (*Chimaphila maculata*), 142, 153
Pitcher plant, 153
Pittosporum, 18; *P. tobira*, 19
Platycodon grandiflorus mariesii, 102, 164
Plukenet, 219, 224, 225
Plum, purple-leaf, 13
Plumbago (*Ceratostigma plumbaginoides*), 132, 171
Plum-yew, Japanese (*Cephalotaxus harringtonia* var. *drupacea*), 172
Poke-root (*Phytolacca americana*), 142
Polianthes tuberosa, 48
Pompon de Paris (*Rosa chinensis* 'Minima'), 202
Poppy, 100; California, 8, 106, 110, 111; Iceland, 11, 99, 161; Matilija (*Romneya*), 212; Oriental, 5, 101, plume, 119; Shirley, 111
Portulaca, 8, 106, 108, 111

Potentilla canadensis, 152; *P. recta* 'Warrenii', 105
Prickly box (*Ruscus aculeatus*), 31
Primrose (*Primula*), 13, 195
Primula 'Golden Plover', 195; 'Munstead Strain', 13, 195; *P. veris*, 99
Privet, Japanese (*Ligustrum*), 18, 25
Prunella, 171
Prunus caroliniana, 19; *P. laurocerasus*, 19, 241
Pudding grass (*Hedeoma pulegioides*, *Mentha pulegium*), 144
Pulsatilla patens, 239
Purdy, Carl, 162, 207–9, 210, 211, 212, 224
Pyracantha, 22–23; *P. coccinea*, 23; 'Lalandei', 23; *P. crenatoserrata*, 23; *P. crenulata*, 23
Pyrethrum, 42, 101
Pyrola, 153
Pyxidanthera barbulata, 167; *P. brevifolia*, 167
Pyxie moss (*Pyxidanthera barbulata*), 167

Quince, Japanese (*Chaenomeles japonica*), 12, 13

Rabbit bells (*Crotalaria rotundifolia*), 118
Ratsbane (*Chimaphila maculata*), 142
Rattle box (*Crotalaria*), 118
Rattle root (*Cimicifuga racemosa*), 142
Rattlesnake master/root (*Cimificuga racemosa*), 142
Rattlesnake weed (*Hieracium venosum*), 152
Rawlinson, Elizabeth, 77, 229
Redbud (*Cercis*), 168
Red-hot poker plant (*Kniphofia* 'Pfitzeri'), 50
Rhaphiolepis, 187
Rhodea japonica, 237
Rhododendron catawbiense, 228; *R. indicum*, 17; *R. molle*, 203
Rhodophiala advena, 65; *R. bagnoldii*, 95; *R. bifida*, 95, 227; *R.* × *huntiana*, 227; *R. pratensis*, 65
Ricinus, 146
Ridgway's color chart, 63, 96, 126, 149, 157, 175, 181n, 223, 225
Robin, Clyde, 211
Robinia hispida, 34; *R. kelseyi*, 34; *R. viscosa*, 34

Robinson, William, 193, 197, 208
Rock Garden in the South (Lawrence), xvi, 245
Rock gardens, 159–87; construction of, 168–69
Romanzoffia sitchensis, 205
Romneya, 212
Rose (*Rosa*), 7, 10, 202, 213, 238; Banksia (*Rosa banksiae*), 10; memorial (*Rosa wichuraiana*), 10; Radiance, 7
Rosa 'American Beauty', 7; 'American Flower Guild', 7; 'Antoine Rivoire', 7; 'Duchess of Wellington', 7; 'Duchesse de Brabant', 7, 213; 'General Jacqueminot', 213; 'Kardinal Piffl', 7; 'Killarney Queen', 7; 'Madame Caroline Testout', 213; 'Mrs. Charles Bell', 7; 'Papa Gontier', 213; 'Paul Neyron', 213; 'Pink Radiance', 7; 'Red Radiance', 7; *R. banksiae*, 10; *R. chinensis* 'Minima', 202; *R. gallica officinalis*, 238; *R. wichuraiana*, 10; *R.* × *centifolia* 'de Meaux', 202
Rosebay (*Rhododendron catawbiense*), 228
Rosemary, xi, xvii, 9
Rowntree, Lester, 71, 157, 206, 210–11, 229
Royal Horticultural Society, xiv, 51n, 52, 55, 90, 227, 230
Rudbeckia, 106, 108
Ruscus 18, 19–20, 31–32; *R. aculeatus*, xvii, 18, 19–20, 31–32; hermaphrodite 32; var. *angustifolus*, 32; *R. hypoglossum*, 32

Sage: Mexican (*Salvia patens*), 240; pineapple (*S. elegans*), 240
Saint John's wort (*Hypericum*), 142
Salpiglossis, 106
Salvia azurea var. *pitcheri*, 105; *S. elegans*, 230; *S. farinacea*, 105; *S. leucantha*, 238; *S. patens*, 240; *S. pratensis*, 101
Sandhills spiderwort (*Callisia*), 149
Santolina, 9
Sanvitalia, 108, 111
Saponaria, 170; *S. officinalis*, 241
Sassafras, 243
Saxifraga stolonifera, 132
Scabiosa, 106; *S. caucasica*, 108; *S. japonica*, 105
Schizanthus, 192

Schizostylis, 89
Sedum, 130–31; *S. acre*, 131, 165; *S. album*, 165; 'Purpureum', 165; *balticum*, 165; *S. anglicum*, 165; *S. anopetalum*, 164; *S. diffusum*, 165; *S. glaucum*, 165; *S. hispanicum*, 165; *S. kamtschaticum ellacombianum*, 165; *S. lydium*, 131, 164; *S. moranense*, 164; *S. nevii*, 165; *S. pulchellum*, 165; *S. reflexum*, 165; *S. sarmentosum*, 165; *S. sediforme*, 165; *S. sexangulare*, 131, 165; *S. spathulifolium* 'Purpureum', 205; *S. spectabile*, 237; *S. spurium*, 165; *S. ternatum*, 130–31, 165
Selaginella rupestris, 226
Sempervivum arachnoideum ssp. *tomentosum*, 166; *S. longifolium*, 166; *S. marmoreum*, 165; *S. montanum*, 166; *S. tectorum*, 166
Senecio millefolium, 150
Senna corymbosa, 9; *S. marilandica*, 9
Shadblow (*Amelanchier*), 168
Sherrard, Drew, 178, 201, 202, 203
Shinn, Bruce, 156
Shinn, Tom, 142, 149, 156
Shortia, 158
Silene, 106, 111; *S. armeria*, 108
Sisyrinchium, 87–88; *S. bermudianum*, 88
Skunk cabbage, 153
Small, John K., 146, 150, 155, 157, 220
Smilax, southern (*Smilax laurifolia*), 10
Smilax laurifolia, 10
Smith, Louise G. "Weesie" (Mrs. Lindsay), 146, 147, 155, 225
Snapdragon, 106
Snowdrop (*Galanthus*), 3, 10, 12, 70, 185, 241
Snowflake (*Leucojum*), 12, 70, 100
Solomon's plume, 154
Solomon's seal, false, 154
Southern Garden (Lawrence), xi, xvi, xvii, 245
Southern Garden History Society, 230
Southern Home and Garden, xiv
Sparaxis, 90
Spiderwort, Sandhill (*Callisia griminea*, *Callisia rosea*), 167
Spirea, Thunberg's, 13
Spiraea venusta, 80
Spotted wintergreen (*Chimaphila maculata*), 142
Spray (*Leucothoë axillaris*), 154
Sprekelia formosissima, 72, 73

Spurge, wild (*Euphorbia corollata*), 5
Squill, 12; Siberian, 171
Starflower, spring (*Ipheion uniflorum*), 49–50, 171
Starker, Carl, 184, 186, 201
Statice, 106, 108
Sternbergia, 202; *S. lutea*, 41, 61, 72, 92, 93, 206, 230
Stewartia, Mountain (*Stewartia ovata*), 33
Stewartia malacodendron, 33; *S. ovata*, 27, 33
Stokesia, 80
Stonecrop (Sedum), 164; cliff (*S. nevii*), 165; common (*S. ternatum*), 130; Old World (*S. acre*), 165
Sunflower (*Heliopsis, Helianthus*), 103, 105
Sweet olive (*Osmanthus fragrans*), 20, 28
Sweet rocket, 238
Syringa × *laciniata*, 6

Tansy, 119
Taxus baccata 'Repandens', 172
Tea olive (*Osmanthus*), 18, 20, 28; Fortune's (*Osmanthus* × *fortunei*), 20; holly-leaved (*Osmanthus* × *fortunei*), 28
Tea plant (*Camellia sinensis*), 22
Terraces, The, 207–8
Texas windflower (*Oenothera*), 165
Thalictrum, 170; *T. aquilegiifolium*, 122, 123
Thorn apple (*Datura stramonium*), 142
Through the Garden Gate (Lawrence), xvi, 245
Thuja, 18
Thunbergia, 110, 111; *T. alata*, 110n, 128–29
Thyme (*Thymus*), 131, 170
Thymus herba-barona, 131
Tigridia, 88, 174; *T. herbertii*, 175; *T. pavonia*, 89
Tithonia, 106, 110, 111
Titi (*Cyrilla racemiflora*), 36
Totten, Henry, 157
Torenia, 48, 109, 111, 116; *T. flava* (*T. baillonii*), 109, 116; 'The Bride', 119; *T. fournieri*, 109, 116
Traub, Hamilton, 95, 125n
Trillium, Ozark (*Trillium pusillum* var. *ozarkanum*), 147
Trillium, 155–58, 170; *T. catesbaei*, 156; *T. cernuum*, 156; *T. cuneatum*, 157; *T. decumbens*, 147, 155; *T. discolor*, 156; *T. erectum*, 156; *T. grandiflorum*, 156;
T. kamtshaticum, 158; *T. ludovicianum*, 157; *T. luteum*, 157, 158; *T. ovatum*, 156, 157; *T. persistens*, 155; *T. pusillum* var. *ozarkanum*, 147, 155; *T. pusillum* var. *ozarkiana*, 155; *T. pusillum* var. *virginianum*, 155; *T. rivale*, 205; *T. rugelii*, 156; *T. sessile*, 157; var. *rubrum*, 157; var. *californicum*, 157; *T. smallii*, 158; *T. stamineum*, 155; *T. tschonoskii*, 158; *T. underwoodii*, 157; *T. vaseyi*, 156; *T. viride*, 157, 158; *T. viridescens*, 157
Triteleia bridgesii, 71; *T. crocea*, 50; *T. hyacintha*, 71; *T. ixioides*, 71, 209; *T. laxa*, 50, 209; *T. peduncularis*, 71;
Tritoma, 42
Tritonia, 42, 49, 88–89
Trumpet vine (*Campsis radicans*), 129
Tuberose (*Polianthes tuberosa*), 48
Tulip (*Tulipa*), 13, 110, 237; botanical, 181; lady (*T. clusiana*), 167, 171; species, 181; waterlily (*T. kaufmanniana*), 166, 182
Tulipa, 100; 'Clara Butt', 100; 'La Tulipe Noire', 100; 'Moonlight', 100; *T. acuminata*, 181; *T. agenesis*, 182; *T. aucheriana*, 181; *T. australis*, 181; *T. batalinii*, 181; *T. biflora*, 181; *T. celsiana*, 166, 167, 181; *T. clusiana*, 166, 167, 182; var. *chrysantha*, 182; *T. fosteriana*, 182; 'Cantab', 182; 'Defiance', 182; 'Princeps', 182; *T. hageri*, 181; *T. kaufmanniana*, 166, 182; 'Bellini', 182; 'Cesar Franck', 182; 'Coccinea', 182; 'Fritz Kreisler', 182; 'Henriette', 182; 'Solanus', 182; *T. linifolia*, 182; *T. marjoletti*, 182; *T. ostrowskiana*, 182; *T. praecox*, 182; *T. sylvestris*, 182; *T. tarda*, 182; *T. turkestanica*, 182
Turkey beard (*Xerophyllum asphodeloides*), 154
Turtlehead, 153
Twayblade (*Liparis liliifolia*), 154
Twin sisters (*Narcissus* × *medioluteus*), 58

Ulmus parvifolia
University of North Carolina at Chapel Hill, 227; Library Extension Service, xvi

Veined-leaf hawkweed (*Hieracium venosum*), 151, 152

Venus fly trap, 153
Verbascum olympicum, 101
Verbena, 105; *V. rigida*, 99
Veronica, 101, 102, 103, 105, 170; *V. austriaca* ssp. *teucrium*, 163, 170; 'True Blue', 101, 163; *V. pectinata* 'Rosea', 163; *V. prostrata*, 163, 166; *V. repens*, 163; *V. spicata*, 102; ssp. *incana*, 101, 161, 163; *V. spuria*, 102; *V. subsessilis*, 102
Vesper iris (*Pardanthopsis dichotoma*), 87
Viburnum tinus, 21
Vinca major, 99; *V. minor*, 99, 131
Viola, 49, 100, 110; *V. blanda*, 177; *V. dissecta*, 176; *V. glabella*, 204; *V. jooi*, 176; *V. nuttalii*, 177; *V. odorata*, 185, 204; *V. patrinii*, 176; *V. pubescens* var. *eriocarpa*, 153; *V. walteri*, 177
Violet (*Viola*), xii, 12; Bird's-foot, 170; Chinese (*Viola patrinii*), 176; yellow (*Viola pubescens* var. *eriocarpa*), 153
Virginia creeper, 129
Virgin's bower (*Clematis virginiana*), 129

Walking iris (*Neomarica gracilis*), 91
Wallflower (*Erysimum*), 100, 101; alpine (*E. linifolium*), 162; Siberian (*E.* × *allionii*), 99, 162
Warley Place, 197, 208
Watsonia, 42, 48–49, 88, 89
Wells, Bertram W., 149, 167
Welty, Eudora, xi, 235, 242
Wherry, Edgar T., 146, 147, 149–50, 218–26
White, E. B., 244
White, Katharine, xi, 244

White hoop petticoat (*Narcissus bulbocodium*), 184
Widow's cross (*Sedum pulchellum*), 165
Wild-cucumber vine (*Echinocystis lobata*), 128
Wilder, Louise B., 166, 182, 209, 224
Wild ginger, 170
Willmott, Ellen, 197, 199, 208
Wintergreen, spotted, 153
Wisteria, xv, 13, 100
Withers, Hannah, 141, 238
Woodlanders Nursery, 218, 219, 223, 224
Wood sorrel (*Oxalis*), 206, 192

Xerophyllum asphodeloides, 154

Yarrow (*Achillea*), 163
Yellowwood (*Cladrastis lutea*), 33
Yew, dwarf English (*Taxus baccata* 'Repandens'), 172
Yucca, 237
Yulan (*Magnolia denudata*), 240

Zenobia, 21, 149; *Z. pulverulenta*, 21, 187; forma *nitida*, 21; *nuda*, 21
Zephyranthes, 45, 48, 68–69, 92–93, 175; 'Ajax', 69, 93; *Z. atamasca*, 48, 68, 151, 170; *Z. bifolia*, 69; *Z. candida*, 41, 48, 68, 69n, 92, 93, 184; *Z. citrina*, 68, 69n, 93; *Z. grandiflora*, 68, 92–93; *Z. longifolia*, 68–69; *Z. macrosiphon*, 69; *Z. pulchella*, 68; *Z. rosea*, 41, 69, 93; *Z. simpsonii*, 69; *Z. smallii*, xiii, 96; *Z. treatiae*, 69
Zinnia, Mexican, 109
Zinnia, 9, 105, 106, 108, 109, 111; 'Lilliput', 109

PERMISSIONS

"Elizabeth Lawrence—An Autobiography" was originally published in *Herbertia*, the journal of the International Bulb Society (formerly the American Plant Life Society and the American Amaryllis Society), vol. 10 (September 1943), p. 13, and is reprinted with the society's permission.

"Twenty-One Plant Facts for Gardeners in the Middle South" was originally published in *House & Garden*, January 1936, pp. 42, 68, 70). It is reprinted courtesy of *House & Garden*, copyright 1936 (renewed 1964) by the Condé Nast Publications, Inc.

"The Onset of Spring" was originally published in *The Home Garden*, February 1943, pp. 23–25, and is reprinted courtesy of Home Service Publications, Inc., Minneapolis, Minnesota, and with the permission of Warren Way and Elizabeth Rogers.

"Broad-Leaved Evergreens for the Mid-South" was originally published in *House & Garden*, October 1937, pp. 100–105. It is reprinted courtesy of *House & Garden*, copyright 1937 (renewed 1965) by the Condé Nast Publications, Inc.

"Here Are Blossoms for Southern Evergreens" was originally published in *The Home Garden*, February 1946, pp. 24–27, and is reprinted courtesy of Home Service Publications, Inc., Minneapolis, Minnesota, and with the permission of Warren Way and Elizabeth Rogers.

"*Pinckneya pubens*" was originally published in *The American Horticultural Magazine*, a publication of the American Horticultural Society, April 1961, pp. 232–33, and is reprinted with the permission of Warren Way and Elizabeth Rogers.

"Butcher's-Broom—*Ruscus aculeatus*" originally appeared in *The American Horticultural Magazine*, a publication of the American Horticultural Society, April 1963, p. 126, and is reprinted with the permission of Warren Way and Elizabeth Rogers.

"Some Trees and Shrubs of the Southeast" originally appeared in *The American Horticultural Magazine*, a publication of the American Horticultural Society, October 1964, pp. 214–16, and is reprinted with the permission of Warren Way and Elizabeth Rogers.

"Summer-Flowering Bulbs" was originally published in *Garden Gossip*, December 1933, pp. 5–6, and is reprinted courtesy of the Garden Club of Virginia and with the permission of Warren Way and Elizabeth Rogers.

"Outdoor Hardy Crinums" is a composite of two articles that were originally published in *Garden Gossip*: "Outdoor Hardy Crinums," December 1934, p. 7, and "Milk-and-Wine Lily," January 1938, p. 13. This material is reprinted courtesy of the Garden Club of Virginia and with the permission of Warren Way and Elizabeth Rogers.

"Diverse Bulbs for the South" was originally published in *House & Garden*, September 1936, pp. 46, 91–93. It is reprinted courtesy of *House & Garden*, copyright 1936 (renewed 1964) by the Condé Nast Publications, Inc.

"Narcissi for Next Spring's Garden" was originally published in *The American Home*, October 1937, pp. 42–43, 107–12, and is reprinted with the permission of Warren Way and Elizabeth Rogers.

"Amaryllids in a Southern Garden" was originally published in *Herbertia*, the journal of the International Bulb Society (formerly the American Plant Life Society and the American Amaryllis Society), vol. 10 (September 1943), pp. 14–23, and is reprinted with the society's permission.

"In Quest of Autumn-Blooming Bulbs" was originally published in the *Bulletin of the American Rock Garden Society*, September/October 1945, pp. 74–75, and is reprinted with the society's permission.

"Ornamental Alliums in North Carolina" was originally published in *Herbertia*, the journal of the International Bulb Society (formerly the American Plant Life Society and the American Amaryllis Society), vol. 11 (September 1944), pp. 313–28, and is reprinted with the society's permission.

"Hybrid Crinums" was originally published in *Home Gardening for the South*, September 1946, pp. 434, 436–37), and is reprinted with the permission of Warren Way and Elizabeth Rogers.

"Further Notes on Hybrid Crinums" was originally published in *Home Gardening for the South*, February 1947, p. 44, and is reprinted with the permission of Warren Way and Elizabeth Rogers.

"A Review of the Iris Family" was originally published in *Home Gardening for the South*, April 1947, pp. 102–4, and is reprinted with the permission of Warren Way and Elizabeth Rogers.

"Tender Bulbs for Summer Bloom" was originally published in *Plants and Garden*, Summer 1948, pp. 94–95, and is reprinted with permission of the Brooklyn Botanic Garden.

"Habranthus" was originally published in *The American Horticultural Magazine*, a publication of the American Horticultural Society, October 1961, pp. 354–55, and is reprinted with the permission of Warren Way and Elizabeth Rogers.

"*Zephyranthes smallii* in North Carolina" was originally published in *The American Horticultural Magazine*, a publication of the American Horticultural Society, April 1963, pp. 125–26, and is reprinted with the permission of Warren Way and Elizabeth Rogers.

"Perennials Suitable for the Mid-South" was originally published in *House & Garden*, July 1936, pp. 57, 83–84. It is reprinted courtesy of *House & Garden*, copyright 1936 (renewed 1964) by the Condé Nast Publications, Inc.

"Annuals Down South" was originally published in *House & Garden*, December 1936, pp. 61, 94, 96–97. It is reprinted courtesy of *House & Garden*, copyright 1936 (renewed 1964) by the Condé Nast Publications, Inc.

"Garden Phlox" was originally published in *Southern Home and Garden*, April 1938, p. 3, and is reprinted with the permission of Warren Way and Elizabeth Rogers.

"*Torenia bailloni*" was originally published in *Garden Gossip*, October 1938, p. 11, and is reprinted courtesy of the Garden Club of Virginia and with the permission of Warren Way and Elizabeth Rogers.

"Some Crotalarias for the Mid-South" was originally published in *Garden Gossip*, March 1939, pp. 5–6, and is reprinted courtesy of the Garden Club of Virginia and with the permission of Warren Way and Elizabeth Rogers.

"Permanent Perennials" was originally published in *Flower Grower*, September 1943, pp. 414–15, and is reprinted with the permission of Warren Way and Elizabeth Rogers.

"My Best Twenty-Five Daylilies" is a composite of three daylily reports that were originally published in *Herbertia*, the journal of the International Bulb Society (formerly the American Plant Life Society and the American Amaryllis Society)—"Daylily Trials in North Carolina," vol. 12 (September 1945), pp. 149–51; "Daylily Trials in North Carolina," vol. 14 (September 1947), pp. 52–55; and "My Best Twenty-Five Daylilies," vol. 15 (September 1948), p. 40—and is reprinted with the society's permission.

"The Curtain in Your Garden" was originally published in *Popular Gardening*, May 1957, pp. 36–37, 68, and is reprinted with the permission of *Amateur Gardening/Popular Gardening* magazine, London, England.

"Groundcovers" was originally published in *Popular Gardening*, April 1958, pp. 50–51, 98, and is reprinted with the permission of *Amateur Gardening/Popular Gardening* magazine, London, England.

"Ivy: Cool Green in Summer, Warm Green in Winter" was originally published in *Popular Gardening*, August 1960, pp. 40–41, 51, and is reprinted with the permission of *Amateur Gardening/Popular Gardening* magazine, London, England.

"Handsome Wild Indigos" was originally published in *Horticulture*, November 1943, p. 421, and is reprinted courtesy of *Horticulture*, the Magazine of American Gardening, 20 Park Plaza, Suite 1220, Boston, MA 02116. Copyright 1943, Horticulture Limited Partners.

"Native Plants for the Country Doctor's Garden" was originally published in *The Newsletter of the North Carolina Wild Flower Preservation Society, Inc.*, Fall

1971, pp. 24–26, and is reprinted courtesy of Linda Mitchell Lamm, editor emeritus, and with the permission of Warren Way and Elizabeth Rogers.

"Pennyroyal" was originally published in *The Newsletter of the North Carolina Wild Flower Preservation Society, Inc.*, Spring 1972, pp. 9–10, and is reprinted courtesy of Linda Mitchell Lamm, editor emeritus, and with the permission of Warren Way and Elizabeth Rogers.

"Southern Endemics" was originally published in *The Newsletter of the North Carolina Wild Flower Preservation Society, Inc.*, Spring 1973, pp. 22–24, and is reprinted courtesy of Linda Mitchell Lamm, editor emeritus, and with the permission of Warren Way and Elizabeth Rogers.

"Neglected Natives" was originally published in *The Newsletter of the North Carolina Wild Flower Preservation Society, Inc.*, Spring 1974, pp. 13–14, and is reprinted courtesy of Linda Mitchell Lamm, editor emeritus, and with the permission of Warren Way and Elizabeth Rogers.

"Morrow Mountain" was originally published in *The Newsletter of the North Carolina Wild Flower Preservation Society, Inc.*, Fall 1974, p. 5, and is reprinted courtesy of Linda Mitchell Lamm, editor emeritus, and with the permission of Warren Way and Elizabeth Rogers.

"A Wildflower Garden in August" was originally published in *The Newsletter of the North Carolina Wild Flower Preservation Society, Inc.*, Fall 1976, pp. 12–13, and is reprinted courtesy of Linda Mitchell Lamm, editor emeritus, and with the permission of Warren Way and Elizabeth Rogers.

"Trilliums" was originally published in *The Newsletter of the North Carolina Wild Flower Preservation Society, Inc.*, Spring 1979, pp. 15–21, and is reprinted courtesy of Linda Mitchell Lamm, editor emeritus, and with the permission of Warren Way and Elizabeth Rogers.

"Rock Garden Plants for the Mid-South" was originally published in *House & Garden*, May 1937, pp. 117–21. It is reprinted courtesy of *House & Garden*, copyright 1937 (renewed 1965) by the Condé Nast Publications, Inc.

"Rules for Rock Gardens" was originally published in *Southern Home and Garden*, November 1938, pp. 7, 23, and is reprinted with the permission of Warren Way and Elizabeth Rogers.

"Rock Garden Conifers in Southern Nurseries" was originally published in the *Bulletin of the American Rock Garden Society*, January/February 1945, p. 10, and is reprinted with the society's permission.

"Some Small Members of the Iris Family" was originally published in the *Bulletin of the American Rock Garden Society*, January/February 1946, pp. 6–7, and is reprinted with the society's permission.

"More about Violets" was originally published in the *Bulletin of the American Rock Garden Society*, September/October 1947, p. 94, and is reprinted with the society's permission.

"A Review of Little Daffodils" was originally published in the *Bulletin of the*

American Rock Garden Society, July/August 1950, pp. 65–67, and is reprinted with the society's permission.

"Some Notes on Species Tulips" was originally published in the *Bulletin of the American Rock Garden Society*, July/August 1951, pp. 59–61, and is reprinted with the society's permission.

"Rock Gardens in Winter" was originally published in the *Bulletin of the American Rock Garden Society*, Spring 1955, p. 84, and is reprinted with the society's permission.

"Two Wonders" was originally published in the *Bulletin of the American Rock Garden Society*, Winter 1959, p. 42, and is reprinted with the society's permission.

"Miss Jekyll of Munstead Wood" was originally published as the introduction to *The Gardener's Essential: Gertrude Jekyll*, by Gertrude Jekyll (1964), copyright 1964, 1986, reprinted by permission of David R. Godine Publishers.

"Friends in Oregon" was originally published in *Pacific Horticulture*, Summer 1977, pp. 3–6, and is reprinted with the permission of Warren Way and Elizabeth Rogers.

"Letters from the West" was originally published in *Pacific Horticulture*, Spring 1978, pp. 3–7, and is reprinted with the permission of Warren Way and Elizabeth Rogers.

"Brothers of the Spade" was originally published in *Pacific Horticulture*, Winter 1981–82, pp. 12–14, and is reprinted with the permission of Warren Way and Elizabeth Rogers.

"In Memory of Dr. Edgar T. Wherry: No Phlox without a Salutation" was originally published as "The Woodlanders and Dr. Wherry" in *The Newsletter of the North Carolina Wild Flower Preservation Society, Inc.*, Fall 1982, pp. 13–26, and is reprinted courtesy of Linda Mitchell Lamm, editor emeritus, and with the permission of Warren Way and Elizabeth Rogers.

"On William Lanier Hunt" was originally published as the introduction to *Southern Gardens, Southern Gardening*, copyright 1982 by William Lanier Hunt, and is reprinted with the permission of William Lanier Hunt.

"A Garden of One's Own: Letters from Elizabeth Lawrence to a Friend" was originally published in an Elizabeth Lawrence memorial issue of *The Trillium*, the newsletter of the Piedmont Chapter of the North American Rock Garden Society, September 1992, and is reprinted courtesy of Linda Mitchell Lamm, Warren Way, and Elizabeth Rogers.

www.ingramcontent.com/pod-product-compliance
Lightning Source LLC
Chambersburg PA
CBHW030108010526
44116CB00005B/146